DIETLAND

This Large Print Book carries the
Seal of Approval of N.A.V.H.

Dietland

Sarai Walker

KENNEBEC LARGE PRINT
A part of Gale, a Cengage Company

A Cengage Company

Farmington Hills, Mich • San Francisco • New York • Waterville, Maine
Meriden, Conn • Mason, Ohio • Chicago

Copyright © 2015 by Sarai Walker.
Kennebec Large Print, a part of Gale, a Cengage Company.

Kennebec Large Print® Superior Collection.
The text of this Large Print edition is unabridged.
Other aspects of the book may vary from the original edition.
Set in 16 pt. Plantin.

LIBRARY OF CONGRESS CIP DATA ON FILE.
CATALOGUING IN PUBLICATION FOR THIS BOOK
IS AVAILABLE FROM THE LIBRARY OF CONGRESS

ISBN-13: 978-1-4328-5229-0 (softcover)

Published in 2018 by arrangement with Houghton Mifflin Harcourt Publishing Company

Printed in Mexico
1 2 3 4 5 6 7 22 21 20 19 18

To my parents,
for believing in me

and to my foremothers,
who didn't always have a voice

She waited for a few minutes to see if she was going to shrink any further: she felt a little nervous about this; "for it might end, you know," said Alice to herself, "in my going out altogether, like a candle. I wonder what I should be like then?"

— Lewis Carroll,
Alice's Adventures in Wonderland

■ ■ ■ ■

Rabbit Hole

■ ■ ■ ■

It was late in the spring when I noticed that a girl was following me, nearly the end of May, a month that means *perhaps* or *might be.* She crept into the edges of my consciousness like something blurry coming into focus. She was an odd girl, tramping around in black boots with the laces undone, her legs covered in bright fruit-hued tights, like the colors in a roll of Life Savers. I didn't know why she was following me. People stared at me wherever I went, but this was different. To the girl I was not an object of ridicule but a creature of interest. She would observe me and then write things in her red spiral-bound notebook.

The first time I noticed the girl in a conscious way was at the café. On most days I did my work there, sitting at a table in the back with my laptop, responding to messages from teenage girls. *Dear Kitty, I have stretch marks on my boobs, please help.*

There was never any end to the messages and I usually sat at my table for hours, sipping cups of coffee and peppermint tea as I gave out the advice I wasn't qualified to give. For three years the café had been my world. I couldn't face working at home, trapped in my apartment all day with nothing to distract me from the drumbeat of *Dear Kitty, Dear Kitty, please help me.*

One afternoon I looked up from a message I was typing and saw the girl sitting at a table nearby, restlessly tapping her lime green leg, her canvas bag slouched in the chair across from her. I realized that I'd seen her before. She'd been sitting on the stoop of my building that morning. She had long dark hair and I remembered how she turned to look at me. Our eyes met and it was this look that I would remember in the months to come, when her face was in the newspapers and on TV — the glance over the shoulder, the eyes peeking out from the thick black liner that framed them.

After I noticed her at the café that day, I began to see her in other places. When I emerged from my Waist Watchers meeting, the girl was across the street, leaning against a tree. At the supermarket I spotted her reading the nutrition label on a can of navy beans. I made my way around the cramped aisles of Key Food, down the canyons of colorful cardboard and tin, and the girl trailed me, tossing random things into her shopping basket (cinnamon, lighter fluid) whenever I turned to look at her.

I was used to being stared at, but that was by people who looked at me with disgust as I went about my business in the neighborhood. They didn't study me closely, not like this girl did. I spent most of my time trying to blend in, which wasn't easy, but with the girl following me it was like someone had pulled the covers off my bed, leaving me in my underpants, shivering and exposed.

Walking home one evening, I could sense that the girl was behind me, so I turned to face her. "Are you following me?"

She removed tiny white buds from her ears. "I'm sorry? I didn't hear you." I had never heard her speak before. I had expected a flimsy voice, but what I heard was a confident tone.

"Are you following me?" I asked again, not as bold as the first time.

"Am I *following* you?" The girl looked amused. "I'm afraid I don't know what you're talking about." She brushed past me and continued on down the sidewalk, being careful not to trip on the tree roots that had burst through the concrete.

As I watched the girl walk away, I didn't yet see her for who she was: a messenger from another world, come to wake me from my sleep.

When I think of my life at that time, *back then,* I imagine looking down on it as if it were contained in a box, like a diorama — there are the neighborhood streets and I am a figurine dressed in black. My daily activities kept me within a five-block radius and had done so for years: I moved between my apartment, the café, Waist Watchers. My life had narrow parameters, which is how I preferred it. I saw myself as an outline then, waiting to be filled in.

From the outside, to someone like the girl, I might have seemed sad, but I wasn't. Each day I took thirty milligrams of the anti-depressant Y——. I had taken Y—— since my senior year of college. That year there had been a situation with a boy. In the weeks after the Christmas break I slipped into a dark spiral, spending most of my time in the library, pretending to study. The library was on the seventh floor and I stood at the window one afternoon and imagined jumping out of it and landing in the snow, where it wouldn't hurt as much. A librarian saw me — later I found out I had been crying — and she called the campus doctor. Soon after that pharmaceuticals became inevitable. My mother flew to Vermont. She and Dr. Willoughby (an old gray man, with gray hair, tinted glasses, a discolored front tooth) decided it was best for me to see a therapist and take Y——. The medication took away my sadness and replaced it with something else — not happiness, but more like a low dull hum, a weak radio frequency of feeling that couldn't be turned up or down.

Long after college ended, and the therapy ended, and I'd moved to New York, I continued to take Y——. I lived in an apartment on Swann Street in Brooklyn, on the second floor of a brownstone. It was a long and skinny place that stretched from the front of the building to the back, with polished blond floorboards and a bay window that overlooked the street at the front. Such an apartment, on a coveted block, was beyond my means, but my mother's cousin Jeremy owned it and reduced the rent for me. He would have let me live there rent free if my mother hadn't nosed in and demanded I pay something, but what I paid was a small amount. Jeremy worked as a reporter for the *Wall Street Journal.* After his wife died he was desperate to leave New York and especially Brooklyn, the borough of his unhappiness. His bosses sent him to Buenos Aires, then Cairo. There were two bedrooms in the apartment and one of them was filled with his things, but it didn't seem as if he would ever come back for them.

There were few visitors to the apartment on Swann Street. My mother came to see me once a year. My friend Carmen visited sometimes, but I mostly saw her at the café. In my real life I would have more friends, and dinner parties and overnight guests, but my life wasn't real yet.

The day after my confrontation with the girl, I looked up and down the street but I didn't see her, so I set off, relieved not to be followed. A day of work at the café awaited me, but first I would stop at my Waist Watchers meeting, taking the long route so I could bypass the boys who congregated at the end of my block and often made rude comments.

My Waist Watchers meetings were held in the basement of a church on Second Street. The gray-rock church sat between a dry cleaner and a health club, the outline of its stained-glass window a daisy shape. Inside the church I walked down the circular steps to the basement, where I was greeted at the door by the usual woman with the clipboard. "Hello, Plum," she said, and directed me to stand on the scale. "Three hundred and four pounds," she whispered, and I was pleased that I was two pounds lighter than last week.

At the table by the door I signed the register and collected the weekly recipes, moving quickly so I could leave before the meeting began. I had been a Waist Watcher for years and didn't need to attend the meetings; if I never attended another one I would still be able to recite the tenets of the program on my deathbed.

There were only women at these morning meetings, and most of them were slightly older than me, with babies or toddlers they bounced on their laps. They were doughy from past pregnancies, but not big. Around them I felt much larger, as well as much younger. I was more like one of Kitty's teenage girls compared to them, even though I was almost thirty. When I was around women who had grown-up lives, the kind of life I thought I should have, I felt suspended in time, like an animal floating in a jar of formaldehyde.

I made my way back up the stairs and put the recipes, which were printed on thick card stock, into my laptop bag. At home I had a collection of more than a thousand Waist Watchers recipes, which I arranged by snacks, main courses, desserts, and so on. After I cooked a dish, I rated it on the back with a star. Five stars was the best.

I tried to be a good Waist Watcher, but it was difficult. I would start off each day with the right breakfast and snacks, but sometimes I would grow so hungry that my hands would shake and I couldn't concentrate on anything. Then I'd eat something bad. I couldn't stand hunger. Hunger is what death must feel like.

Given my failure at dieting, my plan was to trade Waist Watchers for weight-loss surgery. The surgery was scheduled for October, little more than four months away. I was excited about it, but also terrified at the thought of having my internal organs cut up and rearranged and of the possible complications that might follow. The surgery would make my stomach the size of a walnut; afterward I'd only be able to eat spoonfuls of food each day for the rest of my life. That was the horrible part, but the miraculous part was that I would lose between ten and twenty pounds a month. In one year it would be possible to lose more than two hundred pounds, but I wouldn't go that far. I wanted to weigh 125 pounds, and then I would be happy. Waist Watchers could never give me that. I'd been devoted to the program for years and I was bigger than ever.

When I exited the dark church, blinking into the sunshine, I expected to see the girl leaning against the tree, but she wasn't there. I hurried across the street so I didn't have to pass in front of the health club windows, where the smug spinners could have gawked at me.

Since I hadn't seen the girl that day, I assumed I had scared her away, but when I arrived at the café she was there. Rather than follow me, she had begun to precede me. Perhaps she could claim that I was following her.

As I passed her table, she chewed the cap of her ballpoint pen, feigning thought. I ignored her, heaving my laptop bag up onto my usual table. With her nearby it was going to be difficult to concentrate on my work, but I logged into my account and downloaded the new messages, then opened the first one:

From: LuLu6
To: DaisyChain
Subject: step brother

Dear Kitty,

I'm 14 and a half. I hope u can help me. My mom got married last year to this guy Larry. My real dad is dead. Larry has two sons they are my step brothers Evan and Troy. I'm rilly scarred and I don't know what to do. So many times I have woke up in the middle of the nite and Troy is in my room watching me sleeping. When he sees me awake he leaves. He's 19. I think maybe he touches me but I don't know. One time he came in to the bathroom when I was taking a shower naked and he saw me. He said he likes my boobs. I told my mom and she says I'm making this up so she will get divorced from Larry (cuz I hate him). What should I do?

Luv,
LuAnne from Ohio

LuAnne was my first girl of the day, so I wasn't yet working at the height of my powers. I stared out the window to avoid the anxiety brought by the blinking cursor and started my response in my head. *Dear LuAnne, I'm sorry your mother doesn't believe you. Your mother shouldn't be allowed to call herself a mother.* The mothers of Kitty's readers often chose men over their daughters, the desire for romance overwhelming the need to protect their child. I was tempted to respond to LuAnne by asking for her telephone number so I could call her mother and tell her that she was a horrible person. *I'm glad you came to me for help, LuAnne. Contact your school guidance counselor immediately. He or she will be able to help you with your problem.* No, that wouldn't do. LuAnne deserved better than to be passed off like a baton.

With the strange girl in my peripheral vision, like a tiny bug, I placed my hands on the keyboard and began to type, channeling Kitty's voice:

From: DaisyChain
To: LuLu6
Subject: Re: step brother

Dear LuAnne,

I'm *very* upset that your mom doesn't believe you. I believe you! I would

22

definitely lock your door before going to bed at night. If your door doesn't have a lock, then put a chair or a piece of furniture in front of it. Pile books or other heavy items on top of the furniture. If Troy still gets into your room, scream as loud as you can when you see him. It wouldn't hurt to keep a baseball bat or other such weapon with you at night. Do you have a cell phone? If so, call 911 in an emergency like this.

The next thing I want you to do is tell a trusted adult (your best friend's mom or your favorite teacher) what's going on and she will be able to help you with your problem. If you can't find someone like this to help you, you will need to contact the police. Do you know where the police station is in your town? You could go there and explain what's happening to one of the officers. Ask to speak to a woman.

I'm glad you reached out to me, Lu-Anne. I'm sending you courage through this email.

Love,
Kitty xo

I read through my response and sent it off. I would try not to think of LuAnne again, of her bedroom door with the chair in front of it, of her stepbrother slipping under the covers with her and sentencing her to a lifetime of therapy or worse. I needed to put her out of my mind, and the Internet was convenient in that way — people could be deleted, switched off. I responded to each girl only once, and if she wrote again, I usually ignored her; with the volume of messages I received each day, I didn't have time to become a pen pal. To survive my job I needed the callousness of an emergency room doctor.

Next.

There were hundreds of messages in my inbox. Before continuing on, I wanted to order my lunch, the usual low-fat hummus and sprouts on oatmeal bread (300), but the girl was standing at the counter, paying for her fruit smoothie. Carmen served her without knowing there was an invisible tether connecting the girl to me; wherever I went, so went she.

Carmen's café looked like a 1950s kitchen, with walls painted turquoise, and vintage jadeite teacups on display. The front of it was entirely glass, presenting a view of Violet Avenue that was a moving tableau of people and cars. Carmen needed extra help occasionally and I would work behind the counter or bake for her, arriving before dawn to make cupcakes and banana bread. Despite the temptations, I loved to bake, but I didn't allow myself to do it often.

I met Carmen in college, and although we were merely acquaintances then, we connected again in New York. She allowed me to use the café as an office. We were friends, since our relationship extended beyond the café to phone calls and occasional outings, but with Carmen pregnant, I couldn't help but worry that things were going to change.

The girl returned to her table with the smoothie and sat down. She didn't write in her notebook, which sat unopened in front of her. Instead, she twisted the silver rings she wore on each of her fingers, moving from one finger to the next, looking bored. I had bored her.

Was the girl actually following me? She had seemed genuinely surprised when I confronted her. I couldn't think of a reason why she'd want to follow me, unless Kitty had sent her to spy on me, to make sure I was doing my work. The girl didn't seem like the type of person who would work for Kitty, but then neither did I.

From: AshliMcB
To: DaisyChain
Subject: big problems

Dear Kitty,

This is going to sound strange, but I like to cut my breasts with a razor. It's something I started doing last month, but I don't know why I do it. I like to trace around my nipples and watch the blood seep through my bra. It's an embarrassing problem and there's no one else I can tell it to. I hate my breasts, so I don't care if they're scarred. They're small and mismatched. I've seen porn websites and I know I'm not normal but I can't keep cutting myself because I might bleed to death or get infected. Please help. I can't stop. I know it's weird, but I do it because it feels good. It hurts, but it feels good too.

Your friend Ashli (17 years old)

A cutter. I felt a momentary blip of dismay at the thought of such troubled girls writing to a magazine editor for help, but if they didn't I'd be out of a job. I looked through my computer files and copied and pasted my standard response about cutting, adding a few personalized tweaks.

From: DaisyChain
To: AshliMcB
Subject: Re: big problems

Dear Ashli,

I'm very worried that you're cutting yourself. Many girls do this, so please don't feel that you're weird, but as your friend Kitty, I ask that you stop doing this immediately. I'm not legally qualified to give you advice on this topic, but at the bottom of this message there is a web address that will give you a lot of information and options for getting help from professionals in your local area.

The next paragraph of my message would focus on breasts and porn. I looked through my files: My Documents/Kitty/Breasts/Porn.

Many of us have breasts that don't match. Please remember that women in porn aren't normal. *You* are normal!

To make her feel better, I could have told her that I dared not show my own breasts, nipples pointed toward the floor, to anyone.

I hated to even show them to the doctor, though when I was lying down on the examining table it wasn't so bad; only when standing up could one see the full, hideous effect. I couldn't tell Ashli this because I was pretending to be Kitty, whose perfectly symmetrical breasts stood at full salute, I was sure.

For most of the afternoon, the messages I answered fit into predictable categories (dieting, boys, razor blades and their various uses). There was also a string of complaints from Canadian readers of the magazine. (*Dear Tania: Now, let's be reasonable here, I didn't refer to Quebec as a country on purpose.*) There were a few more difficult letters (*Dear Kitty: Have you ever fantasized about being raped?*) but nothing I couldn't handle. As fast as I answered the messages, more of them flooded in, so I rarely felt a sense of accomplishment. While girls in far-off lands had their genitals trussed like Thanksgiving turkeys, Kitty's girls had their own urgent problems. (*If Matt doesn't call me, I'LL DIE.*) I wasn't good with questions about boys.

There was no end to these pleas. They came from the heartland, from north and south and east and west. It seemed there was no part of the American landscape that was not soggy with the tears of so many girls. After writing an email that explained the difference between a vulva and a vagina (*Your vagina is the passage to your cervix. It provides an opening for menstrual blood. To answer your question, no, you cannot shave a vagina. There is no hair there!*), I looked up and noticed that the girl was gone. Relieved, I opened the next message, not expecting something of interest or anything to restore my faith in girl-kind. (*Every night after dinner I go into the bathroom and throw up.*) Before I could slip into despair, which usually happened every afternoon around three o'clock, Carmen surprised me with a cup of black coffee (FREE FOOD) and an oatmeal cookie (195).

She was wearing a maternity top in a pastel shade; her enormous belly looked like an Easter egg. She sat down across from me, letting out a huff of air, running her fingers through her clipped black hair. "Go on, read me one." The messages from Kitty's girls had a car-crash allure.

I looked down at my computer screen. "Dear Kitty, is it always wrong to have sex with your father?"

"You're making that up. *Please, God.*" She was unsure and waiting for a sign from me. When I started to laugh, she laughed too, and I felt wicked, like a therapist mocking her patients. Carmen rubbed her belly and said, "We used to want a girl, but now I'm not so sure. You've scared me. Girls are *scary*."

"Not on the surface," I said. "Only when you dig deep."

"That's even scarier."

While I had Carmen's attention, I decided to ask her about the strange girl. I hadn't mentioned her before, not wanting to seem paranoid. "Did you see that girl sitting over there?" I said, pointing to the empty chair.

"The one with the eyeliner? She's been coming in a lot lately. Why, was she bothering you?"

"She seems a bit strange, don't you think?"

Carmen shrugged. "Not particularly. You see the people who come in here." She paused, and I hoped she was recalling something important about the girl. Instead, she asked if I would cover a shift for her next week while she went to the doctor. I hesitated. I was trying to be good on my diet. Sitting at my normal table wasn't bad if I blocked out the sights and smells around me and drank my coffee and tea, but behind the counter was another matter.

"Sure," I said. On some days, Carmen was

the only person I spoke to. It was only small talk, but at the right moments, she brought me out of my head. For that, I owed her.

Carmen went back to work, and since I was being good, I took only a small bite of the oatmeal cookie. Two teenage girls at the next table smirked as they watched me. I set the cookie down and decided to work more quickly so I could leave. The best way to work was to dive headlong into the water, feeling my way in the darkness, not letting anything stick to me, just letting the current carry me along:

Why are all the models in your magazine so skinny girls are so lucky I'll never be anything but fat ass bitch he said to me after class but I still like him and I know that is crazy cuz he is so mean to me and my friend want to get rid of these gross red bumps on our arms can you help me please cuz my legs look so fat in a swimsuit so should I quit the swim team or what should I do if no guy asks me to the dance cuz my cousin asked me to go with him but is that incest or not every guy likes girls with red hair on my vagina is not sexy tits my history teacher said to me when I wore my purple shirt so he is a perv and now I'm afraid I'm going to gain weight on

31

vacation what can I do if I can't afford a nose job no guy will ever like me with this nose I am sure of it is a mystery to me how you can sleep at night you fucking bitch but why did he say that to me I am not a bitch so I don't understand why my mom won't let me use tampons because I told her I would still be a virgin if I use a tampon will you email her for me and my boyfriend had sex because he made me do it but then he said he was sorry so does that count as rape cuz I still love him but I am confused about why every time I wear red lipstick it gets stuck to my front teeth.

And one last message, from a man in prison: *I like to masturbate while looking at pictures of you. Will you send me a pair of your panties?*
Delete.

At home there was a package. I sat on my bed, the straps of my purse and laptop bag still tangled around me, and ripped open the puffy brown parcel. Inside was a knee-length poplin shirtdress, white with purple trim. It was even prettier than the photographs in the catalog had been.

In the corner of my bedroom was a floor-length mirror in a brass frame. I kept it covered by a white sheet, which I tossed aside so I could hold the dress in front of me, imagining what it would look like when it fit. When I was done I put it in the closet with the other too-small clothes.

My regular clothes, the ones I wore on a daily basis, were stuffed into the dresser or flung on the floor. Stretchy and shapeless, threaded with what must have been miles of elastic banding, they were not in fashion or out of fashion; they were not fashion at all. I always wore black and rarely deviated from the uniform of ankle-length skirts and long-sleeved cotton tops, even in the summer. My hair was nearly black too. For years it had been shaped into a shiny chin-skimming bob, with blunt bangs cut straight across my forehead. I liked this style, but it made my head look like a ball that could be twisted from my round body, the way a cap is removed from a bottle of perfume.

Inside the closet, there was nothing black, only color and light. For months I had been shopping for clothes that I would wear after my surgery. Two or three times a week the packages arrived — blouses in lavender and tangerine, pencil skirts, dresses, a selection of belts. (I had never worn a belt.) I didn't shop in person; when someone my size went into a regular clothing store, people stared.

I had done it once after I'd spotted a dress in a store window that I couldn't resist. I went inside and paid for it, then had it gift-wrapped as though it were for someone else.

No one knew about the clothes, not even Carmen or my mother. Carmen didn't even know about the surgery, but my mother did and she was against it. She was worried about the potential complications. She sent me articles that outlined the dangers of the procedure, as well as a tragic story about children who were orphaned when their mother died post-surgery. "But I don't have any children," I said to her on the phone, unwilling to indulge her.

"That's not the point," she said. "What about me?"

This isn't about you, I had wanted to say, and refused to discuss the surgery with her again after that.

After straightening and rearranging the clothes, I shut the closet door. I knew it was foolish to buy clothes I couldn't try on. They might not fit right when the time came, but I bought them anyway. I needed to open the closet door and look at them and know this wasn't like the other times. Change was inevitable now. The real me, the woman I was supposed to be, was within my reach. I had caught her like a fish on a hook and was about to reel her in. She wasn't going to get away this time.

Carmen called to ask if I wanted to join her and her girlfriend at a pizzeria for dinner, but I didn't like to eat at restaurants when I was following my program, so I said no. From one of the new Waist Watchers recipe cards, I made lasagna, which used ground turkey instead of beef and fat-free cheese and whole-wheat pasta. While it was cooking it smelled like real lasagna, but it didn't taste like it. I gave it three stars. After I ate a small portion (230) with a green salad (150), I cut the rest into squares and put them in the freezer. My hands were still slightly trembly from hunger, but I would be good and not eat anything more.

After changing into my nightgown and brushing my teeth, I took my daily dose of Y—— from the bottle, the pink pill. It was my ritual before bed, like saying a prayer. As I finished my glass of water, I went to the window in the front room and pulled back the curtain, looking to see if the girl was sitting on the stoop, listening to her music, but she wasn't there.

I stayed home for most of the holiday weekend, the unofficial start of summer, leaving only to go to the library and to see a movie. The girl was nowhere around. On Tuesday morning I walked to the café, and as I turned the corner onto Violet Avenue, I wasn't looking where I was going and bumped into someone — or maybe she bumped into me. "Sorry," we both said at the same time, and then to my surprise, I saw the girl standing before me, with her Halloween eyes and cherry-red legs.

"It's you," I said. My heart was a moth flapping around a lampshade.

The girl smiled and said good morning, then opened the door and held it for me as I followed her inside. "Plum," Carmen said, rushing past the girl, waving her hands at me. As she approached, her massive belly covered in yellow and pink polka dots, I remembered I was supposed to cover for her while she went for her checkup. "I won't be gone long," she assured me as she hurried out the door.

The girl walked ahead of me and I watched as she sat at my table. I was annoyed but didn't show it and went behind the counter to help Carmen's assistant. When I set my laptop bag down I felt the tension release from my shoulder as I rid myself of the computer and its endless cries for help. Surrounding me in the kitchen were flour and butter and eggs, the stuff of life; there wasn't a line of text in sight. I breathed in the sugared air and savored it, then felt a twinge of hunger. My Waist Watchers granola bar (90), like sawdust mixed with glue, hadn't provided much sustenance.

It had been a while since I'd helped out at the café, but I soon remembered how things were done. I poured cups of tea and sliced carrot cake. I set delicate cupcakes into pink cardboard boxes, licking the icing and sprinkles from my fingers when no one was looking. It was a relief to engage in work that didn't involve angst, that allowed me to speak with three-dimensional people who asked for simple things like coffee and a slice of pie, not how to fix their cellulite or decipher the behavior of an emotionally stunted boy.

While I was working I glanced at the girl, who was sitting at my table with a makeup bag in front of her. She pulled a silver clamshell compact and a lip pencil from the shimmery pouch. I watched through the glass lid of a cake stand, blurrily, as she lined her lips and smacked them in the mirror.

Distracted by an order, I turned around and busied myself with the espresso machine and three tiny cups. When I returned to the counter I saw the girl in line behind the woman who'd ordered the espressos. My coworker had gone into the kitchen, so I would have to serve the girl. We would have to speak.

The girl stepped forward when it was her turn and we stood face-to-face. "Give me your hand," she said. Startled, I did what she asked. She took the cap off a lip pencil and turned my right hand so that my palm was facing her, my thumb at the top. Then she began to write. I couldn't see what she was writing, but I felt the point of the pencil digging into my skin.

When she finished, I pulled my hand back. "DIETLAND," I read aloud.

"DIETLAND," the girl repeated.

I stared at the penciled letters on my

palm. Was the girl telling me to go on a diet? So much mystery, and there it was: she simply wanted to make fun of me.

In the absence of any comment from me, for at this point I was too embarrassed to speak, the girl quickly gathered her belongings from the table and left the café. Just then my coworker reappeared. I wiped my hand on my apron and excused myself to go to the kitchen. The bottom of the white sink filled with a faint pink color as I put my hand under the cold water and tried to rinse the lettering off.

When I emerged from the kitchen, I saw that the girl had left the lip pencil sitting on the table. I went to collect it. It was a Chanel pencil in a shade called "Pretty Plum."

In the aftermath of my encounter with the girl, I needed to prepare for a visit to Kitty. The visit only came once a month, like my period, and I greeted it with the same level of enthusiasm.

On the subway ride from Brooklyn to Manhattan, I retraced the word DIETLAND on my palm, using my fingertip. What did it mean? I had thought the girl was ridiculing me, but she didn't seem cruel. What I knew for certain was that she was weird. If she bothered me again, I would have to go to the police, but I feared that in a city full of murderers and terrorists they weren't likely to care that a girl in colorful tights was trailing me.

I exited the subway station in Times Square, stopping at the top of the stairs to catch my breath in the heat. With my employee badge I entered the Austen Tower, a glistening silver tree trunk. Austen Media was an empire, publishing magazines and books, running a range of websites, and broadcasting two lifestyle channels. If someone had flown a 747 into the Austen Tower and it crumbled to the ground, American women would have had far fewer entertainment options.

Before my job with Kitty I had worked for a small, not-very-prestigious publishing imprint that was owned by Austen but located in a drab building twenty blocks south. We produced novels about young career women looking for love. The covers of the novels were in springtime shades, like the walls of a baby's nursery. I didn't have anything to do with the content, but worked in production, tracking manuscripts, liaising with editors, helping to usher the books into the world. After college, I had wanted to write essays and feature stories for magazines, but I couldn't find a job doing that, so I settled at the publisher. I loved words and the publisher offered me a chance to work with words all day long, even if they were someone else's. It was a place to start. A foot wedged in the door of the word industry.

My coworkers at the publisher were middle-aged women who wore tennis shoes to work with their skirts and nylons. I soon became comfortable in their world of Tupperware lunches and trips to the discount shoe mart after work, so I made no effort to move on and find the writing job I had dreamed about. One day, after I'd spent more than four years at the publisher, my boss called me into her office to tell me the bad news. We were going out of business.

"I'm sorry I couldn't say anything sooner, but you probably heard the rumors." A vase of hydrangeas sat on her desk, blue pom-poms in brown water, dropping their shriveled petals onto her Filofax.

"Well," I said. The rumors hadn't reached me.

"It's not just us. They're cleaning house. It's the whole building." The whole building was a mail-order book club and a few small magazines, one about cats, another about doll collecting. We had gone unnoticed for years, the dregs of the Austen empire, hidden in an annex on Twenty-Fourth Street. At long last, Stanley Austen had looked down from his perch in the silver tower and noticed us in a tiny corner of his kingdom. Then came banishment.

After the publisher closed, I was unemployed except for random shifts at Carmen's café, but eventually a woman named Helen Rosenblatt from Austen's Human Resources department called to schedule a meeting with me. I went to the Austen Tower as directed, and rode the elevator to the twenty-seventh floor. Helen was a middle-aged woman with a tumbleweed hairdo and a gummy smile. I followed her to her office, noticing that her linen skirt was wedged between her buttocks.

Helen said that my boss from the publisher had told her all about me. "We're old friends," Helen explained, and I wondered what had been said. Helen wanted to talk about *Daisy Chain,* the magazine for teens. I had read *Daisy Chain* when I was in high school. Even my mother and her friends had read it when they were that age. It had been published since the 1950s and was such a part of Americana that the first issue was displayed in the Smithsonian, alongside *Seventeen* and *Mademoiselle.* I guessed that the old issues of *Daisy Chain* on display at the museum weren't like the current issue on Helen's desk, with a cover that read POPPING YOUR CHERRY — IT'S NOT THAT SCARY!

Helen told me that Kitty Montgomery was the new editor of *Daisy Chain.* Austen's other teen magazines had ceased publication, so Kitty was carrying the flag for the teen demographic. "She's a huge hit," Helen said. "Mr. Austen's so pleased, he's had her up to his place on the Vineyard twice." Helen explained that in her monthly column, Kitty was fond of sharing photos and tragic stories from her teenage years, when she was a gangly, pebble-chested misfit from the suburbs of New Jersey. As Helen took a phone call, I perused several of Kitty's columns and read about her being beat up by other girls and shoved into lockers by boys. Her mother compounded her misery by never letting her wear makeup or use a razor. In contrast, at the end of each column there was a photo of Kitty as a glamorous grownup, one who had miraculously shed her hideous adolescent skin and emerged, victorious, like a grand white snake. In her current photos she was perched on the corner of her desk in the Austen Tower; visible behind her were the plains of New Jersey, the land of her former tormentors, so small and insignificant.

"Given Kitty's popularity, she's swamped with correspondence from readers," Helen explained when she finished her call. "They're inspired by Kitty and how she transformed herself. They desperately want her advice and contact her through the Dear Kitty section of the website. It's like a flood." I waited for Helen to explain what any of this had to do with me. I knew there was the prospect of a job, but I assumed it was something tucked away in the subscription department.

"The legal department would prefer that we send out cookie-cutter form responses to the readers, but Kitty won't hear of it. We've decided to indulge her and hire someone to take on the responsibility of responding to her *girls,* as she calls them, by offering big-sisterly advice and encouragement, that sort of thing. This is private correspondence, so it doesn't appear in the magazine." Helen looked at me and paused. "I think you might be perfect for this. I've sent others up there and none of them have worked out, but you," Helen said, putting her glasses on and eyeing me, "you're different."

I knew what my former boss had said about me.

"You want someone to respond to these readers while pretending to be Kitty?"

"I wouldn't think of it as *pretending.* You'd be a team." Helen folded her arms across her chest, which was not two separate breasts but just an enormous shelf. "You're older than the other girls we've considered for the job, and you're different from them in many ways. Most of them are — Well, you know the type. I hear that you're smart, but I don't mind that. You'd write in Kitty's voice. You wouldn't have to believe what you'd write; it only matters that Kitty would believe it and write it if she had time. I think you'd have insight into the problems our girls have — that's what's important."

I should have been grateful for the possibility of a job, but I felt defensive and was trying to hide it. "What makes you think I'd have such insight? You don't even know me."

"I'm guessing," she said, and we both knew what she meant. I hated it when others alluded to my size, despite the obviousness of it. It was as if they were confirming that there was something wrong with me when I'd hoped they hadn't noticed it.

I appreciated Helen's offer, but the thought of working in the Austen Tower every day was unappealing. I imagined it was like a fifty-two-story high school, full of cliques and whispers. Helen must have begun working at Austen Media decades before she morphed into the large postmenopausal woman who sat before me.

My instinct was to flee. I initially refused Helen's offer to meet with Kitty, but both of them were insistent. When I finally met Kitty in her office, she suggested I could work from home. "It was human resources' idea," she said. "As you can see, my assistant has his desk out in the hallway. We're a bit tight for space." Working from home made the job more appealing, but I said I would need to think about it. I had never been the type to offer advice, and I wasn't sure I had the right qualifications for the job. Kitty thought my reluctance meant I was playing hard-to-get, so she began to pursue me with heartfelt emails, flowers, even a scented candle that was delivered via messenger. I was not used to being courted and sought-after. The feeling was mildly intoxicating.

It had been three years since I'd taken the job, three years of responding to messages in the café. I arrived for my monthly meeting with Kitty, stepping off the elevator onto the thirtieth floor, where I was greeted by massive *Daisy Chain* covers, which might have been meant to intimidate enemies, like the buildings and monuments in Washington, D.C. I sat on the lip-shaped loveseat outside Kitty's office and waited. Our meetings rarely lasted more than ten minutes, but I never managed to leave the Austen Tower in fewer than two hours, thanks to Kitty's frenetic schedule. I would have preferred to catch up by phone, but Kitty demanded that we meet.

As I waited on the sofa, her assistant, Eladio, played video games on his computer. The first time I visited the office, he took me to the conference room with the panoramic windows and pointed to the stickpin people on the sidewalk below. "What I love about working here," he'd said, "is that we get to look down on everyone."

He was the only male on a staff of twenty-one white women; he was also Latino and gay, a triple hit of diversity. He told me once that he became irritable and moody at certain times of the month, prone to outbursts of unprovoked rage, caught up in the synchronized menstrual cycles of the women in the office and pulled along for the hormonal ride by mistake. He kept a box of Midol Menstrual Complete on his desk, but it was filled with jelly beans. Kitty once told her readers that the cycles of the women in the office were linked by the moon. She claimed the mass bloodletting each month left the trash receptacles in the ladies' room filled to overflowing.

While I waited, I browsed the latest issue of *Daisy Chain,* checking the masthead for my name, which would be printed over a million times and distributed across North America: *Special Assistant to the Editor-in-*

Chief: Alicia Kettle. Alicia was my real name, but no one ever called me that.

Kitty finally appeared, rushing into her office and dropping a pile of magazines and files onto her desk. "Plum, come in!" She was wearing black slacks and a cropped T-shirt that revealed part of her midriff. There was a red crystal nestled in her bellybutton, like a misplaced bindi. I sat across from her as she moved the clutter around on her desk. "Be with you in a minute," she said, studying a green Post-it note intently.

A traffic helicopter hovered outside her office window, black and buglike, a giant fly. I closed my eyes. In the Austen Tower I always felt uneasy, sometimes even dizzy and nauseated. I didn't like being so high off the ground, suspended in the air by nothing more than concrete and steel. With my eyes closed, I imagined the floor beneath my feet giving way, sending me sailing back to earth.

"Plum?" Kitty was standing behind her desk, looking at me, her brow pinched in confusion. She was a mesmerizing presence, probably better viewed from afar. With the afternoon sunlight streaming in through the windows, casting her mostly in silhouette, the sight of her — Medusa-like red curls atop a slender body — made me think I was hallucinating or looking at something drawn by Edward Gorey.

She launched into chatter about the September issue, handing me a packet of information about the articles, columns, and fashion spreads. It was the back-to-school issue, the biggest of the year. She always shared these details with me even though none of my work appeared in the magazine. I had pitched ideas for articles, hoping to jump-start a writing career, but Kitty had never assigned me anything.

When it was finally time to discuss her correspondence, she sat behind her desk, ready to take notes. I described the tenor of the messages over the past month. I didn't keep formal records but gave her my general impression.

"We've had a lot of cutters."

"Cutters," Kitty repeated, writing something down.

"Purging," I said.

Kitty wrote on the pad again. "Purging," she repeated, and nodded for me to continue.

"Confusion about female anatomy."

Kitty waved her hand, as if what I'd said could be swatted away. "There's nothing I can do about that. Those parental groups said they'll target us if we use the word *vagina.* Better just to avoid it. Of course, it makes our article on tampons difficult to write. I just remembered that." Kitty leaned back in her chair, appearing overwhelmed. "Euphemisms, that's what we need." She looked through the doorway to where Eladio sat.

"Think of some euphemisms for *vagina,*" she shouted to him.

"Poontang?"

"No, nothing sexual. Medicalized terms. Come up with a list and send them to the author of the tampon article. Tell her she can't say *vagina.* Send the list to Plum, too, in case she wants to use it."

It was difficult to believe we were all engaged in real work, for which we were paid. I would have to tell Carmen about this later.

Kitty turned back to me. "Good, glad that's done," she said, even though I hadn't finished going through my mental list. "Between you and me, I know parts of the magazine are silly, but my readers are *real* girls with *real* problems. I truly believe we can help them. I like to think the work that you and I do is an anecdote to all the bad things in the world. Wait, I mean *antidote.*"

When she said that, I imagined a bite on a girl's ankle, as if from a snake, its fangs hav-

51

ing penetrated deep into her flesh.

Kitty always made the girls seem like real people, whereas for me they were too often an army of annoying and persistent ants. "I always say, 'Plum is our link to the girls,' and your work is just as important as everyone else's, even though it's not in the magazine." She continued on with these sentiments for another thirty seconds. They flowed from her mouth in a stream of spun sugar.

"Now, there's something else we need to discuss and then I'll let you go," she said. "For an upcoming issue the staff is testing all sorts of beauty stuff like razors, deodorant, lip-gloss, hairspray, whatever. We'll tell the girls what works best. I want to include you in this."

"You don't have to include me."

"Oh, no, we have to! Just because you work at home doesn't mean you aren't one of us. You know, the strangest thing happened to me last night when I was testing out some shaving gel. I'm sitting on the edge of the tub and I have my leg stretched out so that my foot is resting on the sink. Are you picturing it?" Kitty was nearly six feet tall and I imagined her white leg stretched over the expanse from tub to sink, like an ivory bridge.

"I'm shaving my leg and I don't realize that I nicked a tiny scab I had on my calf. So I'm shaving and this tiny droplet of blood falls from my leg and splashes onto the white tile floor. My bathroom is totally white and this tiny drop of red is, like, the only color. And I'm staring at it and it's just so — now, don't laugh — but it's just so *beautiful*. I just sat there staring at the blood. I thought, *That's my blood.* As women we see our own blood every month, but this wasn't gross like that, you know? So I ran the razor along the little scab again and there were more drops of blood on the floor and some of it ran down my calf. If my boyfriend hadn't knocked on the door, I would've kept doing it all night."

Kitty went on talking about the blood on the white tile, and as she spoke, all I could think was: *Dear Kitty, I like to cut my breasts with a razor . . . I like to trace around my nipples and watch the blood seep through my bra . . . I know it's weird, but I do it because it feels good. It hurts, but it feels good too.*

Kitty left and I sat on the lip-shaped love-seat again, waiting for the beauty editor. After a while I started to feel dizzy and sick, as I had in Kitty's office, so I went to the ladies' room, winding my way through the corridors lined with the huge magazine covers — the models, with their glazed-over looks, like the heads hanging on a hunter's wall. I stared at the carpet until I made it to the bathroom, where there were several girls standing at the mirrors and sinks. I locked myself into one of the salmon-colored stalls at the end and breathed in and out slowly. The nausea was increasing and I felt something churning inside, tumbling like a lone sock in the dryer. I began to gag and choke and leaned over the toilet bowl, but nothing came out. The girls at the sinks stopped talking, and I felt ashamed of the noises I was making.

When the sick feeling passed, I sat on the floor of the stall, lacking the energy to stand, staring into the pinkness. The girls resumed their conversation, which was punctuated by the sound of water, the spray of sinks. Then the talking stopped.

The door to the bathroom opened and closed.

I rested my head against the side of the stall, taking deep breaths of sour bathroom air, which made me gag again. I ran my hand under the three elastic bands that were around my waist, from my skirt and tights and underpants.

The door to the bathroom opened and closed.

"Are you okay in there?" a voice said from the other side of the stall door. The voice sounded familiar. Under the door I saw legs that were green, like the rind of a watermelon, and black combat boots with the laces undone.

Could it be?

"I left something for you in the kitchen," she said, and then she was gone.

After I heard the door close, I struggled to my feet and went to the sink to wash my hands, breathless from the shock of encountering the girl in the Austen Tower. I wondered if she might be in the staff kitchen waiting for me, but when I walked over, no one was there. I looked around, at first not knowing what the girl could have left, but then I noticed the freebie table.

What wasn't used in the magazine was dumped onto a table in the kitchen, available for the taking. I dug through the pile: there was a purse with a broken bamboo handle, a tangle of cheap plastic earrings, tubes of lipstick — nothing that seemed to be for me. Next to the table on the floor was a box filled with books. I bent over to browse through the titles — a few teenage romance novels, the unauthorized biography of a pop star — and then I saw it.

Adventures in Dietland.

It was a book by Verena Baptist. Her name wasn't familiar to me until I read the description on the back. When I realized who she was, I squeezed my eyes shut. I might have been in the Austen Tower, suspended in the air by nothing more than concrete and steel, but in my mind I traveled to Harper Lane, back in time to my childhood home. I felt a pang, the kind that memories bring. How did the girl know? She couldn't have known.

I opened the book to see if there was a note from the girl or anything to let me know I'd found the right clue on her treasure hunt, but there was nothing. I had stuffed the book into my bag and was moving toward the door when suddenly it opened.

"I've been looking for you everywhere." The beauty editor's assistant handed me a bag filled with the products I was supposed to test.

"Do you know if there's a girl working here who wears combat boots and colorful tights?" I asked, taking the bag. "She uses thick black eyeliner. Maybe she's an intern?"

The assistant shrugged.

I left the kitchen, hurrying to the elevators. Once I was on the subway headed for home, I opened *Adventures in Dietland.* As I read Verena's words for the first time — *Before my birth, Mama was a slim young bride* — the train pulled away from the platform and nosed into the tunnel, moving me away from the Austen Tower.

Already, it had begun.

■ ■ ■ ■

ALICIA AND PLUM

■ ■ ■ ■

After fourteen hours in the car, driving from Boise to Los Angeles in a single day, my mother and I arrived at 34 Harper Lane, our faces and arms colored pink. My great-aunt Delia and her second husband, Herbert, lived in the small stone house, its front door obscured by coral vines and bougain-villea, its yard green with lemon and palm trees. "You'll go home to your daddy soon," Delia whispered as I climbed out of the car. "Just give your mom some time."

Delia had lived alone in the house on Harper Lane after her son Jeremy moved east for college, but then she married Herbert and then she welcomed us. My mother set herself up in the study, with the black-and-white television and sofa bed. I was given the spare bedroom at the front of the house that had a view of a date palm, or mostly its trunk, which was patterned in triangles like a giraffe's neck.

After telephone calls to my father and the promised trip to Disneyland, my mother retreated to the study and rarely left it for the rest of the summer. If I wanted to see her I would tiptoe inside and curl next to her in bed. With the curtains closed it was dark; I couldn't see her but I could feel her hand on my head, playing with my hair. I listened to the tick of the fan in the corner, my nose filled with the smell of her sweat.

Delia managed a restaurant during the day. Herbert was retired and sat on the sofa watching "his shows," beginning with *The Price Is Right* in the morning and lasting until dinnertime. He wasn't to be disturbed. He'd taken me to Kmart and bought me a stack of books, plus Color-forms, paper dolls, new roller skates, and a jump rope, expecting me to entertain myself.

One afternoon I sat in the front yard under the palm tree and read one of my new books. It was hot in California, much hotter than in Idaho, and I began to fantasize about a cherry Popsicle. As I was about to stand up, a blue car with two women inside stopped in front of the house. One of the women leaned out the passenger window with a bulky black camera and snapped the button several times. When she was finished, she eased back into the car and it sped away, the sound of the women's laughter trailing behind it.

I looked around, searching for something photo worthy, but saw nothing. Had she been taking a picture of me? I went into the house and peeked from behind the living room curtains to see if the women would return.

Herbert didn't register my presence as I sat down next to him on the sofa. On the coffee table, his reading glasses, in their snakeskin tube, rested on top of the open *TV Guide.* I tried to read my book again, but the game-show clapping made it difficult to concentrate. Pushing the curtains aside, I peered into the street but there was no one there. I went out with my Popsicle and sat under the tree, peeling down the sticky plastic wrapper and licking the red drops from my fingers.

A yellow convertible stopped. A girl leaned out the passenger window and snapped several photographs. She looked at me and laughed, then the convertible sped away, the wind blowing the girl's blond hair straight up like a flame.

When the sound of the car disappeared and everything was quiet again, I dumped my Popsicle in the dirt. What had the girl seen? I wanted to run to my mother, but she was inside the dark room.

"Herbert?" I said, stepping into the house. He shooed me away. For the rest of the afternoon I stayed hidden in the backyard, sitting with my books inside the small swimming pool, a concrete shell with no water.

I avoided the front yard for several days, but I didn't like being at the back of the house, which was cramped, with a collection of bamboo stalks in one corner, patio furniture in the other, and a concrete hole in the middle. When I was bored of reading and my crayons became soft in the heat, I strapped on my roller skates, thinking the dimpled concrete of the empty pool could serve as the perfect skating rink. Herbert saw me from the kitchen window and shouted that I would break my leg.

He kept a stash of Twinkies and fried fruit pies hidden behind the breadbox in the kitchen, so I took a Twinkie and went to the front yard in my skates. As I was sailing to the mailbox, my mouth full of yellow sponge and cream, a car stopped and I knew what was going to happen. A man stepped out of the car and took a series of photos, then drove away.

Delia came home that evening and saw me sitting at the kitchen table, reading my book. "Why aren't you outside, doll?" I shrugged. I didn't want to tell her that people were looking at me, that they stared and took photos and some of them even laughed.

On most nights, our dinner came from the restaurant. Delia unloaded Styrofoam containers from a brown paper bag and set them on the table. I ate my Reuben sandwich and coleslaw, weird food my mother never made at home. She didn't join us for dinner and I was left alone with Herbert and Delia, who talked about grown-up things. I looked out the front window from the table, watching for more cars. None came.

After dinner, Delia and Herbert sat on the back patio with wine and I was allowed to watch television in the front room, sitting in the crater left by Herbert on the green sofa. I watched two sitcoms and before the third came on, I went into the kitchen to get a glass of milk. On my way back to the living room, holding the glass to my lips, I saw a man standing outside the front window. He was large and looming. We locked eyes and then he rushed to his car and drove away.

I set my glass down on the coffee table, splashing milk onto Herbert's *TV Guide,* and ran to my bedroom. In my bed, from underneath the covers, I wondered: Who are these people? And why are they staring at me?

Before we moved into the house on Harper Lane, I had feared there was something wrong with me. Back home when we visited cousins they would laugh and call me Miss Piggy, until a chorus of mothers went *Shhh-hhh.* In first grade, in Mrs. Palmer's class, the two girls who sat next to me, Melissa H. and Melissa D., told me they weren't inviting me to their Halloween party because I had fat germs. When I asked my mother what this meant, she said to ignore them.

I didn't know what other people saw when they looked at me. In the mirror I didn't see it. Now at Delia's house, things were even worse. People were taking photos and I didn't know why. During the day I hid in my bedroom and watched for them. Once when I was making a mess in the kitchen with peanut butter and jelly, two girls climbed over the fence into the backyard. I dropped the knife and screamed for Herbert, who flew out the back doors and chased the girls away. "Goddamn tourists," he screamed. I looked outside in horror. Herbert came back into the house and tousled my hair. "Just ignore 'em, kiddo."

Ignore them. That's what my mother had said.

I stayed away from the windows so that no one could see me. For most of the day I sat on the living room floor, wrapped in a blanket to protect me from the chill of the air conditioner, and watched Herbert's shows with him. When my mother left her room to go to the kitchen, she said I was spending too much time indoors. "She's not the only one," Herbert said.

He and Delia took me to Sears and bought me a bicycle with purple tassels that dangled from the rubber handles. When we got home with the bike, they expected me to ride it up and down the street. I lasted for an hour, until a man and a woman in a silver van stopped outside the house. "Hello, *leetle* girl," the man said in a weird voice.

When I went inside the house I was crying.

"What's wrong, sweet pea?" Delia asked, coming over and running her acrylic nails down my back. "Did you fall off your bike?"

"People are looking at me."

"Who is?"

"People in cars. They stop in front of the house and take photos of me."

Delia began to laugh, holding her hand over her mouth, her frosty pink nails hiding a wide smile. "They're not taking photos of you, doll. They're taking photos of the house. A famous lady used to live here. I've been in the house so long, I don't notice those crazy people anymore."

Delia told me about Myrna Jade, a silent film star of the 1920s. Delia said she hadn't heard of Myrna Jade when she bought the house. "It was an absolute wreck. Completely falling apart. You never would've imagined a movie star had lived here." Myrna Jade had been forgotten, her films out of circulation, until a historian wrote a book about her in the 1970s, which was turned into a popular film in the 1980s. "Myrna mania," Delia called it. "Now my house is on one of them *star maps* and people drive by at all hours of the day and night. It's mostly Europeans. I know it's annoying, doll — believe me, I know, but there's nothing I can do about it, so don't pay 'em any attention."

I wasn't sure I believed Delia, thinking a movie star would live in a castle, not a small stone house. I wondered if she was trying to make me feel better. I went to my bedroom for the rest of the evening and when it was time for bed, I put on my pajamas and peeked outside. A flashbulb. *Pop.* Then two more. *Pop. Pop.* Electric flowers in the night sky.

The women who came before me were black-and-white. My grandmother, mother of my mother, died before I was born, but there are photographs of her. In my favorite one she is a young woman, standing next to her sister on the Boardwalk in Atlantic City, the two of them clasping their arms and smiling as they look into the camera lens. I like to think that my grandmother was looking through time toward my mother and me, though she couldn't have imagined us then. She's a teenager in the photo, her hair bobbed in the style of the 1920s. She and her sister are wearing polka-dotted dresses and both of them are round all over. Even as a girl I saw myself in them. I knew we were connected, like a string of round white pearls stretching into the past.

When my mother was little she was black-and-white like them, but not round like them. On the day I was born, she looked at me and knew she would call me something other than the name she'd put on my birth certificate. "You had the darkest hair," she said, "long enough to wrap around my fingers. Your skin was rosy pink. You were so succulent and sweet, my little Plum."

A pearl, a plum — roundness defined me.

Every year on the first day of school the teacher would take attendance, and when she reached my name, she would say, "Alicia Kettle?" and then I'd have to tell her I was called Plum.

Plum. Plump. Piggy.

Alicia is me but not me.

We lived in the house on Harper Lane for five months and then we moved to our own apartment. My father stayed in Idaho and my parents got divorced. My mother's salary as a secretary in a university biology department afforded us a place with dark woodwork that sucked up the sunlight, and carpet a vomitous orange. We lived in the apartment for a few years, until Herbert died of a stroke. Delia was so unhappy living alone that she begged us to move back to the house with the starers, the gawkers, the photograph-takers.

The schools near Delia's house were better for me, my mother said, and she was

71

excited about the possibility of escaping the apartment complex with the dirty diapers floating in the pool. She had made up her mind to go, and so we went.

In the house on Harper Lane we were under constant surveillance. Sitting at the breakfast table, I'd look up from my oatmeal to see a figure outside the front window, which would bolt away like a frightened mouse when my slipper hit the glass. In my bedroom I kept the curtains closed, but I knew they were out there. Delia and my mother didn't seem to mind the strangers' stares and camera lenses. When they were away from home they could escape — for them it was only temporary.

At school, there was nowhere for me to hide. I was surrounded. There were so many of them that I never knew for certain who was looking. All day I felt the urge to turn away, to close up like a flower in the shade.

I kept what happened at school to myself. Sometimes at the end of the day I would find spit in my hair or a note taped to my back that read DO ME A FAVOR, POP ME! My first year of high school, after an older classmate was raped in the vacant lot behind Von's, the school offered self-defense classes for girls. When I showed up, two girls snickered and said, loudly enough for everyone else to hear, "Who'd want to rape her?"

On the telephone to Idaho, I said: "Daddy, do you think I'm pretty?" I knew he would say yes because he was my father.

During my sophomore year of high school, a boy asked me to the homecoming dance. I was suspicious of boys, since they never paid me any attention unless it was for name-calling or worse, but my mother insisted that I go. She dropped me off outside the school gym and I waited for the boy in the parking lot for more than an hour, the wispy ends of my homemade lavender gown dragging in pools of motor oil. The boy never came and everyone knew. They had seen.

I wanted to become smaller so I wouldn't be seen.

If I was smaller they wouldn't stare. They wouldn't be mean.

At Carmen's café, my laptop opened before me, I couldn't concentrate on the messages from Kitty's readers. I'd set Verena Baptist's book on the empty chair next to me, having read a few chapters the day before. I kept glancing at it: *Adventures in Dietland*. It wasn't the type of book I'd normally read, but I had the urge to go home and devour its pages. I didn't know why the girl had left the book for me or why she'd been in the Austen Tower. It seemed impossible that she could be part of Kitty's world and yet she'd been in Kitty's office. I hadn't seen her since then, so I wondered if her little game was finished.

Ever since I'd laid my eyes on the book, and the name Verena Baptist, I'd been transported to Harper Lane. The girl couldn't have known anything about my past, or that I'd been a Baptist, but thanks to her I couldn't stop thinking about that time, when I was the age of Kitty's girls. I pushed my laptop aside and began to read again. The memories weren't welcome, but the book pulled me back.

I became a Baptist during the spring of my junior year of high school. I was sick with the flu and stayed home from school for three days, doing nothing but watching television. The personalities that populated the daytime airwaves were unfamiliar to me, particularly the smiling spokespeople advertising products I hadn't known existed. I had never heard the name Eulayla Baptist before, but she appeared in a series of commercials for Baptist Weight Loss. I had never heard of that, either.

In each commercial, an old photograph of Eulayla Baptist filled the screen. She was enormous in a pair of faded jeans, trying to shield her face from the camera. In a voice-over, she said: "That was me, Eulayla Baptist. Back then I was so fat, I couldn't even play with my daughter." Sad violins swelled in the background, reaching a crescendo as thin Eulayla burst through the photograph, ripping it to shreds. She stood in a *ta-da!* pose, her arms extended toward the heavens.

Cut to Eulayla sitting at a sun-dappled

kitchen table covered with a red-checkered tablecloth: "By choosing to eat the Baptist way, you'll never have to starve yourself again. For breakfast and lunch, enjoy a Baptist Shake, flavored with real Georgia peaches. For dinner, the possibilities are endless. Right now, I'm enjoying chicken 'n' dumplings." Eulayla, her blond hair in a tight French twist, her ever-present gold cross around her neck, set down her fork and stared into the camera, which moved in for a close-up. "On the Baptist Plan, there's no need to grocery shop or cook. My program provides you with everything you need, except for willpower. That special ingredient has to come from you."

Every twenty minutes or so this woman appeared on the screen, bursting through her enormous jeans. She was accompanied in the ads by other successful photo-bursters. There was Rosa, age twenty-three: "If I had to look fat in my wedding dress, then I'd rather die an old maid." Sad violins, then *Burst!* Rosa was thin. Marcy, age fifty-seven: "My husband wanted to take a cruise, but I said 'No way, buster! These thighs aren't getting into a pair of shorts.'" Sad violins, then *Burst!* Marcy was thin. Cynthia, age forty-one: "After my husband was killed on American Airlines Flight 191,

I ate at least ten thousand calories a day. If Rodney were still alive, he would have been so ashamed of me." Sad violins, then *Burst!* Cynthia was thin.

For hours I watched TV, waiting for the ads, mesmerized. I dug out my yearbook from tenth grade, looking at a snapshot of me on page 42. The caption read: "Alicia Kettle works on her science project in the library." I imagined seeing that photo on TV, me in my ever-present black dress, the roll of fat under my chin. *Burst!* I'd obliterate that hideous girl.

I wrote down the toll-free number, determined to become a Baptist, though I knew my mother would try to stop me. She had a play-the-cards-you're-dealt mentality when it came to matters of the body, be it height or weight or hair color. She saw these things as fixed, for the most part. "You're beautiful the way you are," she would always say, and it seemed as if she meant it. Once when we argued about dieting, she said, "You look like Grandma," meaning: "You look like Grandma *and there's nothing you can do about it.*"

No matter how much I had pleaded, she would never let me diet. My friend Nicolette's mother was a member of Waist Watchers, and I photocopied her materials, keeping them hidden. I tried to follow the diet on my own, but I didn't know how many calories were in the dishes that Delia brought home from the restaurant, whether it was lasagna or chicken potpie. There were too many ingredients to count. I took smaller portions and sometimes skipped lunch at school, but I didn't like being hungry. There were girls at school who starved themselves, but I didn't know how they did it. When I was hungry I couldn't concentrate, and I needed to concentrate so I could get good grades.

The ads on television said: *A Baptist is never hungry!* That was part of the appeal. I didn't know how I would pay for the Baptist Plan, but I would find a way. I was high on my secret plan. On the night of the junior prom my mother took me out for dinner. When we arrived home, we found a man kneeling in the front yard, paying homage to Myrna Jade. When he saw me he snapped a photo. "*Preeeetty* girl," he said. No one except my parents and Delia had ever called me pretty. I was pleased. Since I had decided to become a Baptist there was a change in me. Just the thought of it had made me lighter.

I didn't care that I wasn't at the prom that night. I didn't need proms or the boys at my school. Summer vacation was approaching and then my senior year, at the end of which I would go to college in Vermont. Thanks to the Baptist Plan I would be thin when I arrived at college. No one would know that fat Plum had existed. I wouldn't even call myself Plum. I would be Alicia, since that was my real name.

If people asked about Plum, I'd say, "Plum who? Plum doesn't exist."

Burst!

In the hours after school, I didn't see friends or attend clubs. I did my homework. I was always diligent about it, never needing to be prodded. In the afternoons, alone in the house on Harper Lane, I sat at the dining table with the curtains drawn and worked by lamplight. Sometimes people knocked on the door and threw rocks at the windows. They'd jiggle the door handles. I did my best not to be seen.

When my mother arrived home from work she'd fling open the drapes, allowing in the light. "The weather is beautiful," she'd say, but I'd escape to the darkness of my bedroom. One day Delia suggested that I come to the restaurant in the afternoons to do my homework. I assumed she had discussed the plan with my mother, but she made it seem spontaneous.

Between lunch and dinner the restaurant was practically empty. Delia and I sat in a red vinyl booth in the back, she with her paperwork, me with my schoolwork, both of us sipping Diet Coke in tall glasses packed with lemon and ice. I would sit for hours doing geometry and reading thick Russian novels for my advanced literature class. Sometimes Nicolette would join us and she and I would work together on chemistry or French.

I'd been going to the restaurant every day for a couple weeks when I had an idea. I'd been secretly thinking of ways to pay for the Baptist Plan and wondered if I could use the restaurant to my advantage. I began to go into the kitchen and watch Chef Elsa prep for dinner, expressing interest, asking questions. As I'd hoped, she allowed me to help out, teaching me to chop and sauté. When I asked Delia for a job she agreed, and so for a couple hours a night I worked in the kitchen, where opera played on the radio.

After nearly a month on the job, with school about to let out for the summer, I had enough money to become a Baptist. When I told my mother, we argued. "It's too radical," she said. Behind closed doors, I heard her and Delia discussing it. "Be reasonable, Constance. Life isn't easy for her," Delia said. I would have gone even without my mother's permission. I was seventeen years old and she couldn't stop me.

There was a branch of Baptist Weight Loss near the restaurant, its windows covered in white curtains so no one could see inside. I had passed two health clubs, plus Nutrisystem and Jenny Craig, on my way there, but I wasn't interested in any of them. The Baptist approach was the right one for me. On the first day of summer vacation, the money from my job in my wallet, I opened the door to the Baptist clinic and was greeted with a life-size portrait of Eulayla Baptist holding up her enormous jeans. Two chimes rang out as I entered, announcing the start of my new life.

With the other new members I was led to a darkened room, where we watched a documentary about Eulayla called *Born Again.* There was footage of Eulayla as Miss Georgia 1966 and of her competing in the Miss America pageant. After she married and had a baby she gained a lot of weight, which she couldn't lose. She tried every diet, and even anorexia, but nothing worked long-term. On her child's fifth birthday, she weighed more than ever. The former beauty queen became suicidally depressed and begged her husband to pay for stomach stapling surgery, but he refused. A neighbor had died after the same procedure and he wouldn't let Eulayla risk her life.

Allen Baptist, founder of a thriving evangelical church in suburban Atlanta, which he hadn't been allowed to name The Baptist Church for legal reasons, was devoted to his wife and desperate to help her. He hired his cousin to move in with the family, to cook for Eulayla and make sure she didn't eat too much. He decided she needed to be completely removed from the world of food. His cousin prepared all of Eulayla's meals so she didn't have to shop for food or go into the kitchen. Allen Baptist even took the drastic step of padlocking the refrigerator shut. He kept Eulayla away from restaurants and she stopped socializing with friends and even attending church. Rumors spread around the neighborhood that Eulayla was dead.

After nine months of hell, with Eulayla eating nothing but hard-boiled eggs and lean roast beef and cottage cheese with canned peaches, she lost the 115 pounds that had been ruining her life, likening the process to rebirth. That's when she felt a calling to help others overcome their appetites and realize their full potential, as she had done.[1]

With her husband's reluctant support, Eulayla conceived of an idea to start a diet clinic that would provide its patrons with low-calorie shakes, frozen dinners, and a special exercise program. Baptists wouldn't cook or grocery shop; they wouldn't think about food at all, except when it was time to drink or heat up their next meal. The first Baptist Weight Loss clinic opened in Atlanta in 1978. By the late 1990s, when I was ready to join, there were more than a thousand branches worldwide.

When the documentary ended and the lights came back on, we waited for the orientation to begin. Meanwhile, the photo-bursting commercials played on a loop.[2]

1. Within a year, Mama began to regain the weight she'd lost. Since she had invested our family's savings in Baptist Weight Loss, Daddy foresaw disaster and agreed that Mama needed her stomach stapled. It was the only answer. After the surgery, Mama developed an anal leakage and had to wear diapers. (*Adventures in Dietland,* Chapter 1: "The Birth of Verena, the Birth of an Empire," p. 27.)

2. Baptist Weight Loss pioneered the "photo-bursting" technique. See J. Lucas, "Ripped to Shreds: Advances in Weight Loss Advertising," *Ad-*

There were only women in the group of new members, and several of them were quite slender. I didn't understand why they were there, but they were all friendly with me, behaving as if we had something in common.[3]

Our group leader, Gladys, arrived to introduce herself. She was a black woman with an old-fashioned bouffant-style hairdo. She wore pumps that made a squishing sound as she walked. She smiled nonstop as she handed out the binders and Baptist handbooks and laminated cards printed with the Baptist Oath, which we were supposed to put in our wallets and on our refrigerators:

---

week, June 9, 1986. See also H. Whelan and M. Burns, "Baptist Weight Loss and the 'Before and After' Photograph," *Journal of Female Psychology* 4, no. 2 (1993): 42–65. (*Adventures in Dietland,* Chapter 1: "The Birth of Verena, the Birth of an Empire," p. 54.)

3. Memorandum: From senior vice president [name redacted] to Eulayla Baptist (October 24, 1982): "People who only imagine they're fat are a huge market for us. Fat, thin . . . these are meaningless distinctions, except at the extremes. What is fat? What is thin? Who cares." (*Adventures in Dietland,* Baptist Weight Loss Internal Memo Index, p. 329.)

> Baptists must treat their bodies like temples. Successful Baptists must incorporate the Three Tenets into their lives. First Tenet: I will not pollute my body with fattening and unhealthy foods. Second Tenet: I will exercise regularly. Third Tenet: I will spread the Baptist message to others.
>
> © Baptist Weight Loss, Inc.

I collected the handouts, cards, and pamphlets and placed them in my shiny new binder, so thrilled to be part of Eulayla's family. That's what she called us: a family.

After the meeting was under way, a woman rushed through the door, apologizing for being late and taking a seat next to me in the back row. Janine was tall and bigboned, with cottony blond hair, and her appearance shocked us all, as much as if she'd been naked. She was wearing a radiant dress, floral patterned, with pink tights and boat-size heels on her feet, like Minnie Mouse shoes. None of the other new Baptists were dressed in bright colors, but instead wore the depressing shades of an overcast day. Looking at Janine was like looking directly into the sun.

I wished she hadn't sat down next to me,

since we looked like two Humpty Dumptys seated together. During the part of the meeting where we were supposed to chat with our neighbor, Janine spoke as if the two of us were the same. She even invited me out for coffee after the meeting, but I said I was busy. I had never had a fat friend and I didn't want one.

Throughout the meeting, Janine spoke up, saying things like, "My whole family is fat and they think dieting is a waste of time." Gladys shuddered at Janine's words and continuously corrected her. We learned to say *overweight* or *obese,* not *fat.* We were never to say *diet,* either, but instead use terms such as *the plan, the program,* or *eating healthily.*

Toward the end of the meeting, Gladys handed each of us a booklet with "When I'm Thin . . .™" printed on the cover. There was a photograph of two smiling women carrying shopping bags. Gladys said that we would write in our "When I'm Thin . . .™" journals each week. Inside, at the top of the first page, it said, "When I'm Thin . . .™" and then there were five blank lines underneath with suggested topics such as romance, careers, and fashion. Gladys directed us to close our eyes and imagine ourselves thin. She told us to write down five things that our thin selves would be able to do that our overweight selves couldn't.

The other women and I began to write, but Janine looked stunned. "You've got to be kidding," she said. "I came here to lose a few pounds because of back pain. What kind of sick, self-loathing mindfuck is this?" She was flipping through the booklet, red in the face, breathless from rage.

"Watch your language," Gladys said. "Baptists do not use vulgarity."

Janine looked at Gladys, her eyes blazing behind her rhinestone-studded cat glasses. "Are you for real?" She flung her "When I'm Thin™" booklet at Gladys, who seemed terrified, holding up both hands to shield herself. Janine made a door-slamming exit. In her wake there was silence in the room, leaving us to contemplate the departure of the loud, angry woman, disagreeable and huge, what none of us wanted to be.

When it was my turn to meet with Gladys individually, she apologized multiple times for the "unfortunate incident." "What we're doing here at the clinic is radical and life affirming," she said. "We're taking care of our bodies. People like *that woman* find this very threatening. She's like an alcoholic or drug addict, completely in denial. She'll probably be dead soon." Gladys seemed to savor the thought.

She gave me a tour of the exercise room, with pink dumbbells bearing the Baptist name scattered on the floor and a woman in a modest leotard leading a group in jumping jacks. In the privacy of her cubicle, Gladys snapped a Polaroid of me and told me to stick it in my binder and bring it to the clinic each week. This was my *before* picture. She then weighed me and, using a software program developed by Eulayla's brother, a computer scientist, calculated that I needed to lose 104 pounds, which would take only nine months on the Baptist Plan. "In nine months, you'll be looking foxy!" she said, her silver charm bracelet clanking on the keyboard. Gladys made it seem so easy that I wanted to hug her. I would be thin in nine months. Software doesn't lie. I carried my first week of shakes and frozen dinners home in two shopping bags, puffed up with Gladys's words of encouragement.

At home, my mother looked on coolly as I put my food away. The six-packs of shakes and the pale pink trays of frozen food filled most of the space in our fridge and freezer. I also had a packet of Baptist Supplements.

"Why do you need these?" My mother examined the pebble-colored tablets.

"Gladys said I have to take one each day."
She'd been emphatic.[4]

At breakfast and lunch, I drank a foamy
peach shake from a can. At dinner, I micro-
waved my designated meal, then peeled
back the silver plastic to reveal beef stew, its
chunks of meat and peas floating in a
lukewarm bath of brown gravy, or a turkey
meatball, like a crusty planet surrounded by
red rings of pasta. The meals were small,
merely a scoop or two of food, and they
seemed to lack a connection to actual
foodstuffs; I thought it was possible the
"food" was constructed of other elements,
like paper and Styrofoam, but I didn't care,
as long as eating it led to thinness.[5]

4. Some Baptists claimed to have suffered kidney
problems as a result of the diet, but this was never
proven in a court of law. Mama threatened to sue
her accusers for slander, but she never did. Under
oath she couldn't have denied that the diet gave
some Baptists bad breath and constipation and
made their hair fall out. (*Adventures in Dietland*,
Chapter 2: "The Baptist Plan: Not Everyone Is a
Believer," p. 138.)

5. Mama's personal assistant, [name redacted],
blackmailed her in the summer of 1990. She had
recorded a phone conversation between Mama
and her, in which Mama said that the Baptist

My first week as a Baptist, I was filled with energy and motivation. I'd been instructed to avoid people who were eating, those unruly mobs with their knives and forks, but given my job at the restaurant this was impossible. It didn't matter. I was experiencing transcendence from the grotesque world of mastication and grazing. The sight of people eating made me sick.

Before my shift at the restaurant, I would stop by the Baptist clinic to do aerobics. At work I moved faster than ever. One night I chopped twenty-five onions in record time, leaving Chef Elsa to marvel at my speed. Red peppers, celery, and garlic lay in colorful heaps on my chopping boards. I'd finish early and take on extra projects, such as reorganizing the grain cupboard and alphabetizing the spices.

When I returned home from work one night I was greeted by ten Italian pilgrims sitting in our yard, lighting candles and playing the guitar. I opened the curtains in my bedroom to listen to them sing. They waved and smiled, and I didn't mind that

---

meals "tasted like shit" and "you couldn't pay me to eat them." (*Adventures in Dietland,* Chapter 2: "The Baptist Plan: Not Everyone Is a Believer," p. 141.)

they were looking at me. Nothing could dampen my mood. I was a jailed girl about to be released from a long sentence.

By the end of the week, I was twelve pounds lighter. Gladys and the other women clucked around me, admiring my shrinking figure.[6]

In nine months, you'll be looking foxy!

Like most highs, mine was not to last; as I entered week two, I crashed. If school had been in session, I wouldn't have made it. I skipped aerobics class and had to force myself to leave the house to go to the

6. Memorandum: From senior vice president [name redacted] to Eulayla Baptist (August 1, 1980): "A diet that produces slow and steady weight loss will not hook new customers, Eulayla. How many times do I have to spell this out? People want immediate results, and an 850-calorie-a-day regimen will give them just that. Baptists will lose a significant amount of weight in the first few weaks [*sic*] and become addicted to the high of dropping pounds. When they fail to keep up this momentum, they'll only blame themselves. Trust me on this. I worked at [name redacted] for five years, remember? That's why you hired me!" (*Adventures in Dietland*, Baptist Weight Loss Internal Memo Index, p. 332.)

restaurant, which I had to do to pay for the Baptist Plan. In Chef Elsa's kitchen, I became prone to staring off into space without blinking. "Are you sick?" she asked me. The week before I'd been a wind-up toy spinning around furiously; now I had fallen over, silent and still.

I called Gladys. "What's wrong with me?" I whispered into the phone, too weak to even speak.

"It's sugar withdrawal. You're an addict, honey. That poison is leaving your system."

"But I'm so hungry."

"I know, sweetie," said Gladys. *Sugar. Honey. Sweetie.* Gladys wasn't helping.

I kept waiting for the horrible feeling to go away, but it didn't. At night I dreamed about éclairs. Hunger pangs woke me, traveling through my body like the reverberations of a bell. I held my hands over my ears and rolled back and forth in bed, hoping the sensations would go away.

Between meals, I dealt with my hunger by dipping lettuce leaves into mustard (a tip from Gladys), which was practically a zero-calorie snack, about as effective as eating air. Still, it gave me something to chew and swallow. Gladys's other tips for fighting hunger included doing jumping jacks, even in public places, drinking liters of water, and writing in my food journal:

> 1. After eating, I feel: Very satisfied, somewhat satisfied, hungry, or starving: _starving_
> 2. My mood right now is: Positive, neutral, discouraged, or irritable: _positive_
> 3. Today I am thinking about food: Only at mealtimes, occasionally, or constantly: _constantly_

On the Baptist Plan, I nearly passed out from hunger. Once in the kitchen, I was slicing a bell pepper, but then there were two on my cutting board, then three. They were multiplying. I set down my knife and stumbled backwards, bumping the handle of a skillet on the stove, sending hot oil and scallops crashing to the floor. Elsa insisted I go home, but I went back to my peppers, trying to chop while my hands shook.[7]

7. Memorandum: From senior vice president [name redacted] to [name redacted] cc: Eulayla Baptist (February 3, 1982): "Pay attention, [name redacted], we're not going to get sued! (That lady in Tucson notwithstanding.) 850 calories a day is adequate for human survival. Ignore those World

I wanted to stuff myself with the food that surrounded me in the restaurant, but in my mind I pleaded with my hungry self to be sensible. Nicolette's mother, a Waist Watchers obsessive and borderline anorexic, had a bumper sticker on her car that read NOTHING TASTES AS GOOD AS SKINNY FEELS. I didn't know how it felt to be skinny, but if I ate the pink trays of food and the packaged snacks and nothing more, I would find out in only nine months. The fact that my misery had an end date, a parole date, kept me going. Once or twice I thought about jumping off the roof of the restaurant, but I kept these fantasies to myself.

When I returned to the house on Harper Lane after work, I ate my dinner quickly and crawled into bed, since being awake was torturous. In the morning I would try to soothe myself with a hot shower, but I grew increasingly worried as the drain filled with clumps of my hair.

At the Baptist clinic, Gladys would say,

Health Organization stats. There's a big difference between a starving African and a fat American. Besides, our literature says it's a 1,200 calorie-a-day regimen, which is perfectly safe." (*Adventures in Dietland,* Baptist Weight Loss Internal Memo Index, p. 333.)

"You must have been good this week!"[8] She and the other women were interested in my progress, pulling up my shirt to get a better look at my hips and tummy. The weigh-in was the highlight of my week. I was good for a whole month and lost twenty-nine pounds.

When July came, my father sent my yearly airline ticket, Los Angeles to Boise, but I told him I couldn't visit. There was no way for me to transport my Baptist frozen meals, and I couldn't eat normal food. "You're not coming to visit me because of a *diet*?"

8. Memorandum: From senior vice president [name redacted] to Eulayla Baptist (November 12, 1985): "I cannot emphasize enough the importance of using moral terms when talking about dieting to our clients and the media. The Baptist name makes this even more effective. When Baptists lose weight, they're 'good'; when they stray from the plan, they're 'bad,' as in: 'Were you good or bad this week, Rosemary?' Every clinic must implement this language immediately." (*Adventures in Dietland*, Baptist Weight Loss Internal Memo Index, p. 337. N.B. See also D. Montrose, "American Dieting Culture and Its Roots in the Christian Narrative," *Journal of Weight Loss Studies* 1, no. 2 [1999]: 124–46.)

"I can't, Daddy. You'll be proud of me when this is finished, I promise." I was his only child. He had married again, but his new wife couldn't have children, so I was his only hope for grandkids. If I was fat, no one would want to marry me. I wanted to tell him this, to explain that this wasn't just a *diet,* that everything in my future and his depended on it, but I couldn't say the words.

With my summer cleared of all obligations except for my job at the restaurant, I spent most of my time alone at home. When I went out, I didn't have the energy to care if people took photographs of me. Nicolette invited me to the mall and to movies, but I couldn't be surrounded by such fattening food. Every evening at the restaurant I was exposed to non-Baptist food, and those were the worst two hours of my day.

In our weekly meetings, Gladys expressed her worries about my job. "You need to separate yourself from temptation, Miss Kettle."

"If I don't work at the restaurant I can't afford to be a Baptist."

"Well, we don't want *that,*" Gladys said. There was a newspaper on her desk and she began to look through the classifieds to help me find a job that didn't involve food.

"Here's an ad for a dog walker."

"I don't have the energy to walk."

"Babysitting?"

I imagined being passed out from hunger on the kitchen floor and a toddler with a phone, trying to dial 911.

"No, I'm better off at the restaurant. I can handle it."

Except that I couldn't. One evening I had to stir a massive pot of macaroni and cheese, then serve it up on plates for thirty-four children celebrating a birthday. There must have been thousands of pasta tubes in the pot, glistening in the gluey cheese. The intoxicating smell filled my nose and my mouth, even penetrating my brain and wrapping its orange tentacles around every conscious thought. *Nothing tastes as good as skinny feels,* that's what I told myself. I wondered how many calories were in the pot. A hundred thousand? A million? The thought was repulsive.

When the plates came back to the kitchen, a few of them were scraped clean, but there were many with lumps of macaroni and cheese stuck to them. A few of the plates looked as if they hadn't been touched. The dishes were lined on the counter, waiting for Luis to clean them, but he had gone out back for a smoke.

I paced in front of the plates, looking around to see if anyone was watching me. With my fingers I scooped up some of the pasta tubes and placed them on my tongue. It was the first real food I'd had in more than a month. The texture was different, like cashmere instead of a scratchy polyester.

After the initial moments of bliss, the gravity of what I was doing began to spread over me in a feverish heat. I ran to the bathroom and spit the glob of food into the toilet, my eyes filling with tears. Stupid, stupid, stupid. Gladys had given me pamphlets on every eventuality: *Dieting After the Death of a Loved One* and *The Dangers of Carnivals, Circuses, and Fairs.* I had piles of these pamphlets, but they hadn't been powerful enough to restrain me against the siren song of pasta and melted cheese. In the face of that, I decided I'd done well. I hadn't even swallowed.

I started wanting to call in sick to work. I *was* sick, or at least I felt that way practically every moment of the day, but I couldn't admit it. That would have given my mother a sense of satisfaction. If I told her how I felt she would try to ban me from Baptist Weight Loss. I began to worry about what would happen when school started and whether my grades would suffer, but I decided that I wouldn't think that far ahead.

At work I continued to pick scraps off plates, delighting in the taste and then spitting the food out in the toilet or into a paper towel. Sometimes, though, when Luis was in the alley, I'd eat a few french fries off dirty plates, chewing and then swallowing. Just a few in my belly eased the pain in my head.

On the night of a retirement party, I worked extra hours to help Chef Elsa prep. The woman who did the baking in the restaurant had prepared macaroons earlier in the day, which Elsa asked me to arrange on platters. Alone in the kitchen, my hands sheathed in crinkly plastic gloves, I stacked the macaroons in a pyramid formation. Six weeks of systematic starvation had weakened me. For every macaroon that made it onto the platters, another went into my apron pocket. When I finished, Delia took the macaroons into the dining room, noticing neither the slightness of the pyramids nor the bulges in my pockets.

I went to the bathroom, but two waitresses were there, styling their hair and putting on makeup, so I went into the back alley and sat down on the concrete steps next to the trash cans. When my hand first grazed the macaroons in my pocket, I could have stopped for a moment and used my training; I could have written in my food journal or done jumping jacks, but I didn't. One macaroon slipped into my mouth, and then two, and then as many as would fit. I consumed them so hurriedly that at first I didn't enjoy the shock of creamy coconut against my tongue. I stuffed three macaroons into my mouth before stopping to catch my breath, and then I made room for two more. My face flushed and burned and I began to cry. I knew what I was doing was wrong, but I couldn't eat the macaroons fast enough. A ball of coconut formed in my throat. I paused to swallow, then continued working through my stash, wiping my nose with my sleeve as I chewed. I was still wearing plastic gloves. I felt like a criminal.

As I swallowed the last cookie, my face stained with tears and mascara, I saw Luis and Eduardo nearby in the alley, smoking. I didn't know how long they had been there. They were looking at me — they had seen.

After so many weeks without much food, my stomach, shriveled like a raisin, was struggling to absorb the explosion of calories. I felt a sharp pain at my center as I made my way home. I expected to be sick, but once the pain was gone, I felt better than I had in ages. My headache disappeared. I had grown so accustomed to having a headache that not having one felt strange; there was a feeling of release, as if a belt that had been fastened tightly around my head was suddenly loosened. I slept through the night for the first time since becoming a Baptist.

The next day when I awoke, the hunger was there again. I had slept late and missed breakfast, so I drank two Baptist Shakes, but they didn't satisfy my hunger beast, and when he wasn't satisfied he gnawed at me. I couldn't bear being trapped in the house with him and decided to eat my dinner, though it was only one o'clock. Then I ate a second dinner, then drank another shake; then I heated up a Baptist pizza, which was just shavings of plastic cheese on a crust as thin as matzo. The kitchen counter was littered with empty pink trays and bottles and pieces of silver plastic, which were gummy and stuck to the countertops. I gathered up the evidence and took it outside to the garbage can so that no one would find out. As I made my way back into the house, I saw a woman with a camera pointed at me. She had seen.

I didn't feel full or happy after my binge. With the macaroons, I'd had a taste of real food, and now I wanted more. I called Nicolette. "I thought you were dead," she said. That's what people had said about Eulayla Baptist, too.

"I'm not dead, I've just been removed from the world of food." We went to the mall, Nicolette's mother driving us in her gold Mercedes with her bumper sticker: NOTHING TASTES AS GOOD AS SKINNY FEELS. Nicolette could eat whatever she wanted and never gain weight — that's why her mother hated her, she said. At the mall, we ate chili dogs and nachos with extra jalapeños and washed it all down with sugary cherry lemonade. We bought soft pretzels and funnel cakes dusted with powdered sugar and ate it all. We made a point of browsing CDs and shoes, but we were only at the mall for the food.

Before leaving, I bought half a dozen donuts from Winchell's to take home, topped with white icing and rainbow sprinkles.

After bingeing on donuts at 2 a.m., I feel:
euphoric

At my next meeting with Gladys, filled with guilt, I confessed everything. She held my hand, urging me to find the strength to transcend my bodily cravings. "A Baptist isn't afraid to admit she failed," Gladys said, "but a Baptist never loses faith in herself either." As I listened to her, it almost seemed possible. She gave me a pamphlet with Eulayla on the cover, entitled "I Don't Want to Be Thin — I Choose Health!"[9] There were sections on high blood pressure,

9. Memorandum: From senior vice president [name redacted] to Eulayla Baptist (February 14, 1998): "Pursuant to our last meeting, those fat feminist cunts in Michigan with their 'Love Your Body' bullshit are still chanting outside our clinic in Ann Arbor. This movement cannot be allowed to spread. We'll counter them with our health jargon (did you approve those pamphlets yet?). They won't be able to refute our death stats with their feel-good crap. We might want to get a couple MD-for-hire types on the payroll to farm out to the media. That cardio guy in Miami would be perfect for this. Can you authorize payment, please?" (*Adventures in Dietland,* Baptist Weight Loss Internal Memo Index, p. 351. N.B. See also A. Adamson, G. Hoyt, and O. Rodgers, " 'I Don't Want to Be Thin — I Choose Health!': Baptist Weight Loss Advertising and the Birth of Obesity Epidemic Rhetoric," *Eating Disorder Quarterly* 14, no. 7 [2004]: 97–119.)

diabetes, and heart disease. Gladys said I was at risk for all these diseases if I quit the Baptist Plan. "Do you want to die before you're forty, hon?" She told me about her sister who was the same size as me and infertile.

I cried as Gladys weighed me and I discovered I had already gained back half the weight. All of the suffering I'd endured was for nothing and the new life I'd envisioned was slipping away, all because I was a pig. I resolved to do better and become a good Baptist again. I wasn't going to meet my goal weight on schedule, but Gladys assured me this was normal, that it happened to everyone, including her.[10]

The Baptist lifestyle consumed me again. I hid in my bedroom, accepted feeling sick, avoided my friend, and in my head repeated the phrase *the pink trays, the pink trays,* like

10. Memorandum: From [name redacted] to senior vice president [name redacted], cc: Eulayla Baptist (March 1, 1990): "Did you get that memo from the lawyer? She says the 'Results Not Typical' disclaimer on our posters of Eulayla needs to appear in much larger font. Christ, is there any way around this? We don't want people to notice it." (*Adventures in Dietland,* Baptist Weight Loss Internal Memo Index, p. 357.)

a mantra, reminding myself that if I only ate what was in the pink trays and nothing more, I would become thin and I wouldn't die before age forty.

Each week as I left the clinic with my pink trays and shakes, I promised myself I'd be good. But it didn't matter. I wouldn't remain a Baptist for much longer.

When I arrived at the clinic one afternoon, the women were crying. A distraught Gladys told me that Eulayla Baptist and her husband had been killed in a car accident in Atlanta. "There was a rainstorm," Gladys managed to say. "They lost control of the car. *She's gone.*"

I looked at the poster of Eulayla holding up her fat jeans. "*Gone?* You mean *forever*? That's impossible." I steadied myself against a chair.

Within days, Gladys called with the bad news. "Eulayla's daughter is shutting us down," she said through her sobs. "The company is closed. We're finished."

I went immediately to the clinic with the intention of hoarding food, but when I got there the doors were already padlocked. There was no sign of Gladys or any of the other staff. "No," I cried, pounding on the doors. Other women milled around on the sidewalk, gaunt and dejected, probably on the verge of meltdowns but too weak for histrionics.

"Why?" howled one of the distraught women, placing her hands on my shoulders. "Why does Eulayla's daughter hate us?"

When I arrived home, my mother was sitting on the front steps, peeling an orange. I sat down next to her.

"What's wrong?"

"No more Baptist Weight Loss. Eulayla's daughter closed all the clinics."

"Good for her."

I watched my mother drop the curls of rind onto the ground between her feet. I was in mourning and she was nothing but pleased. From my bag, I pulled the *before* picture that Gladys had taken of me. I was twenty-five pounds lighter than that, but still fat. School was starting soon, and without the Baptist clinic, my plans for my last year of high school and then college in Vermont were going to unravel. I feared I would stay a *before* picture forever.

A vintage car stopped in front of the house, probably from the 1960s, small and black like a bug. A man sat in the driver's seat and next to him a teenage girl, who stepped out of the car with a camera. She stood on the sidewalk before my mother and me and raised the camera to her eye. They were always going to be looking at me. That was my destiny.

"Go away," I screamed, rising to my feet. The girl turned back toward the car and raced to open the door. As it sputtered away I chased after it, grabbing the lid off one of our metal trash cans as I leapt off the curb, hurling it into the middle of the street and letting out a roar. It landed in the street with a cymbal crash, rumbling the pavement where I stood. The car disappeared around the bend at the end of the road.

When I turned around, my mother was standing on the sidewalk in front of the house.

"Plum?"

I faced her from the street, standing where the starers normally stood, a brief moment of reversal. The house was nothing special from the outside, but I had lived there for much of my life. If the photos from all the tourists were collected and placed in chronological order, I could have flipped through them to see the girl under the tree become a young woman, one who grew larger and larger, moving into the house, standing behind the curtain — half in the frame, then nothing but shadow.

■ ■ ■ ■

DRINK ME

■ ■ ■ ■

Two days after finding *Adventures in Diet-land* at Kitty's office, I had nearly finished reading it. I should have been at the café answering messages, but I'd abandoned my work for the book. I soaked in a bath while reading, careful not to dampen the custard-colored pages.

Twelve years had passed since I was a Baptist. I had rarely thought of that time over the years, but as I read, the memories of the Baptist Plan came alive in my mind. I could taste the food: the metallic, watered-down tomato of the pizza and pasta, the casseroles that tasted the way carpet cleaner smells. I remembered the Baptist Shakes, their chalky texture, their medicinal, sour aftertaste. When the company closed, I knew only the most superficial details: Verena Baptist inherited the company and as the sole shareholder she had the power to shut it down, which she did within days of her parents' fiery car crash. I had hated Eulayla Baptist's daughter then, but I had never known her name. Now, thanks to the girl, I held her words in my hands.

Verena wrote that after she closed the company, she was left with "gallons of Baptist Shakes, vats of beef stew, and truckloads of chicken breasts slathered in a mysterious goo," all of which were given to soup kitchens and homeless shelters, "to people who were starving by no choice of their own." Verena described this as an act of charity, and I supposed the Baptist meals were slightly better than nothing.

I couldn't help but feel disgusted and angry while reading about Eulayla Baptist. Like all Baptists, I'd been destined to fail, but I blamed myself when I did. I may have hated Eulayla's daughter once, but as I read the book I was glad that she'd exposed her mother. I knew my failure as a Baptist wasn't my fault.

I did wonder why Verena turned on her mother so publicly. Verena slipped through the pages of the book for the most part, but in the first paragraph she was there, most tellingly: "Before my birth, Mama was a slim young bride. She and Daddy set up house in Atlanta and for one shining year things couldn't have been better. Then one tipsy night after martinis on the veranda with the Ambersons from across the street, Daddy impregnated Mama with a bomb that took nine months to blow up, leaving her fat and scarred, with stretch marks and a waistline that looked like an inner tube."

That bomb was Verena. She had ruined her mother's figure, which led to an obsession with dieting, which led to the horror of Baptist Weight Loss being inflicted on the world. I wondered if this was why Verena had decided to disgrace her dead mother in print and reveal her secrets: She'd been made to feel guilty for being born.

The book wasn't only about Baptist Weight Loss. Verena attempted to expose the entire weight-loss industry. She wrote extensively about the many weight-loss authors and gurus, diet drugs, even the surgery I was planning to have. She devoted a whole chapter to liberating oneself from what she called Dietland. "Dietland is about making women small," Verena wrote. I thought my mother would enjoy her book. I was sure she would have sent me a copy if she knew of its existence.

Inside the book were photographs of Eulayla, one from her beauty queen days and another from her fat years, as well as the famous photo of thin Eulayla holding up her fat jeans. In one photo, her face was taut and her legs were slim, but she was still slightly roomy in the hips. I looked at the photo and thought that in death, Eulayla had finally achieved what had eluded her in life. As a corpse she was as thin as she could ever hope to be. Just skin and bones, I imagined.

There was a short author bio on the back of the book: "Verena Baptist lives in New York City, where she manages Calliope House, a feminist organization." That was it. There was no photograph of her, no way to put a face to the name of the woman whom I had once hated so much for ruining my dream.

I closed the book and tossed it onto the bathroom floor, not wanting to think of my Baptist days any longer. After I was forced off the Baptist Plan, I spent most of my senior year of high school eating. I couldn't stop. At Delia's restaurant I served as an apprentice to the woman who did the baking, and I gorged on cakes and cookies and pies. By the time I started college I had gained back all the pounds I'd lost and added many more. In college I joined Waist Watchers, since they held meetings right on campus. When I became disillusioned with their program I followed the diet plans outlined in books and magazines. I took diet pills, including one that was later recalled by the FDA after several people died. I took a supplement from a company in Mexico, but gave it up after it caused violent stomach pains. For all of my junior year, I drank a chocolate diet shake for breakfast and lunch, which turned my bowel movements into stones, causing hemorrhoids, and which tasted even worse than the Baptist Shakes had tasted. I was too squeamish for bulimia and lacked the masochism needed for anorexia, so once I had cycled through every diet I could find, I went back to Waist Watchers.

In the years that had passed since I'd joined Baptist Weight Loss, I'd gained nearly a hundred pounds. After reading *Adventures in Dietland,* I felt certain that surgery was the right option for me. Verena would have been horrified by this response, since she railed against weight-loss surgery except in life-threatening situations, but her intentions in writing the book didn't matter. She had proven that dieting doesn't work. I was grateful to her for that.

The memories exhausted me, and I relaxed for a while in the tub, the water lukewarm but not unpleasant. I no longer thought the girl was trying to be mean by giving me Verena's book, but I still didn't know what she wanted. When the phone started ringing, I didn't want to get out of the water. Whoever it was didn't leave a message, but a few minutes later the ringing started again. Annoyed, I left the bath and stomped naked down the hallway, leaving pools of water behind me on the floor.

"Is this Ms. Kettle?"

"Yes."

"Is this Plum?"

"Who is this?"

"This is Erica calling from Austen Human Resources. We need you to come to the office on Monday at ten a.m. to sign a form."

"What form?"

"A form you need to sign. There's a problem with your health insurance."

"All right," I said, irritated at the thought of another trip to Manhattan.

"Please come to the Human Resources office on the twenty-seventh floor. Thank you, goodbye."

Austen Media was the furthest thing from my mind. Since starting Verena's book I had ignored Kitty's girls. They were trapped inside my laptop — a Pandora's box I refused to open.

On the twenty-seventh floor of the Austen Tower, I stepped off the elevator and walked down a long carpeted corridor. At the end was a floor-to-ceiling window, revealing the breadth of midtown Manhattan in a blaze of sunlight. The corridor was like a diving board perched above a sea of buildings. I placed my toes and forehead against the glass and looked down at the streets below.

Erica, the woman who'd pestered me on the phone, greeted me in the Human Resources office. She produced a clipboard with a form that had the logo of Tri-State Health at the top. "Please read this and sign," she said, sitting next to me in the waiting area. The form contained little content and only asked me to confirm the insurance plan I'd chosen when I began working for Kitty.

"Terrific," Erica said when I handed the clipboard back to her. "I'll walk you to the elevator."

"That's it? I came all the way from Brooklyn."

"You don't want your insurance to expire, do you?"

I wanted to reply to her in the same snotty tone, but it wasn't worth it. I gathered my things and she escorted me out of the office, which I thought was unnecessary.

As we waited for the elevator, I looked out the window and thought of the diving board again. The idea of lifting off, of diving into midtown, absorbed me until I heard a crinkling sound. The corridor was so bright that I had to strain to see that Erica had removed my insurance form from the clipboard and was stuffing it into the mouth of a trash can.

"Hey, that's my form."

"Go to Basement Two," she whispered. "B-Two. You'll have to change elevators at the lobby."

"What's going on?"

She held her arm between the elevator doors, preventing them from closing. "Go on, hurry up. I have to get back to work."

I was in the elevator and descending, my vision splotchy from the sunlight, when only one thing came to mind: the girl.

In the lobby, I hesitated, but then couldn't

resist finding out what was going to happen if I followed Erica's directions. I looked for the bank of elevators that would take me to B2. When I reached the basement, two floors beneath the Austen Tower, I was standing before a set of double doors, a tarnished silver portal with a sign attached to it that read BEAUTY CLOSET. There was a keypad to the right of the doors, and a button, like a doorbell.

The elevator doors closed behind me. I stepped to the silver doors and rang the bell. A number of seconds passed, but there was no sound or hint of a human being on the other side.

I was about to ring the bell again when I heard the faintest noise. I pressed my ear to the door. *Click-clop, click-clop.* The sound grew steadily louder. *Click-clop, click-clop,* like a horse in a Western film. *Click-clop.* I listened for a minute longer and realized it was the sound of someone wearing high heels, approaching from a great distance. *Click-clop.*

"Coming," a voice called, and then one of the doors opened slightly and a head popped out. "I am Julia Cole, manager of the Beauty Closet. How may I help you?"

"I'm Plum. I don't know why I'm here."

The woman opened the door, allowing me

entry, but she didn't speak. I stepped inside and what I saw made me gasp. The Beauty Closet was hardly a *closet*. You could easily fit a 747 inside it, perhaps two. For as far as I could see were steel shelves reaching to unknown heights, with blinding lights overhead; it was like a supermarket on the grand scale of a temple constructed by the Babylonians. Ladders on wheels were positioned in each aisle, extending so high that the tops of them were whited out by the lights, as if they were ascending into the sky. There were signs at the end of each aisle — LIPS, LIDS, LASHES, HAIR, and so on — and each shelf was lined with black lacquered trays filled with products.

"You call this a *closet*?"

The woman stood before me, wearing a silky mauve blouse and cream-colored slacks that ended just above her ankles, with heels on her feet. Around her slender waist was a black canvas tool belt, filled with brushes and tubes of lipstick.

"For you," she said, handing me a metallic tube. On the bottom it said, "Juicy Plum."

Julia motioned for me to follow her. We walked down the Lips aisle, which was subdivided into sections for lipstick, gloss, liner, and balm; each of these sections was subdivided by color, with swatches on display, like the inside of a paint store. Taped to one of the shelves was a handwritten sign: LIPS: MINORA AND MAJORA, with an explicit illustration of a vulva. "Just a little humor," Julia said when she saw me looking.

In the middle of the aisle were two stools on wheels, where Julia and I sat. "To answer your question, we call this the Beauty Closet for old times' sake. When the Austen Corporation was founded on this site in 1928, Cornelius Austen's daughter was put in charge of organizing the cosmetics for the two fashion magazines Austen published at that time. It was just a way to keep her busy until she found a husband. She was well liked, always offering tea to those who visited her in the closet. The Beauty Closet became an Austen tradition."

Julia adjusted her tool belt to prevent some makeup brushes from slipping out. Above her head was a shelf labeled LIPSTICK/MATTE/BURGUNDY.003LMB. I wondered if Julia had devised this Dewey Decimal System for cosmetics.

"What's all this makeup for?"

"There are fifty-two stories on top of us. We publish nine fashion magazines, known collectively as the Nine Muses, as you know, and we also produce many television programs and all sorts of other things. There are a lot of women on our pages and on our air, and all of them need makeup. That's what we provide here."

I glanced around, trying to take it in, and shivering slightly.

"It's chilly in here so the makeup doesn't melt. I'm used to it by now," she said. "Before we go any further, you must agree that what I say to you here is confidential."

I nodded.

Julia reached into her belt and withdrew a folded paper. "On May eleventh, writing under an assumed name, I sent this message through the Dear Kitty portal of the *Daisy Chain* website: *Dear Kitty, I consider you to be one of the great intellectual minds of our time, so I would like to ask you a question. Who is more oppressed — a woman covered from head to toe in a burka or one of the bikini-clad models in your magazine?*"

I thought for a moment, and then the memory of it swam to the surface. "I remember. That wasn't the usual type of message."

Julia continued. "Three days later, I received this reply: *It pleases me that you think about such issues. I don't normally receive messages from girls like you! You pose an interesting question, one that I'm not sure I can answer. One woman covers her body, while the other exposes herself. You could think of it as two sides of the same coin. Thanks for writing to me!"*

Julia folded the paper and slipped it back into her tool belt. Hearing her read the words of Plum-as-Kitty made me self-conscious.

"I knew this message was not written by Kitty. I had no expectation that she would reply personally, of course, but it was immediately clear that this message was not written by the regular sort of person Kitty would hire, one of the beauty bots who make up her staff. I wanted to find out who had written this message, which wasn't difficult. I called her assistant, Eladio, who blabbed all in a matter of minutes. Once I knew who you were, and that you worked from home, I sent Leeta to learn about you. She's my intern. I lured her away from *Glamour Bride* last fall."

Leeta. At last, she had a name. "She doesn't strike me as the *Glamour Bride* type," I said, envisioning the combat boots and scary makeup.

"She has no interest in glamour or brides, I can assure you. Her internship there was purely a means to an end."

"Is she here?" I hoped that she wasn't. She knew too much about me. She had seen.

"Leeta had to go out of town unexpectedly. Now, let me take this opportunity to apologize for her behavior. Yes, I sent her to follow you, but you must understand that the work I do here is highly sensitive. I wanted Leeta to scope you out, to get an idea of your daily routine, to see if she could tell what kind of person you are. I can't trust just anybody, and I wanted Leeta to see if you'd be friendly to our cause."

"What cause?"

"My point is that after speaking with Leeta and reading the journal she kept, I fear that she might have behaved inappropriately, that she might have intruded upon your life and . . . unsettled you." Julia reached deep into her tool belt and withdrew the red spiral notebook that Leeta always wrote in while she was following me.

"Let me see that," I said, grabbing for the notebook, but Julia put it back in her tool belt.

Rebuffed, I said: "I could have called the police."

"Then why didn't you?"

I had no good answer.

"Again, I'm sorry for what happened," she

said. "You weren't supposed to notice Leeta."

"But sending her to spy is okay?"

"She was not spying. She was getting to know you."

"Without my knowledge?"

"In the beginning, yes."

I wondered if I was the victim of a practical joke. If so, Julia was quite an actor. "Why did she give me Verena Baptist's book?"

"Leeta took it upon herself to do that. She grew fond of you and wanted to reach out. She thought you might appreciate the message of the book."

"Do you know Verena?"

The doorbell rang. Julia was startled and slid back her chair, hitting the shelf behind her; tubes of lipsticks rained on her head and spilled all over the floor. "Shit," she said. "Come with me." Julia ran in a trot toward the entrance, as fast as she could in the heels. Someone was banging on the door. "It's Tamryn Suarez-O'Brien," a woman shouted. "Is anyone in there? Open this door!"

"She's a producer on *Lingerie Live,*" Julia whispered to me.

Tamryn Suarez-O'Brien teetered into the closet on purple snakeskin heels, drumming the fingers of her right hand on her enormous pregnant belly. "What took you so long? You know I can't stand up for very long," she said to Julia, but she was looking at me.

"Who are you?" Tamryn rolled her eyes over me.

"She works for Kitty," Julia said. "She came down to get some lipstick."

"Yeah, well, I hate to pull rank, but I need some perfume and I can't wait. All morning I've smelled something horrible. You know, *BO.* I was wondering who it was that smelled so bad, then I realized it was me."

Julia led Tamryn to the perfumes, leaving me alone. I picked up the clipboard hanging at the end of the Lips aisle:

[New Arrivals — Week of June 4, 2012]
Afghan Red.00379 All Night Long.00380
Amaretto.00381 Amber Rose.00382
Amorous. 00383 Angel.00384 Apache
Red.00385 Apple Brandy.00386 Arabian
Night.00387 Areola.00388 Aroused.00389
Baby Doll.00390 Baby's Bottom.00391
Baked Earth.00392 Bare.00393 Beauty
Queen.00394 Beige Beauty.00395 Belle
de Jour.00396 Bitchy.00397 Bite
Me.00398 Black Honey.00399
Blackberry.00400 Blaze.00401
Bleed.00402 Blonde Honey.00403 Blonde

Venus.00404 Blood Red.00405 Bloomin'
Pink.00406 Blush.00407 Blushing
Rose.00408 Bohemian Bronze.00409
Brandy.00410 Brownest. 00411 Bruised
Algerian.00412 Bubblegum.00413
Burgundy Babe.00414
Butterscotch.00415 Buzzkill.00416
C-Word.00417 Café Crème.00418 Candy
Apple.00419 Catfight.00420 Cheery
Cherry.00421 Cherry.00422 Cherry
Bomb.00423 Cherry Popper. 00424
Cherry Red.00425 Cherrywood.00426
Chili.00427 Cinnamon.00428 Cinnamon
Rose.00429 Cobweb.00430 Cocktease.
00431 Coconut.00432 Coffee
Addict.00433 Cola.00434 Copper
Coin.00435 Copper Dust.00436 Coral
Rose.00437 Corpse.00438
Cosmopolitan.00439 Cotton Candy.00440
Cranberry.00441 Crème Brûlée.00442
Crush.00443 Crushed Berry.00444
Daddy's Girl.00445 Dark Diva.00446 Dark
Side.00447 Decay.00448 Deep
Coral.00449 Devil Woman.00450
Diva.00451 Do It to Me.00452 Dolce
Vita.00453 Dominatrix.00454 Dreamy
Peach.00455 Dusty Rose.00456 Edible
Rose.00457 Empowered.00458 F**k
Me.00459 Fairest One.00460 Fire
Engine.00461 Flame.00462 Flesh.00463

Forbidden. 00464 Foreplay.00465
Freckle.00466 Fresh Moroccan.00467
Frosted Grape.00468 Gash.00469 Girl
Trouble.00470 Girlish.00471 Girly.00472
Gold Digger.00473 Gold Dust.00474
Grape.00475 Guava Kiss.00476 Harlow
Gold.00477 Hit Me.00478 Honeyflower.
00479 Honeyplum Glow.00480 Hot
Pink.00481 Hussy.00482 I'm Easy.00483
Indecent.00484 Ingenue.00485
Jailbait.00486 Jilted.00487 Juicy.00488
Jungle Red.00489 Just Peachy.00490
Just Red.00491 Kiss of Death.00493 Kiss
Me.00492 Kitten.00494 Lady Like.00495
Lickable.00496 Lolita.00497 Lusty
Lady.00498 Maiden.00499 Maple
Sugar.00500 Marilyn.00501
Menstrual.00502 Merlot.00503 Mexican
Spice.00504 Misfit.00505 Mocha
Honey.00506 Mocha Maiden.00507
Mocha Mama.00508 Mochalicious.00509
Moll.00510 Moulin Rouge.00511 Nail
Me.00512 Naughty Girl.00513 Nearly
Red.00514 Nipple.00515 Only Pink.00516
Orgasm.00517 Pale Pink.00518 Parole
Violator.00519 Perfect Plum.00520
Peroxide. 00521 Perv.00522
Pigalle.00523 Pink Berry.00524 Pink
Burst.00525 Pink Champagne.00526 Pink
Flamingo.00527 Pink Heart.00528 Pink

Lemonade.00529 Pink Parts.00530 Pink Princess. 00531 Pink Rose.00532 Pink Sugar.00533 Pinkapalooza.00534 Pinkest.00535 Plum Brandy.00536 Plum Nude.00537 Plum Passion. 00538 Plum Rose.00539 Pomegranate.00540 Porn Star.00541 Pretty in Pink.00542 Prey.00543 Princess.00544 Punk.00545 Pussy Galore.00546 Raisin 'n' Rose.00547 Ramblin' Rose.00548 Raspberry Kiss.00549 Raspberry Swoon.00550 Rated X.00551 Raven.00552 Ravishing Red.00553 Red Apple.00554 Red Devil.00555 Red Grape.00556 Red Indian.00557 Red Lizard.00558 Red Queen.00559 Red Rage.00560 Red Roses.00561 Red Rubies.00562 Red Scare.00563 Red Sherry.00564 Red Velvet.00565 Red Wine.00566 Reddest.00567 Rockin' Raisin.00568 Roman Holiday.00569 Rose Blush.00570 Rose Bouquet.00571 Rose Lust.00572 Rose Pink.00573 Rose Red.00574 Rouge.00575 Ruby.00576 Ruby Addict.00577 Ruby Kiss.00578 Rum Honey.00579 Sangria.00580 Scarlet Diva.00581 Scarlet Harlot.00582 Scheherazade.00583 Screw Me.00584 Seeing Red.00585 Sex Me.00586 Sex Offender.00587 Sexy.00588 Shrinking

Violet.00589 Silver Haze.00590 Silver
Moon.00591 Skinny Rose.00592 Sleeping
Beauty.00593 Slutzilla.00594 Smack Dat
Bitch.00595 Spice.00596 Spicy
Apple.00597 Spicy Ginger.00598
Spiderwoman.00599 Starlet.00600
Statutory.00601 Stiletto.00602
Stoplight.00603 Strawberry Kisses.00604
Sugar Plum.00605 Sugared Violet.00606
Sun Kissed.00607 Sunlight.00608
Swollen Angel.0069 Tease.00610
Temptress.00611 Tequila Blossom.00612
That's Amoré.00613 Tickled Pink.00614
Tigerlily.00615 Toasted Citrus. 00616
Tramp.00617 Turkish Delight.00618
Underage Red.00619 Vamp.00620
Violated.00621 Virgin Scary.00622 Violet
Goddess. 00623 Violet Vixen.00624
Vixen.00625 Volcanic Violet.00626
Voodoo Mama.00627 Voodoo
Queen.00628 Watermelon.00629
Wedding Night.00630 Whisky Rose.00631
White Girl.00632 Wicked.00633 Wild
Thing.00634 Wine-oh!.00635
Wounded.00636 Zombie.00637

Tamryn emerged with the desired bottle
of perfume. "It sucks being pregnant," she
said as Julia escorted her out of the closet.
When Tamryn was gone, Julia rested her

forehead on the back of the doors, closed her eyes, and said, "Cunt."

She turned to me. "Two years ago I got my Ph.D. in women's studies. No one in this place thinks anything of the fact that I have a doctorate from a prestigious university but now I sort lipstick and mascara in a windowless closet all day. Look at me," Julia said. "These clothes, these shoes, the highlights in my hair. Please understand that I would never dress this way." Julia was flushed and sweaty despite the chilled air. She wiped her forehead and fanned herself, then adjusted her tool belt again. Her skin was pale and there were dark circles under her eyes, probably from spending her days in a subterranean closet, away from the sunlight. She looked like someone who worked in some sort of fashion-forward coal mine.

"What does Verena Baptist have to do with this?" I asked again.

"Nothing," she said, taking the clipboard from me and putting it back on the hook. "No more questions right now." She moved toward me. "Stand against the wall," she whispered, nudging me back until I was up against the cool cinderblock. We were the same height and stood eye to eye. Julia's hair, brown with caramel highlights, fell to her shoulders in scoops. She placed her hand on my chin and tilted my head back. "Open your mouth," she said.

"Huh?"

"Just do it." With her right hand, she rummaged through her tool belt. Soon I felt a pencil tracing around my O-shaped mouth; it was hard at first, then grew softer. I could feel Julia's breath on my neck as she finished by applying lipstick.

"This color suits you. Your skin is white as a rose." I blushed. "Doesn't anyone ever tell you you're beautiful?" I looked away, but Julia pulled my chin toward her.

"What color are your nipples?" she asked.

"Huh?"

"Your nipples. What color are they?"

No one had ever asked me that before. "Pink."

Julia pulled a compact from her tool belt and opened it up. I looked at the palette of pink blusher. "Lighter than that." Julia reached into her tool belt again and showed me another palette, this one of the palest pink. "Like that."

Julia took a brush and dusted the powder across my cheeks. The brush fell to the floor and she bent over to pick it up. Inside her blouse, I could see she had roses with thorns tattooed all over her chest.

"Now close your eyes," she said. Something tickly and soft, like the tip of a feather, moved across my eyelids. When she finished, I opened my eyes. Julia stood back to observe me.

"All makeup is drag," she said, and folded her arms.

"Why am I here?"

Julia paced in her heels, biting on the wooden end of a brush. "You could go to Kitty right now and tell her about me and then I'd be ruined."

"Tell her what? I don't know anything."

Julia considered this. "Leeta thinks you can be trusted. I want you to do something."

For Shonda

The men were alive when they were placed inside the brown canvas bags. Two men, two bags. During the night, the bags were dropped from the Harbor Freeway interchange, the tallest in Southern California. The bodies fell from the transition road all the way down to the Century Freeway. The drop would have surely killed them, the authorities later said.

Over the next several hours, the bags were hit and dragged by speeding cars and trucks. A highway patrolman spotted one of the bags and called to report a dead animal on the side of the road. Something brown and massive, he said. It wasn't his job to stop.

An hour later a road crew arrived, two crew veterans and a young rap star named Jayson Fox who was doing community service. One night in his Hollywood Hills home, Jayson Fox had beat up his girlfriend, a famous model. The police photos of the battered model's face were leaked online. Jayson Fox's punishment was a short stint in the L.A. County jail followed by this: wearing a khaki jumpsuit and riding around in a dirty City of Los Angeles truck, sitting between two burly men with bad prostates, picking up animal corpses. Two months of this would teach him not to beat up his girlfriend. Or at least not to get caught.

"You're up, Fox," said the driver of the truck as they stopped on the shoulder of the freeway near one of the brown objects. Jayson Fox, accustomed to riding in a Bugatti Veyron, was relieved to get out of the smelly truck. The two men watched him walk away, eating their Egg McMuffins. A car full of girls was parked behind them on the shoulder. Girls followed them everywhere. One of them held a sign out the window that read YOU CAN SLAP ME, JAYSON!

"That don't look like no animal," said one of the men as he watched Jayson Fox approach the brown object with a shovel.

"Nope," said the other man.

As he got closer, Jayson Fox saw that it was a bag, not a mangled animal. He looked back toward the truck in confusion. One of the men, Egg McMuffin in hand, motioned for him to open the bag, which was soaked in what seemed to be blood. Jayson Fox held his breath and opened it. The men in the truck watched as he peered into the bag and then saw the shock spread across his face. He ran to the edge of the road and threw up. The girls filmed him retching with their phones. Within hours the footage was on the Internet.

The second bag was found later, having been dragged by a truck for seven miles. The Century Freeway was temporarily closed in both directions, causing traffic to back up.

Dr. Ormond Brown watched the news coverage at his home in West Texas and wondered if the police would soon be at his door. He had a feeling he knew who was in those bags, and if he was correct, then he was responsible in some way for their deaths. Or lynchings. He and his wife had put the names and photos of Simmons and Green on their website, after the police and the army had refused to act. Now someone had gone and killed them. This made Dr. Brown think of his daughter. He thought of her till he cried.

The death of Dr. Brown's daughter, United States Army private Shonda Brown, had been ruled a suicide. She was the first African American woman from Texas to die in the Iraq War, a distinction her father would rather she didn't have. On her death certificate, the cause of death was listed as *gunshot wound, self-inflicted.* In the three years since she died, this had not been amended.

Shonda had been stationed at Camp Mojave in Iraq. In her letters and calls home, she seemed untroubled, yet army investigators said she had shot herself in the head with an M16, leaving no note behind. After her body was shipped home, Dr. Brown examined her at the local mortuary, where she was in full military dress. The white gloves she wore on her hands were glued to her skin. That was the first sign that something was wrong. Upon close inspection, Dr. Brown saw that his daughter's face was bruised and her teeth broken. The exit wound at the back of her head was small, too; not from an M16, her father reasoned, but from a pistol.

He asked the funeral home to remove his daughter's clothing and to cut the gloves from her skin. Her hands were found to be scraped and burned. There were bruises all over her arms and legs. When he received the autopsy report, he read that her genitals were burned with bleach. Shonda's father had known all along that his daughter hadn't committed suicide. He couldn't understand how such a conclusion was ever reached.

For three years, through their congressional representative and the Freedom of Information Act, Shonda's parents collected evidence about their daughter's rape and murder. In his investigations, Dr. Brown learned of other

American servicewomen who had "committed suicide" in Iraq by seemingly impossible means, such as multiple fatal gunshot wounds or being run over by a truck. Talking to the women's families made him feel as if he was doing something, even if he was powerless in Shonda's case.

Near the third anniversary of Shonda's death, her parents received an unexpected break in their investigation. After he was discharged, Sergeant Lance Pederson committed suicide by asphyxiation in his brother's garage. Before his death, he wrote a letter to the Browns, telling them that their daughter had been raped by two of their fellow soldiers stationed at Camp Mojave — Michael Simmons and Davis Green. He didn't know if they had murdered her, but they had raped her. Everyone knew it.

Shonda's parents turned the letter over to army investigators. Simmons and Green, by this time both private citizens in Los Angeles, were interviewed, but there was no evidence that Shonda had ever been raped, and no rape kit was ever done. Officially: *gunshot wound, self-inflicted.*

In an act of desperation, Shonda's parents put the names and photos of Simmons and Green on the website they'd set up for Shonda. *What if they rape someone else?*

Shonda's mother had asked. *What if they commit another murder?* Simmons and Green threatened to sue and even hired a lawyer, but now it would never come to that.

Dr. Brown sat in his living room, watching the reports that showed aerial footage of the Harbor Freeway interchange, the brown canvas bags, and the videos of Jayson Fox vomiting. Dr. Brown knew who was in those bags, he just knew. The night before, he had received an email with a file attached. On the file were video confessions, one by Simmons, one by Green, admitting what they had done to Shonda in the kind of detail that left no doubt they were telling the truth. The footage was reminiscent of the videos made by suicide bombers. The men sat in front of an American flag and spoke directly into the camera, knowing that death was upon them.

More than a week had passed since my encounter with Julia in the Beauty Closet. She wanted the email addresses of every girl who'd written to Kitty since I'd started my job. There were at least 50,000 of them. When I asked Julia why she wanted them, she said she had her reasons. "It's for a good and noble cause," she said, "but it's better that you don't know the particulars. Then you'll never have to lie."

I knew I could get in trouble if I gave her the addresses, which I couldn't afford, since losing my job and my health insurance before the surgery would derail my plans. I had tried to stop thinking about Julia's request. There was nothing in it for me and it was reckless to even consider it, yet I'd been turning it over, unable to forget our meeting. Julia, Leeta, and Verena's book had disrupted the rhythm of my days.

To distract myself, I heated up a slice of

my turkey lasagna (230), then turned on the television, placing my plate on the coffee table in front of me. *The Cheryl Crane-Murphy Report* was on. She was discussing the murders of Simmons and Green, as every news channel had been doing for days. The Harbor Freeway interchange was a familiar sight.

"Do I think they deserved to be murdered? Well, as a committed Christian I believe murder is wrong, but at the end of the day I'm not shedding any tears over these thugs. Sue me." Cheryl Crane-Murphy was like a middle-aged male politician with a comb-over, except that she was a woman and the comb-over was more of a metaphorical one. Her actual hair was short and dark blond, teased and sprayed into place, stiff like whipped meringue. She spoke with faux folksy charm, the camera lens in front of her a peephole to America that she peered through from her desk in New York as if to say, *I can see you, I'm one of you.*

I scrolled through the channels, looking for something else, and landed on one of the Austen stations, catching sight of Kitty being interviewed.

There was no escaping Kitty.

"Earlier, I showed you how to pose for photographs so that your hips will appear slimmer," she said. "Now we're going to camouflage . . ." I clicked back to Cheryl Crane-Murphy, who said, "We should pass a law stating that any serviceman who rapes a servicewoman should be castrated — *without anesthesia*. I swear, I should run for Congress." I ate my lasagna and watched Cheryl pounding her desk, her eyes wild.

A yellow BREAKING NEWS banner appeared at the bottom of the screen. Cheryl adjusted her earpiece and announced that preliminary autopsy results on Simmons and Green had revealed that each man had a wadded-up piece of paper stuck down his throat with the name *Jennifer* written on it.

"Who is Jennifer?" Cheryl Crane-Murphy wanted to know.

The thought of the paper in the dead men's throats made me queasy, and I pushed my plate aside. I switched off the TV and reached for the phone to call my mother. We spoke every couple of days. If I didn't call, she worried.

"Who is Jennifer?" she asked upon answering the phone, knowing it was me. My mother never missed Cheryl Crane-Murphy's show. "Did I ever tell you that your father wanted to name you Jennifer? Practically every girl was named Jennifer back then." She went on discussing the crime and how she'd been delayed in traffic on the day the bodies had been found.

I let her talk. Since Delia had moved to a retirement home, she was lonely in the house on Harper Lane. I had encouraged her and Delia to sell the house, to rid our family of that horrible place, but they were both too attached to it. No matter how much I emphasized its value as the former home of Myrna Jade, neither of them was persuaded. To them it was home. I had visited Harper Lane so many times in my mind while reading Verena's book that I felt as if I had just been there, but I hadn't set foot in that house for four years.

"I have my own mystery," I said, cutting off her chatter about the murders. I offered her an edited version of recent events in my life. I needed to say it out loud to another person to make sure I wasn't going crazy. I kept the beginning of the story to myself — the story of Leeta was too odd — but I told my mother about the Beauty Closet, Julia Cole, and her request.

There was silence on her end, and then she said, "Are you making this up?"

"Which part?"

"All of it. Is this Beauty Closet for real?"

"Imagine Madison Square Garden filled with cosmetics. That's how big it was."

"I don't know what you've gotten yourself mixed up in."

"I didn't mix myself up in it. They just . . . *found me.*"

"What's the worst that could happen if you give this Julia person the email addresses?"

"I could get fired."

"I said the *worst* thing. Getting fired wouldn't be bad at all." My mother had been against the Dear Kitty job. She wanted me to pursue my writing. "That silly old Kitty" is what she always called her. Having accidentally opened the door to a discussion of my career, or lack of one, I moved to close it. I told her I would decide what to do and let her know.

"Are you feeling okay?"

"What's that supposed to mean?" Every word with her was filled with hidden meaning. *Feeling okay.* She meant the pink pills. Was I depressed? She always worried. It's why she wanted to talk on the phone so frequently.

"You're leaving the apartment regularly, right?"

"Ma, I go to the café every day."

"Besides that. You go *out,* don't you?"

"Sure."

We both knew I was lying.

When I hung up the phone, it took a few minutes to fully inhabit my New York life again. I went to my desk and turned on the computer. The responsible choice would be to forget Julia's request, but I had a vague sense that she might lead me someplace interesting, away from this apartment and this life.

I downloaded the addresses into a spreadsheet, all 52,407 of them. I was stunned at the number, thinking of the thousands of pages I'd written over the years and how that writing could have been put to better use. As the spreadsheet filled, I waited, drumming my fingers on the trackpad, a nervous *tap tap.* I clicked *send* and off it went to Julia's personal account. Once it was gone there was no taking it back.

A few minutes later I received Julia's reply:

From: JuliaCole
To: PlumK
Subject: Re: spreadsheet

Thank you for the spreadsheet. I'll be in touch again soon.

In the meantime, Verena Baptist wants to meet you.

J.

Verena Baptist welcomed me into her cluttered, blood-colored home. "Welcome to Calliope House," she said, but who Calliope was or what the name meant wasn't explained. *You're Eulayla Baptist's daughter,* I wanted to say.

Calliope House was actually two townhouses joined together, sitting on a leafy stretch of Thirteenth Street between Sixth and Seventh Avenues in the West Village. I stepped into the entryway and was enclosed in a womb of red wallpaper. To my left and right there were ruby-hued rooms, one a living room, the other filled with desks, where women sat, working and talking to one another. Chandeliers hung from the ceilings, and on most flat surfaces were stacks of books and papers.

Verena didn't fit into her surroundings, being an entirely vanilla creature with blond skin and hair, a beam of light in the dark.

She was tall and slender. When she reached for my hand, I could feel the bones in her fingers, as fragile as matchsticks. I had expected some resemblance to Eulayla Baptist, who'd had that plasticine, middle-American look of the beauty queen, but no one would have guessed they were mother and daughter. When Verena spoke there was a light undercoat of southernness, just enough to set her apart from the average New Yorker.

"The house is a little overwhelming," she said, almost apologetically. "It was this color when I moved in and I didn't want to change it." I scanned the room with the desks, but the women took no notice of me.

"Is this a house or an office?" I asked, still looking around, noticing something different every time I turned my head. On top of a cabinet, a large orchid was trapped under a bell jar.

"It's both." Verena explained that she lived in the house, but it also served as her office. Most of the women came and went each day, but a few of them lived there with her.

She explained that from the 1920s through the 1970s, the townhouse had been owned by a Catholic charity that used it as a home for unwed pregnant teenagers. The girls had either run away or been cast out by their families. With nowhere else to go, they moved into the house for the duration of their pregnancies. When their babies were born, the infants were adopted by religious families and the girls never saw them again. The young baby-less mothers left the house on Thirteenth Street and reentered the world as if nothing had happened to them — nothing they could talk about, anyway.

When Verena heard about the history of the house on her visit with the real estate agent, she knew she had to have it. There had been other inhabitants between the 1970s, when the charity closed, and when Verena bought it ten years ago, but the walls had always been red. I wondered if the girls had looked at the walls and thought of the periods that had not come: the absence of red, a foreshadowing of doom.

I followed Verena through the living room. A floral-patterned scarf was tied around her head like a headband, its knot and tail disappearing beneath her long hair. She wore a knee-length dress of blue canvas material, with gaping pockets at the front filled with pens and scraps of paper; beneath the blue smock she wore a white T-shirt. The ensemble smelled of laundry detergent, that chemical floral scent not found in nature. She was simple and clean, the type of breezy girl you might see playing tennis in a tampon commercial, only she wasn't a girl. I knew from reading her book that she was close to forty.

As I walked behind her, seeing her hips sway beneath the blue canvas dress, watching her bare calves constrict and release, it was difficult to believe she had sprung from the loins of Eulayla Baptist. Verena's body had destroyed her mother's figure; it was where Baptist Weight Loss had begun, that tiny seed that turned into "a bomb that took nine months to blow up." Verena's body could have been displayed in a museum, a part of American history.

We arrived in the kitchen at the back of the house, which was also red. A round oak dining table filled most of the empty space in the kitchen, with chairs circled tightly around it. On the wall behind the table was a framed pair of old jeans, folded at the knees and pinned to a white silk background. "Is that . . . ?" I pointed, unsure if I should mention the dead mother.

"Yeah, those are Mama's *fat jeans,* the ones made famous in the TV commercials." I placed my hand on the glass, imagining Eulayla bursting through the pants. She had never been as big as she seemed. Her fat jeans certainly wouldn't have fit me. I leaned over to examine them more closely. I had known that Eulayla Baptist was a real woman, but she had always seemed more mythic than human. Now there were her pants, and here was her daughter. I laughed. I couldn't help it.

Verena poured me a glass of sweetened iced tea (105) from a pitcher and invited me to sit down at the table. "I was a Baptist once," I said, still eyeing the legendary jeans.

"It was hell, wasn't it?"

"Worse." I shared the story of my time as a Baptist, about joining after I saw her mother on television and about my group leader, Gladys, and how she cried when she told me Eulayla had died.

"You must have hated me," Verena said. "I still get hate mail more than a decade later. *You took away my dream of being thin!* That's what all the haters say. I got a death threat just last week."

Verena explained that in the first few years after she closed Baptist Weight Loss, there were disgruntled former Baptists who stalked her and even threatened her life. They held meet-ups across the country. There were Baptist Shakes for sale on an online auction website years past their expiration dates, as if they'd aged like a fine wine. Some former Baptists collected old meals and any memorabilia connected to Eulayla. Some went so far as vandalizing Eulayla Baptist's grave with chisels, scratching out the words "Beloved Mother" on the headstone in an attempt to obliterate any link to Verena, even posthumously. Verena had replaced the headstone three times already.

I asked Verena if she had ever followed the diet. Given her slim figure, I doubted it.

"No, I can eat whatever I want and never gain weight," she said. "I take after Daddy. When I was a kid I wanted to be fat, just as a fuck-you to Mama. Fat as a form of subversion. My nanny was fat. She had such a lovely roundness about her. Mama was all bones and hard angles. You couldn't cuddle with her; it would have been like cuddling with a pile of tent poles."

"If you've never been —" I couldn't say the f-word, I couldn't say *fat;* I never said it out loud, hating the way it sounded. I preferred a variety of euphemisms: *overweight, curvy, chubby, zaftig,* even *obese.* I had once described myself as having a dress size in the double digits, but never as fat. "If you've never been —"

"Fat," Verena said.

"Then why do you care so much about dieting? Why did you write the book?"

151

"To tell the truth and undo some of the damage that Mama did, if that's possible. My family made a fortune exploiting vulnerable people and now that fortune is mine. It's ill gotten, of course, and it weighs on me. Sometimes at night when I think of it I can't breathe."

The fortune, I'd read online, was rumored to be close to $200 million. I wanted to joke that at least one brick of the townhouse — maybe more — belonged to me, but I didn't. She seemed pained. She said her extended family had been outraged by the book and most of them had shunned her. "The truth is a lonely place, but it doesn't matter. I have a new family now. A better one."

Verena said she had no intention of writing another book, that *Adventures in Dietland* was her one and only. She said she wasn't a writer, but a philanthropist, an activist. She had also trained as a therapist, but she didn't practice anymore.

I wondered if she was analyzing me. I kept waiting for her to explain why she had invited me over. "Do you work with Julia?"

"Heavens no. Julia and I met at a conference a few years ago. She's interested in my work and stops by the house once in a while for a chat. The last time was just a few days ago. She said that her intern — Lena, is it?"

"Leeta." It was the first time I said her name out loud.

"Oh right, *Leeta*. Julia said Leeta thought we should meet, so here you are."

"Leeta gave me a copy of your book."

"I'm glad she did. I never turn down the chance to meet interesting women. You might say I'm a collector of women." Her house was certainly full of women. She reached across the table and gave my hand an affectionate squeeze. It was rare that someone touched me, but both Julia and Verena had placed their hands on me.

I told Verena about how Leeta had spied on me and how Julia wanted the spreadsheet of email addresses. "What's Julia's story?"

"She inhabits a world of intrigue and secrets that I find exhausting. I do know that she's working on an exposé of Austen Media, among other things. She mentioned something about hoping you could dig up dirt on Kitty."

So that's what Julia wanted. I wasn't the ideal person to *dig up dirt,* given that I didn't even work in the office.

"When she told me that someone like you answers Kitty's mail, I was intrigued," Verena said.

"Someone like me?" I knew what she

153

meant, but I was hurt that she said it.

"People probably attack her for only having thin girls on staff and appearing in the magazine, but she can say, 'Hey, one of my assistants is fat.' It's like the person who says, 'I'm not racist, my best friend is black.' The really sick thing is that Kitty doesn't even want you working in that office."

"She said it was Human Resources' idea for me to work from home," I said.

"Do you really think that's true, hon?"

I stared into the small yard that was ringed with rosebushes and tall trees, hot in the face. I felt like a whale that'd washed up in Verena's red-walled house, a grotesque creature on display. "I don't want to look like this, you know. I hate looking this way. I don't need to be reminded of what everyone else thinks of me."

"They're the ones that have the problem, not you. There's nothing wrong with you."

I didn't respond, my lips pressed together tightly, curled into a frown.

Verena looked confused. "Have I said something wrong?"

"I don't like being called *fat.*"

"I see," Verena said. "I don't think fat is a bad thing, so I didn't realize I had offended you. I thought we were on the same wavelength and that's why Leeta wanted us to meet."

"I don't know why Leeta wanted us to meet."

"I can see that now." Verena apologized, but I was still upset.

"It's easy for you to say that being big isn't a bad thing. You don't have to live this way." She may have had a fat mother once, but that wasn't the same. I told Verena that I wouldn't be overweight for much longer, that I was having weight-loss surgery in a few months. "Dieting doesn't work, you said so in your book. It's time for me to do something else."

"That's the message you took away from my book?" If she weren't so pale, the color would have drained from her face. "Oh, Plum, don't do that. Don't butcher yourself. I beg you to reconsider."

Here we go, I thought. Another thin woman, like my mother, trying to dissuade me from the surgery. "I've already made up my mind."

"The only difference between my mother and the doctor who will perform your surgery is that my mother didn't have a license to practice medicine. They're all charlatans." Rose colored her pale cheeks. She was about to say something else, then caught herself. She placed her palms flat on the kitchen table and inhaled deeply, trying to prevent further upset. I could tell she was the type of person who didn't like to lose her cool. As I watched her, I saw the idea register on her face. The news of my surgery had tightened her features, but now her muscles were loosening. She sat up straight and asked me, "How are you going to pay for your surgery?"

I told her that my insurance was paying for part of it, but that I would owe about $7,000, which I would pay with savings and credit cards.

"What about the expenses that come after — new clothes, plastic surgery? You'll need more surgery, you know. If you lose weight that quickly, your skin will hang off your body."

I had already started buying the clothes, but I knew she was right about needing more surgery. I told her I would find a way to pay for it all.

"Let's make a deal," she said. "I'll give you twenty thousand dollars. You were a Baptist member. You paid your dues and you paid for that horrid Baptist food. With interest, and considering pain and suffering, I'd say I owe you twenty thousand."

I wanted to laugh, thinking she was kidding, but the serious look she was giving me said otherwise. "Twenty thousand dollars is a lot of money to you, but it's nothing to me," she said.

"What do I have to do?"

"I'd like for you to think seriously about the surgery. You can't undo it later."

"I've already thought about it seriously."

"What I mean is that I want you to think about it in a different way."

I needed a psychological evaluation before the surgery, which was a requirement of the doctor and insurance company. Verena was still a licensed therapist, despite not practicing, and suggested she could evaluate me. "We could meet several times over the next few weeks," she said. "I'll give you a series of tasks to help you be sure you're making the right choice."

"What kind of tasks?"

"Nothing too difficult. If at the end you decide to go ahead with the surgery, I'll sign the form and give you the money. If you decide you don't want the surgery, I'll give you the money. Either way, you win."

"Wouldn't it be against the rules for a therapist to pay her patient?"

"Rules don't interest me. Don't think of me as a therapist anyway — think of me as Eulayla Baptist's daughter. When you took the Baptist Oath all those years ago, you became a part of the Baptist family, remember?"

I remembered. I would have grown excited about the thought of $20,000 — it was more money than I could have ever imagined anyone giving me — but it didn't seem real. Only a few weeks before, the idea of sitting under the shadow of Eulayla Baptist's fat jeans and talking to her infamous daughter would have been unimaginable. It was Leeta who had led me here. She had followed me around the neighborhood, but now it was as if she was leading me somewhere.

"I feel protective of former Baptists," Verena said. "It's a guilt thing."

"There are masses of us out there."

"I know, but you're right in front of me. I'm not asking you to sign a contract in blood. You can change your mind at any time."

I thought about the things I could do with the extra money. It would be like winning the lottery. I knew she was going to do everything possible to change my mind about the surgery, but I'd play along. "Okay, why not?"

Verena beamed. "We'll call this the New Baptist Plan," she said. "The original Baptist

Plan failed you, but this time things will be different. The New Baptist Plan will completely transform you, I guarantee it."

Sunset

Every day on page three of the *Daily Sun* there was a full-page color photo of a topless young woman. The British newspaper, which interviewed prime ministers and helped decide elections, had been printing photos of topless young women on page three for decades. These "Page Three Girls," as they were affectionately known, sometimes went on to achieve great things in modeling or reality TV. A couple of them ended up strangled by ex-boyfriends or jealous lovers, but that could happen to any girl. Over the years, there had been halfhearted campaigns to ban the photographs in the newspaper, but they were never successful.

The newly installed CEO of empire Media, who oversaw the newspaper division, was only forty years old and a woman. She represented a new generation in the company, but like her male predecessors, she carried on the page-three tradition in the *Daily Sun* and ignored any complaints she received. Empire Media owned newspapers and television stations in the United Kingdom, the United States, Hong Kong, and Australia. "The sun never sets on empire Media," their founder liked to say. The CEO was aware of what had happened in Los Angeles to Simmons and Green — Empire Media's many publications and news channels had chronicled it all. "Who is Jennifer?" The front page of the *Daily Sun* had asked. In her own way, the CEO was fond of Jennifer, whatever she was. The mystery was good for business. The CEO was fond of her until, one day, she wasn't.

One morning she received news that her twin brother and his young son had been kidnapped on a trip to Scotland. It was several days before the kidnappers made contact and until then the CEO and her family didn't know what they wanted. When their request finally came, it was laughable. The CEO laughed. The kidnappers didn't want money. What they wanted was for the CEO to end the topless models on page three. "No more naked girls," said the note, signed with the name Jennifer. "Show us some cock."

Amateurs, she thought. They didn't know who they were messing with. Her twin brother's wife, unhinged by panic and rage, demanded that the CEO give the kidnappers what they wanted. The CEO thought her sister-in-law was a spoiled woman, prone to irrational behavior. "We have to negotiate," the CEO told her. "We don't give in to terrorists."

"They have my husband and child!" she screamed. "Give them all the cock they want!"

The CEO refused, despite her close relationship with her brother. She had a reputation in the business for being ruthless, which she couldn't afford to lose now. It wasn't easy being a woman in a man's world. She and the police in London waited for further communication from the kidnappers. It came in the form of a blond scalp stuffed inside a Jiffy Pack, delivered by the postman. The whole family was blond, but forensics determined the scalp with the receding hairline was from the CEO's twin brother rather than from her nephew.

The next day on page three of the *Daily Sun* there were no tits, but a naked man instead. Each day after that, a naked full-frontal man appeared in the newspaper, as directed by the kidnappers.

"Savages," the CEO called these criminals. The scalping had convinced her they were American.

When the cocks started appearing on page

three, there were immediate protests from media watchdog groups, from parents and government ministers, who claimed the photos were indecent. Many newsagents began to keep the *Daily Sun* behind the counter, lest anyone be offended. Some of them refused to sell it at all or even touch it. The circulation dropped by half during the first week. In media surveys, men said they were too embarrassed to read the paper. "I'm not gay," said a man who was interviewed. The CEO knew cocks were bad for business. Breasts she could get away with. Women knew their place, but with men it wasn't as simple.

As the cocks continued to roll off the presses, the hunt for the kidnappers intensified, as did the news coverage. Empire Media executives were well connected throughout the Metropolitan Police, Parliament, and MI5. All American Jennifers living in the United Kingdom fell under immediate suspicion.

One such Jennifer appeared on *The Cheryl Crane-Murphy Report* via satellite from London. Jennifer Chu, a thirty-two-year-old from Seattle, was studying for a master's degree in international relations at the London School of Economics. She had been detained by the police for twenty-four hours and interrogated.

Cheryl Crane-Murphy was perched at her desk in New York, wearing an American flag pin on her lapel. "It's not a good time for American Jennies, is it?"

Jennifer Chu nodded. "Talk about needles and haystacks. The name Jennifer is as close to a generic woman's name as you can get. There are tons of us out there."

"What I really want to know is — and I think I speak for all of my American viewers here — what the heck is going on over there in the U.K.? Are there pictures of naked ladies in the daily newspaper or what?"

"Not anymore," said Jennifer Chu, trying to suppress a smile. She explained that when she first arrived in London, she was shocked to see topless models in the newspapers, to see the iconic red telephone booths filled with graphic advertisements for prostitutes, to walk into any corner shop or newsagent and be faced with explicit pornographic magazines. "This city is like one big red-light district. I know these kidnappers are, like, evil and stuff, but I think they've done a public service."

The cocks continued to appear on page three of the *Daily Sun* and as they did, the kidnappers turned their attention to another target. Townsend's was a chain of newspaper and magazine shops spread across Britain, popping up in every train station and shopping center and airport. The front of every shop was stocked with the usual fashion and home decorating magazines, the financial publications and gossip rags, but there were also myriad lads' magazines, as they were called. The lads' magazines weren't on the top shelf, but were at eye-level for everyone to see. The graphic covers featured naked women, often in pairs or even in triplicate, rubbing their barely concealed nipples together, putting their tongues in each other's mouths.

In the wake of the Empire Media Scandal, the CEO of Townsend's received a threatening note, which the police deemed to be credible. The note, signed *Jennifer,* demanded that the lads' magazines be removed from every branch of Townsend's and replaced with soft-core gay male porn. The CEO took immediate action. The lads' magazines were exchanged for those that featured images of buff young men, hairless and muscled and bronzed, with bulging underpants (if they were wearing underpants). The men played with their nipples and flashed their man patches.

After the renovation, Townsend's was filled with women and girls. It was funny to see images of semi-naked, sexed-up men. For women it was like being in a carnival funhouse, where nothing was as it was supposed to be. News reports claimed that men felt uncomfortable going into the shops, since the women were leering and laughing. Businessmen in Armani suits tried to conduct them-selves with dignity, but it was difficult to do with all those perfect male butts in their faces, with those men staring at them with a look that said *fuck me.*

In London, images of men with *fuck me* looks were beginning to proliferate. Threats of kidnap and murder had spread, and images of female bodies were disappearing rapidly and being replaced with male ones. Men's body parts were scattered around the city: men's lips, torsos, legs, and buttocks. Pieces of men would flash by on the sides of buses, enough to brighten any girl's day. Before, the covers of the men's and women's magazines alike had featured women, but now most of them featured men instead. London was be-ing renovated, and the wallpaper covering every surface of the city was no longer deco-rated with women. The default Londoner, the implied viewer of everything, was no longer male.

Tourism increased, with women from many countries anxious to see what was happening firsthand, but there were also unforeseen consequences. London was scheduled to host the G8 Summit, but world leaders complained. The French president commented on a British television advert that featured a man washing his hair with a new floral-scented shampoo;

the man was so excited by the shampooing experience that he made orgasm sounds as he massaged his head. "I cannot be taken seriously in such an environment," the French president said. Other world leaders echoed his comments, and so the G8 Summit was moved from London to Berlin.

The imam of an East End mosque was taken hostage soon after that. While he was being held in captivity, a video was released to the media in which he ordered all good Muslim men to wear blindfolds. "It's not right that women should cover themselves from our gaze. Who has the problem here: women, who have committed the heinous crime of merely existing, or men, who choose to objectify women? If the sight of uncovered women offends you, stay at home or wear a blindfold. Better yet, pour acid into your eyes. Then you'll never have to see anything that offends you again."

Was New York next? That's what everyone wanted to know.

Verena and I sat on a bench across the street from the Austen Tower, watching the workers set up concrete barricades. "That's to prevent car bombs," she said, biting into her sandwich. "They know something we don't."

The events in London had just started to unfold, and rumors were circulating that on this side of the Atlantic, Austen Media had also been threatened. I looked up at the glistening silver trunk. If Austen had been threatened, then it wasn't a good idea to sit on a bench outside the building, but Verena wanted to see what was happening for herself and asked me to join her at lunchtime.

"Listen to this," she said, and read to me from a copy of the *New York Daily* that had been left behind on the bench. "In an internal Austen Media memo leaked to several online sources, Stanley Austen instructs the editors of his nine women's magazines to remove all references to blow-jobs from upcoming issues, which he said is a 'prudent cautionary measure in these volatile times.' In response to this news, lingerie chain V — S — has threatened to withdraw their advertising from several Austen publications, including teen title *Daisy Chain.*" Verena laughed and ripped the article out of the paper, putting it in her pocket.

She had finished her sandwich, but mine was still wrapped in the white paper: tuna with lettuce and tomato on rye bread. I was hungry, having eaten my bowl of oatmeal (105) and green apple (53) hours before, but I was worried about the sandwich. It felt like a brick in my hand. The tuna was loaded with mayonnaise and the whole thing could have easily been packed with five hundred, even six hundred, calories.

"I shouldn't be laughing about any of this," Verena said. "I abhor violence and destruction. My parents died in a fireball of metal and glass."

An image in my mind: Eulayla Baptist's fat jeans, consumed with flame.

She set down the newspaper and saw that I hadn't unwrapped my sandwich. "You're not going to eat that, are you?"

169

"It's not on my plan."

"Must I remind you that you're on the New Baptist Plan now? repeat after me: No calorie counting and no weighing."

For $20,000 I'd say whatever she wanted. "No calorie counting and no weighing."

"That's right. On the New Baptist Plan, absolutely *everything* is on your plan."

"You won't stay in business for long with that strategy."

"The weight-loss industry is the most profitable failed industry in history, did you know that?"

"I read it in your book."

I watched as she got up and went to the newsstand on the corner to buy a candy bar. She wore a faded minidress over a pair of jeans, her hair in a straggly braid down her back. Crowds of Austen employees milled around on the sidewalks, having descended from their heights to graze for food at earth level. I didn't like being in their vicinity and I certainly didn't want to run into Kitty. As I inspected the crowds, searching for her, a woman sat down next to me on the bench. She was wearing a beige trench coat despite the weather: hot with no sign of clouds. Most of her face was covered by black sunglasses, and she held a silver phone to her ear.

"I'm talking to you but I'm not talking to you," the woman said.

"Wh . . . ? Are you . . . talking to me?"

"Of course I'm talking to you." The woman lifted up her sunglasses and it was Julia. She put the sunglasses back down and looked in the opposite direction, still holding the phone to her ear. "Do you have any gossip about Kitty?"

It was startling to see Julia in the light of day. "Why would I have gossip?"

"You're a source now. I need gossip about Kitty. It's for a good cause."

I didn't mention that Verena had told me about the exposé of Austen. I liked that I knew a secret about Julia — and that she didn't know that I knew. "I have her list of article ideas for upcoming issues."

"Aces," said Julia. "Email that to me."

It wasn't a request so much as a command. "How's Leeta?" I asked. I thought of Julia and Leeta as a pair, though I had never seen them together.

"She's finally back at work. She's a bit of a loose cannon, you know." In a weird way, I missed Leeta. She had sprung up from nowhere, haunted my daily life, and then disappeared. I wanted to see her again, but not really.

Verena returned with her chocolate and

171

put her arm around Julia, who wriggled away and stood up, still with the phone to her ear, looking blank and unexcitable. "I should not be seen talking to the two of you, especially not you," she said, pointing at Verena with her foot. She pretended to talk on her phone, moving her lips and laughing, though no sound was coming out. Finally she said, "I have a conference call about lip liner with the West Coast now," and drifted away into the crowd.

"Poor thing, her paranoia must be off the charts," Verena said, motioning to the barricades. When I asked her about Julia, she said there were five Cole sisters, all of their names beginning with *J:* Julia, Josette, Jillian, Jacintha, and Jessamine. Their surname was Coleman, but they had deleted the *man.* The sisters all worked in the media or the fashion and beauty industry, and were all spying like Julia. "They're like a cabal," Verena said. "They live in a massive loft in Tribeca, the Weird Sisters."

I felt a twinge of panic regarding the email addresses, but I tried to push the thoughts from my mind. It was better that I didn't know why she wanted them. *Then you'll never have to lie.*

"I shouldn't tell you this," Verena said, "but none of the Cole sisters have breasts.

Their mother died of breast cancer when the youngest sister was only two. All of them have the gene, so when they turned twenty-one, one by one they had preventative double mastectomies." I remembered looking down Julia's shirt in the Beauty Closet and seeing the roses and thorns tattooed on her chest. She'd been wearing a bra, so I'd assumed there were breasts there too.

I peeled a mayonnaise-free strip of crust off my sandwich and put it in my mouth, then slid one of the tomatoes out from underneath the wedge of lettuce, careful to avoid the tuna. I ate tuna all the time at home, but with fat-free mayonnaise. Real mayonnaise was different. Once I had a taste of real food, I always wanted more. I spent my days tiptoeing around food, the way one might tiptoe into a baby's room while it's sleeping. One wrong move and the baby wakes up and screams. That's how it was with hunger, too. Once it awakes, it screams and screams and there's only one way to quiet it.

"Since you're planning on having surgery, why not just eat everything in sight?" Verena asked. "Pretty soon you'll only be able to eat baby food. You might as well enjoy yourself before doomsday strikes."

"My doctor said I have to stay on my plan

now, otherwise the adjustment will be too difficult later — Oh God, there's Kitty," I said, spotting the red bushel of curls. I turned sideways on the bench, covering my face with my hands. It was impossible for a three-hundred-pound woman to blend into a crowd, but I tried.

Verena told me Kitty was gone and I looked up to see the back of her head gliding through the glass doors. "How do you think Kitty feels about you?" she asked, but I told her I didn't want to talk about Kitty.

"A Baptist isn't afraid to confront hard truths."

"Who cares about Kitty? Once I have the surgery I'm not even going to work for her. She's unimportant."

"I disagree. You spend your days pretending to be her and writing in her voice. I'd say she's very important. I want you to articulate how she really feels about you."

Looking up at the Austen Tower, I imagined Kitty in her office on the thirtieth floor. Despite how friendly she acted, I had always suspected she was disgusted by me, but it was easier not to think about it.

"Come on," Verena said, continuing to prod me. "Let loose, dig deep. If I can trash my own mother in print, you can do this."

I ran my thumb across the top of my

sandwich, feeling the coldness of tuna beneath the bread. I wanted it badly. Instead I channeled my energy into the conversation, directing my crankiness toward Kitty. "If Kitty or any of the women on her staff were given the choice between looking like me and losing an arm or a kidney or even *dying,* they'd probably choose death or dismemberment," I said. "There. Are you satisfied?"

"This is good. Keep going."

"The Austen Tower is there ascending into the sky, filled with magazines and TV shows that tell women how they can avoid looking like me. I'm every American woman's worst nightmare. It's what they spend their lives fighting against, it's why they diet and exercise and have plastic surgery — *because they don't want to look like me.*"

"Keep going."

"Kitty doesn't want me working in her office. I'm the embodiment of everything she hates." It hurt to say it, but it felt good, too.

"You're Kitty's inner fat girl. She leeches off your pain. It's a resource that she's exploiting, like some big oil tanker parked in the Gulf of Mexico. She's sucking you dry."

"I'd rather not think about it. It's easier to

just ignore her." If I ignore it then it isn't real.

"You ignore a lot of things. Say *fat.*"

"I don't like saying that word."

"I know you don't. That's why you need to say it."

I tossed my sandwich into the garbage can next to the bench, where it landed with a thud. "Fat, fat, fat," I said. "Having lunch with you isn't fun."

"Being a Baptist is never fun."

Verena wanted to see where I lived, so we took the subway to Brooklyn. I didn't want her in my apartment, but it was better than sitting on a bench outside the Austen Tower, worrying about being blown up.

She wasn't expecting me to have such a large apartment. I told her it belonged to my mother's cousin Jeremy and that he was a journalist permanently away on assignment. I explained that I had grown up living in his mother's house on Harper Lane. The name Harper Lane made it sound quaint even though it was in Los Angeles. I made no mention of Myrna Jade, the ghost of my childhood. Verena was a therapist and I wasn't willing to offer up that delicious detail.

I assumed this was the official start of the

New Baptist Plan and Verena was preparing to analyze me. The psych evaluation form from the insurance company was sitting on my desk, but I knew Verena wouldn't sign that right away. I waited for the grilling to begin, but she wanted to look around first. My eyes surveyed the apartment, searching for any hidden details that might reveal something unintended. No one besides the super had been inside my apartment for more than six months. My apartment was a secret place, only for me, so intimate that it was full of my scent. I resented Verena for inviting herself over.

She asked if she could peek inside my bedroom and I agreed, believing I had put away my secret clothes, but as soon as I followed her through the doorway I saw a belt on the dresser. I had no use for a belt. Even worse, there was a scarlet dress lying crosswise on my bed, like a gash cut into the white comforter. It had arrived that morning when I was on my way out; I'd opened the package quickly, placed the dress on my bed, and forgotten about it.

Verena had seen the dress — it was impossible to avoid, splashed there on the bed, a slender column. She didn't say anything, but bent over to examine the framed photographs on my dresser. "That woman looks like you," she said, pointing to the photo of my grandmother and her sister on the Boardwalk in Atlantic City.

Verena straightened up. "If you have the surgery you won't look like her anymore."

"She died before I was born," I said, hoping Verena would feel bad.

She didn't comment, but walked back into the living room. We sat down and she removed a pad of paper from her bag and asked if she could take notes. She reminded me of Leeta, poised there with her pen and paper, ready to observe me. All of these new people in my life seemed to find me fascinating. I pointed out the psych evaluation form that needed to be signed before the surgery, but Verena stuffed it in the back of her pad without even looking at it.

Saying she wanted to show me something, she reached into her bag. She pulled out a bottle of pills and placed it on the coffee table between us. She explained that her colleague Rubí had just returned from a trip to Paris, where she had obtained them. Rubí called the pills Dabsitaf, but that wasn't their real name. Dabsitaf was a diet drug, more specifically an appetite suppressant. It had been available in France for two years.

"I've tried diet drugs. They don't work," I said.

"This one does. When Rubí was in France she talked to people who've taken it and lost vast amounts of weight. They're not hungry at all." She said it was manufactured by an American company, but they released it in France first because they knew they couldn't get FDA approval right away.

"It really works?" I examined the bottle with French writing on the label.

"The complete lack of hunger, that's what it gives you. The absence of want. The eradication of desire. Would you want to take it?"

"I'd try it."

Verena said there was evidence from France to suggest that some of the people who'd taken the drug had developed life-threatening complications. Their blood vessels tightened until they couldn't breathe, suffocating them from the inside. The drug company denied any link to their product, and clinical trials in the United States had already concluded. "If it becomes available here, and if you weren't having the surgery, would you take it, knowing the risks?"

If I thought the pills worked, I'd be on the next plane to France, but I kept this to myself. "I'd consider it."

"Why?"

"Because I don't like being hungry. I wish

my hunger would go away."

Verena wrote something on her pad. When she finished, she took back the bottle of pills. She crossed her legs and looked at me, saying nothing more. She wanted me to take the lead now — I knew what therapists were like.

By way of introduction, I said: "I wasn't molested." I thought it was important to get that out of the way. "Doctors always assume I was molested and that's why I'm . . . this way. I wasn't molested or raped, I just want you to know." In my ears I heard those girls from high school: *Who'd want to rape her?*

"I get it," said Verena. "Your fat body isn't the result of some deep psychological trauma. This is *me* you're talking to, remember? I was at a conference recently and an acclaimed psychotherapist said that women become fat because fat protects them from unwanted male attention, like a suit of armor."

I pictured myself as Joan of Arc, whom I had portrayed in a third grade play. "But I've always been this way, from the beginning."

"Like your grandmother, I know. Let's move on."

There was silence again. She was waiting for me to say something more. I thought of the scarlet dress on my bed. I knew she'd seen it. I thought it was best if I brought it up first.

"The dress on the bed is mine." I was like a nervous criminal, blurting out a confession. "What I mean is that it's for me." There was no point in saying the dress was a gift for someone else.

"You're buying clothes for your post-surgery self?"

I nodded. "I have a closet full."

"I'm not surprised. You believe there's a thin woman inside you, waiting to be set free."

"You sound like Eulayla now."

"You've internalized her ideology, haven't you?"

An image in my mind: Eulayla Baptist holding up her fat jeans. *Burst!*

"What's the name of the thin woman who lives inside you, imprisoned under all those layers of fat?"

"She's not a separate person; she's me. Or who I'll be eventually."

"All right, but let's give her a name."

I wanted to scoff, but then I remembered that when I was a teenager on the Baptist Plan I had thought of my thin self as Alicia.

Alicia is me but not me.

"I guess we can call her Alicia," I said.

181

"That's my real name."

"Your real name for the real you." Verena turned to a fresh page of her notepad. "What will Alicia be able to do that Plum can't?"

I immediately thought of the "When I'm Thin . . .™" booklet from my first day as a Baptist member. Ever since meeting Verena and reading her book, these flashes from my past kept coming back. They didn't belong here in my present life. I wished they would go away.

Verena pushed me to answer, so I told her that Alicia would be able to walk down the street and no one would look at her in a bad way or say something mean.

"What do people say to Plum?"

I liked this, thinking of Plum as a separate person, one who would soon be consigned to the past. "They say, *Go on a diet.* They make oink and moo sounds. A few weeks ago I crossed the street in front of a car and the guy shouted out the window, 'I'm glad I didn't hit *you,* girl!' everyone turned to look. People laughed."

"And what do you say to people who make these rude comments?"

"Nothing. I just pretend like I didn't hear it or that it didn't bother me." If I ignore it, then it isn't real.

"In an ideal world, what would happen?"

"I'd like to see them get what's coming to them."

"Such as?"

"Pain and suffering. *Death.*"

"That's honest. Do people often make rude comments?" I told her that I tried to avoid situations where that was likely to happen, but I still had to go out. Every morning before I left my apartment I felt dread.

"What kind of places do you avoid? Be specific."

"Parties, clubs, bars, beaches, amusement parks, airplanes." I told her that I hadn't been on a plane in four years. One time a man asked to be moved because he said I spilled into his seat. I couldn't always buckle the seat belt around me and it was embarrassing if I had to ask for an extension. The flight attendants weren't always nice about it. Once the plane was delayed from taking off because they couldn't find an extension for me and I feared I'd have to disembark in shame. The flight attendant at the back of the plane became so exasperated that she spoke over the loudspeaker to the flight attendants at the front. "Can't you find a seat belt extension for the lady in twenty-eight-B?" Passengers looked in my direction. For more than twenty minutes, the stares and murmurs persisted, until an extender was found on another plane. People complained they'd miss their connecting flights. I offered to get up and leave, but they said I couldn't. My luggage had already been checked. That was the last time I had flown.

"My mother has to come to New York if she wants to see me."

"What about your father?"

"He can't afford to visit New York. I haven't seen him in five years."

"Will Alicia be able to visit her father?"

"Alicia will be able to go anywhere." I felt a momentary, inexplicable flare of resentment toward my future thin self. "Do you understand now why I want the surgery? Don't you see?"

"Of course I see," she said, writing something on her pad. I wished she would leave. I had already decided to have the surgery. There was no need to excavate these depths of humiliation.

"What else can Alicia do that you can't?"

"Everything!" I said, snapping at her. "She won't be alone all the time, she won't spend all of her time in this apartment, she'll dress in pretty clothes, she'll travel, she'll have a job that she likes, she'll host dinner parties." This last comment must have sounded silly, but I had always wanted to host dinner parties, with candles stuck into empty wine bottles, the orange and red wax dripping down the glass like stalactites.

"What else?" Verena was digging for more, scraping out the cavity until she hit the nerve.

"Alicia will be loved," I said, at last.

I hadn't wanted to say it, but she'd pushed me. She knew what she was digging for and I had said it and now it floated in the room between us like a big black cloud of shame. It was so thick, I couldn't see through it.

"Isn't Plum loved?" she asked. I told her that my parents loved me, but I wanted more than that.

"Let's talk about men," Verena said. "Or are you interested in women? Or both?"

"Men," I said. "And what about them?"

"Do you want to be in a relationship with a man?"

"One day."

"When you're Alicia?"

"Yes."

"Do you hope to marry?"

"One day."

"What about babies?"

"One day."

"When *one day* finally arrives, it'll be an

185

exciting time for you."

I looked at her pale, delicate face and felt scorn. She thought she could judge me, but she couldn't last five minutes living in my skin. I remained silent. Sulky.

"I want you to consider something, hon. What if it's not possible for you to ever become thin? What if there is no *one day?* What if this is your *real life* right now? What if you're already living it?"

"I'm not."

"But what if you are? What if this is your real life and you're fat and that's that?"

"Then I wouldn't want to live anymore." As soon as the words escaped my mouth, I knew I shouldn't have said them. "I'm not suicidal."

"I didn't say you were," she said, and then after a few seconds she asked if I took any prescription medication. She was looking for evidence. I told her that I took thirty milligrams of Y—— every night and had done so since college.

"That's a powerful drug. Who prescribes it for you?"

"Just my regular doctor."

"A general practitioner?"

I nodded and Verena frowned. She wanted to know why I had started taking Y—— and I told her it was because of depression, obviously, but she asked if there was a "precipitating event." I told her I didn't want to relive the drama, that it was too long ago. I gave her the short version. "There was a boy in college. It was just silly."

"It couldn't have been silly if it caused you such pain. What did he do?"

"He rejected me," I said. She wanted to know why. I bent over and played with the strap on my sandals, looking at the floorboards. "He liked me but he was afraid to get involved with me."

"Why was he afraid? You don't seem scary to me."

"I think he thought his friends would laugh at him."

"He sounds like an asshole."

"I had a breakdown over it." I thought about the library window and the librarian and the days afterward when I couldn't stop crying. I didn't tell Verena any of these things.

"Why not just find another boy, one who wasn't an asshole?"

"There were no other boys for me."

"There are plenty of boys."

"Maybe for someone like you, but not for me. There wasn't the possibility of another boy."

"Ah." Verena sat back in the chair. She asked if I still cared about him.

"His name is Tristan," I said. "And, no, I don't care about him anymore."

"Then why have you continued taking Y—— ?"

"I don't want those feelings to come back again."

She wanted to know what my love life had been like since Tristan, but I told her I hadn't had one.

"What if you were to get a boyfriend now?"

"I don't want a boyfriend now."

Verena wanted to know if Alicia would take Y——. She sometimes asked such obvious questions. "Alicia won't need Y——," I said.

I was hoping that Verena was ready to leave. I had never admitted such things to anyone. I wouldn't be able to look at her the next time I saw her.

Instead of leaving, she asked for a glass of water. I was a bad hostess, unused to guests. Once her throat was wetted, she started with the questions again, only this time she had my psych evaluation form in her hand. Finally, I thought. She wanted to know why I'd decided on the surgery. I remembered the day I called the doctor, and what had prompted me to call him, but I wasn't willing to share that, so I spoke more generally. I told her that I'd tried everything else, but nothing worked.

"The surgery can change me," I said.

"You'll be malnourished. There could be other major side effects too. You could even die."

"I could die from being fat."

"If you eat healthy food and exercise, then it doesn't really matter what size you are."

"I've heard all of this from my mother. I know you're against the surgery, but I'm going to have it regardless of what you say. I'm not going to let you take away my dream." She had already taken away my Baptist dream as a teenager and now all these years later she was trying to take away my dream of the surgery. "If you don't sign my form, I'll just have someone else sign it. I don't need your twenty thousand dollars, either, even though you promised it to me."

"You'll have it," she said. "I'm not a dasher of dreams, Plum. Your dream, as it were, is to look different. To be *smaller.*"

"I want to look normal."

"You live on the hope of becoming Alicia, don't you? Without the possibility of this transformation, you'd rather die than live, you said."

189

"I didn't mean that."

"You didn't hesitate when I asked you."

"It just came out."

"But where did it come from?"

She left the question dangling and stood up from her chair. She walked to the front window, then back again, considering something intently.

"It's time to discuss the first task of the New Baptist Plan."

"I thought today *was* the first task?"

"I was getting to know you today. Now that I know you better, I want you to consider reducing your dosage of Y—— and then quitting it all together. You said Alicia wouldn't take Y——."

"I'm not Alicia yet."

"*One day I'll do this, one day I'll do that.* That's what I've heard from you all day. Let's start bringing the future and the present together, just a little bit. Alicia wouldn't take Y—— and so neither should Plum."

"I don't know if I'm ready for this."

"If you don't think you're ready to become Alicia, then maybe you shouldn't have the surgery. The weight will come off quickly. You need to be prepared."

She had a point. I had thought of giving up Y—— many times, but whenever I had missed a dose, I'd wake up in the morning feeling as if someone had poured molasses into my head, gumming up all the gears and switches. I explained this phenomenon to Verena.

"That's why you never quit medication like Y—— cold turkey. You can cut your thirty-milligram tablets in half and we'll try the half dose for a month. If things go well, after that you can quit completely. Think it over," she said, gathering up her things. She handed me a card with her contact information, a red card to match the red-walled house.

"Aren't you going to sign my form?"

"There's plenty of time for that," she said. "Today is only the first day of the New Baptist Plan. There are plenty more days to come."

When Verena left, my head throbbed. It was as if she'd been inside my brain, picking through it as if it were a chicken carcass. I lay down on my bed, wrapping the scarlet dress around my neck like a scarf.

I hadn't expected Verena to suggest that I give up Y———. I didn't know what I had expected the New Baptist Plan to be. It had seemed like a joke, but now I knew she was serious. She wasn't going to give me $20,000 for doing nothing. Until our conversation, I hadn't thought of Y——— as a thread that connected me to Tristan and that difficult time in my past, but that's what it was. Verena wanted me to sever it.

Tristan and I had never been anything more than friends, but we were close; at the age of twenty-one I had never experienced closeness with a boy. When our senior year of college started, we began to spend so much time together that to others we quickly became "the two of you." Wherever one of us went, the other was soon to follow.

I thought we were building up to something during those autumn months. For the first time I thought I understood what love was. I had always thought of myself as outside of things; when others spoke of dates and relationships and sex, I knew it didn't apply to me. I hadn't realized the extent of my exclusion until Tristan came along and made me feel included. I was one of them, finally. In the campus bookstore with a friend, I'd point to a funny card with hearts on it and joke that I could buy that for Tristan. As the autumn festival approached, I thought I'd have someone to go with. Tristan was possibility more than anything else; he opened up a world to me that had always been closed. When I saw couples holding hands or kissing, I didn't feel resentful anymore. Tristan hadn't kissed me, but we were moving in that direction. The anticipation of him wanting me brought joy that I'd never known. Every day when I awoke, I thought I didn't deserve to be so happy, that no one did.

I couldn't have sex with Tristan — I was firm in my mind about that. He could never see me naked, and so there was a line between us, and what was beyond that line was out of my reach. What I wanted was for him to want me, for him to touch me. He held my hand sometimes. Once I fell asleep next to him on the sofa, my cheek resting against his white T-shirt, and he put his arm around me. I wanted more than that — I wanted for him to kiss me. I wanted his want.

In the end, he didn't give it to me. Tristan said we shouldn't be friends anymore, that it was "impossible." We'd been on the verge of what I'd wanted, that place of wanting and touching, but he pulled back at the last moment. "You're not right for me," he'd said, and then he refused to talk to me.

When our friendship ended he began to date a girl from my history class. After months of being friends with me, of building up to something that never happened, he began to date her and instantly they were holding hands and kissing as they walked together on campus, and doing other things behind closed doors that I could only imagine. That was the start of the unraveling that would culminate several weeks later with my mother's arrival on campus and Dr. Willoughby prescribing Y——, but I didn't know that at the time.

At the beginning of the new semester in

January, I walked to the campus health center in a snowstorm. I felt that something bad was going to happen to me. "I need help," I said to the disinterested receptionist behind the desk. She asked what was wrong but I didn't have words for it. "Well?" she asked; there was a line forming behind me. "I'm bleeding," I said. It wasn't true, but it seemed to sum up my defectiveness as a female more than anything else I could say.

As I sat in the waiting area, I thought about leaving, but I didn't know where else to go. My friends had tried to be helpful, but I didn't share with them the depths of my pain; they might have laughed. There had never been anything between me and Tristan besides friendship, so they would have thought me foolish. That there had only been friendship between us made it worse. There had been a line between us. It was the line I grieved over, more than I grieved for Tristan. The line would always be there, even after Tristan was gone.

In the examining room I put on a gown and the nurse weighed me and took my blood pressure. The doctor arrived and listened to my heartbeat and then helped me recline on the examining table. He felt around on my breasts, where I had imagined Tristan might have touched me. Then he said something about my cervix and moved my legs apart. I had always avoided gynecological exams, too embarrassed at the thought of exposing my body in such a way. I lifted up my head. "Wait."

"Just lie back and relax," he said in a tone he must have thought would soothe me. He touched me down there with a cold, gloved hand. I had never been touched there before and my knee moved involuntarily and bumped his head. "Are you sexually active?"

I could see the top of his blond head over the curve of my stomach. "No."

"I'm going to insert the speculum now. You might feel a pinch." I looked up at the ceiling tiles, cloudy and white like the surface of the moon, and held the sides of the table as he pushed something hard into me, opening up what felt like a new space. I had never had anything put inside me before, not a penis, a tampon, or a finger. It felt as if he were stabbing me. With Tristan, and then with the doctor, I felt pain in places I hadn't known existed.

"Relax," the doctor said. "Don't clench."

When the doctor finished, he said he'd leave me alone to get dressed. After he was gone, I couldn't move except to put my legs together. I felt pinned down. Tears ran down the sides of my face and into my hair. There was a poster on the wall, an illustration of a see-through pregnant woman standing in profile, her guts like the inside of an aquarium. I had imagined having a baby with Tristan, had fantasized about all sorts of things happening between us, even though I had known it was impossible, that there was a line.

I tried to maneuver myself up from the table, wanting to leave before anyone saw that I was crying. When I stood, blood ran down my legs and into my socks. I hobbled to the counter where there was a roll of blue paper towels, and tried to wipe myself down. Once I got back to my dorm room, I stood in the shower and watched the blood circle the drain. There was a wound somewhere, deep inside of me. It never healed, but after I began to take Y——, I could no longer feel it.

The First Couple

The world's most famous porn star was shot in the head outside a Times Square hotel. A photograph of her corpse appeared in all the morning papers, even the respectable ones. After being shot she rolled into the gutter, a fact that the tabloids chose not to exploit. If not for the wound in her forehead, it would not have been obvious she was dead. She was lying with her eyes fixed in space, her lips slightly parted, which is how she often looked in her films.

Stella Cross was a major star, not some anonymous girl from the Midwest who was plucked before she was ripe, fucked in every orifice, and tossed into the compost heap. Stella Cross, her name a tangle of allusions to Jesus or just being nailed, had sealed her pornographic fame with a series of seven films called *A Cum-Sucking Slut Named Stella,* 1 through 7; the series was halted after the tissue between Stella's vagina and anus was torn from so much "double anal" and "double vag," as she put it, which she had endured for days on end for the seventh film; She was left with a gaping wound that needed reconstructive surgery. "I nearly had to retire my cooch!" She told a radio interviewer, likening it to a baseball player's jersey.

The new vagina was revealed in her comeback film, *Stella De-Flowered,* a reenactment of her rape by a neighbor at the age of fifteen, which was directed by her husband and awarded Best Anal (nonconsensual) by *Adult Film Digest.* A mold of her new vagina was mass-reproduced by a factory in Manila and sold on her website as a sex toy. Stella had a framed photograph of the hair-netted Filipino factory women holding the molds of her ladyparts and smiling.

Stella Cross was an international star whose fame transcended the pornographic world. She was the subject of a documentary that won a prize at Cannes. She was the face of Kiss Me jeans, bought in shopping malls across America by preteen girls. A charity called Help These Children flew her to Guatemala after a mudslide, where she handed out stuffed toys to the kids and cheered everyone up. The name Stella had even been number one in Ghana among baby-girl names, two years running. People who had no idea that Stella Cross made her living on her back and on all fours like a dog knew her name, even if they were not entirely sure how they knew it.

After Stella Cross was shot, her husband was gunned down too. He had been talking on his cell phone at the end of the block, unnoticed by anyone. When the bullet entered his head, he crumpled to the ground with far less attendant excitement. Everyone always said he was a behind-the-scenes kind of guy. At the time of his death he was being investigated for using underage girls in his series of films called *Barely Legal Slumber Party: Daddy's Cumming.*

"Waves of grief for Stella Cross and her husband, Travis, rolled over Silicone Valley yesterday," said an article in the *New York Daily.* "Cross and her husband were known in the industry as the First Couple of Porn. 'They were our Camelot,' said performer Reginald C*********."

Witnesses said Stella had been shot by a woman on a motorcycle. "A crack shot," said a witness when interviewed on TV. The man, wearing a Jets ball cap, was interviewed outside the hotel, which was still festooned with yellow police tape, like a sad sort of Christmas garland.

"She was just shot — *bam!* — like that," he

said. It seemed that he wanted to add "awesome" or a similar exclamation.

Before she was murdered, the appearance of Stella Cross on the sidewalk outside the hotel had caused an outbreak of excitement among the tourists in Times Square. Such was the crush of autograph seekers and photograph takers that ten minutes before the shooting, the chief justice of the United States Supreme Court, after receiving an award in the hotel ballroom, walked out the front door and into a waiting car, unnoticed.

"Do you think the assassin was actually aiming for the Supreme Court justice?" the television interviewer asked the man.

"No way," the man said. "No way. I don't know nothin' about this justice or whatever, but I'm telling ya, this motorcycle pulled up outside the hotel and this woman just aimed right at Stella and shot. It was totally a woman who did it, too."

The blond Stella was shot as she walked away from the crowd of fans, sandwiched between two large black men who were her bodyguards. By the next evening, there were tribute videos posted online by Stella's fans, with clips of Stella having sex spliced together with photos of her dead body — or perhaps they were just stills from her film *Fuck Me Till I'm Dead.*

THE *NEW BAPTIST PLAN,* TASK ONE: WITHDRAWAL

The Nola and Nedra Show played on the radio, broadcasting live from Minneapolis. I listened while lying naked on the sofa, running my fingers through the sweaty curls of my pubic hair.

"My eleven-year-old nephew has a Stella Cross poster on his wall," said Nedra Feldstein-Delaney.

"No!" said her cohost, Nola Larson King.

"Yes. My sister said all of his friends have it and she didn't want him to be left out."

"Oh, Nedra, I'm just sick about this." I could hear the pain in Nola's middle-aged, midwestern voice. She was always the more emotional of the two.

I picked up my glass of water (FREE FOOD) from the coffee table; after taking a drink, I set it over my bellybutton, the black hole amid the swirling stretch marks and deep crevices. Outside it was a boiling July day, and inside my body it felt like July as well. I was baking from the inside. I had the air conditioner running, but it wasn't helping.

The day after meeting with Verena I had begun to cut my tablets of Y—— in half. She was right. Alicia wouldn't be strung out on antidepressants, and if I was serious about becoming her, I needed to start taking more steps in that direction. Within days I began to experience flu-like symptoms and thought I had caught a bug, but Verena told me over the phone that I was suffering from "Y—— flu" and that this was a normal symptom of withdrawal.

She made me sound like a drug addict.

"Y—— won't give up its grip on you easily, but your willingness to change is impressive, hon. This is an important step." She encouraged me to endure the symptoms but said if they became too much I should call my doctor and ask for a low dose of Prozac, which could make Y—— withdrawal easier. I thought another pill was the last thing I needed.

For days I had a high fever and was marooned in my bed, wrapped in the sheets. I was nearly delirious for some of the time and saw things that weren't there, like my dead grandmother sitting at the end of my bed. I began to sweat and experience chills and aches. This went on for days. When the worst of it was over I left my bed and went to the living room to lie on the sofa and watch TV or listen to the radio, feeling leaden and exhausted, sensitive to touch and light. I couldn't recall ever feeling such misery, and yet in a strange way I welcomed the symptoms. They were unpleasant, but they were evidence of the change I was going through, my metamorphosis from Plum to Alicia.

Despite the humiliation of my session with Verena, I was grateful that she'd moved me one step closer to my new life, though I knew she had other intentions. Speaking with her had been painful and embarrassing, but in a way it was a relief to say those things. Afterward I felt as if I were carrying one less burden.

"Stella Cross's father is being released from prison early so he can attend her funeral," said Nedra Feldstein-Delaney.

I wasn't answering Kitty's messages. It'd been at least a week since I'd even opened the Dear Kitty account. In the three years I'd been working for Kitty I had been obsessively disciplined about my job, only taking weekends off, almost never missing a day, even working when I was sick. I had suspected that if I stepped out of Dear Kitty completely, I'd never want to go back.

I had a sudden fear that Kitty might find out I had been slacking off. She didn't have the password to the account, but the IT department could surely find a way in. My anxiety was enough to send me to the computer. I sat on my wooden chair without wearing any clothes, my bottom sticking to the seat, my breasts sagging down to the level of the keyboard. In the computer I saw myself reflected back, but I was too numb to muster disgust.

"In a poll conducted last year, more seven-year-olds had heard of Stella Cross than Martha Washington," said Nola Larson King.

As always, the Austen system was slow to log me in. An hourglass on the screen turned cartwheels while I waited. This ritual always gave me time to brace myself for what would flow into my inbox, like the moment on a cop show before a sheet is pulled back from a mutilated corpse in the morgue. Sharp intake of breath and then . . . *the horror.*

The messages poured in. There were more than a thousand of them. The sight of the massive list was like a collective cry in my ears. I opened the first letter but couldn't summon the mental powers to concentrate. Kitty. Abortion. Blah. Blah. Blah. I wanted to write back to the girl, HaleyBailey80, and say, "Why are you asking me, Kitty Montgomery, whether or not to have an abortion? I flunked out of Brown!" Only after a break did the absurdity of anyone writing to Kitty for advice, and thus the absurdity of my job, become clear.

Nedra Feldstein-Delaney said, "Last Christmas my eight-year-old niece asked Santa Claus for a G-string."

I looked at the next ten messages in the queue and I couldn't face them. Not the next ten, not the next two hundred. I dragged my cursor down the list, highlighted them all, and clicked *delete.* I waited a few seconds to see if I'd feel any guilt, but I didn't feel anything.

THE *NEW BAPTIST PLAN,* TASK TWO: CONFRONTATION

With the Y—— flu subsiding, I soon developed new symptoms, such as the feeling of shocks in my extremities, tiny pinpricks of electricity. I was zapped throughout the day on the bottoms of my feet and my fingertips. Overall I didn't feel right; I was at a remove from life, as if there were a pane of glass between me and everything else.

My apartment was stale with sweat and the remnants of fever — it was like living inside a jar with the lid screwed shut. I was in the middle of washing clothes and linens and preparing to open all the windows when Verena called to explain about the second task of the New Baptist Plan. She wanted me to confront people who made rude comments or stared at me. "Don't ignore them," she said. "Respond."

I was still in the middle of the first hellish

task, and now she was giving me another. "Why bother? I won't look like this for much longer."

"I think you need to stand up for Plum, don't you? Once she's gone, you may regret that you never defended her." Verena spoke about Plum as if she was going to be annihilated. I saw a watermelon dropped from the roof, its remains reddening the sidewalk.

"If you're trying to talk me out of the surgery, then reminding me how much everyone hates me isn't going to achieve that."

"Trust in the process. A Baptist isn't afraid to take risks."

I was glad we were talking on the phone so she couldn't see me roll my eyes. I had no intention of confronting anyone. The only way I could survive my life was to exist in a fog of denial. Acknowledging what happened around me was almost unimaginable. In nearly thirty years of life I'd rarely done it. If I ignored it, then it wasn't real. Still, I told Verena that I would. She'd never know. I'd make up a story, something filled with pathos, like a message from one of Kitty's girls.

The $20,000 would soon be mine. After hanging up the phone, I looked through all my catalogs and ordered more clothes.

■ ■ ■ ■

Verena had said the process of weaning off
Y—— would take more than a month. I
couldn't hide in my apartment for all that
time. I decided that returning to my normal
routine would offer stability and help me
deal with the disorienting symptoms. I
packed my laptop bag and headed to the
café for the first time in weeks. On my way
there I thought more about the second task.
If I had wanted to confront someone I
wouldn't have had to search for opportuni-
ties. I thought about what I'd say to the
mean boys who hung out on the corner.
Nothing came to mind, no witty, zinging
statement to put them in their place. Words
were insufficient. Instead I imagined them
being dropped from the Harbor Freeway
interchange, like those men on the news, or
maybe a bus could swerve onto the sidewalk,
splattering the five of them and sending
their heads rolling down the street like
bowling balls.

"In an ideal world, what would happen?"
Verena had asked during our first session.

In an ideal world, they would bleed.

At the café, I settled at my usual place. At

the table where Leeta had sat, two elderly women shared a slice of cheesecake.

After being at home for so long, I felt the café's onslaught of sensations — the abundance of light through the many windows, the noises from people and machines. I was like a cave-dweller thrust into brightness. My hands fumbled with the clasps on my laptop bag, the electric shocks becoming more bothersome. I felt feeble and fragile, unfit to be in a world of normal people.

On the café radio, Nedra Feldstein-Delaney said: "Stella Cross's real name was Jennifer Rose Smith."

Carmen was pleased to see me, but she was busy with customers and couldn't talk, so I went to work. I'd deleted the backlog of messages, but there were new ones every day. I opened the first one: *deer kittey, i think i have hpv do u know if this is deadley?* I stared at the message the way one stares at a painting: straight on, rather than reading it from left to right. The words were symbols, but I wasn't sure what they meant. *hpv.* Oh, I recognized that. I could have opened my file and copied the relevant material, but deleting the girl was easier.

With great effort, I opened another message: *Dear Kitty, Is it bad that I cut my arms with a razor?* I leaned over, placing my face in front of the screen: *cut. arms. razor.* A cutter. I used to hear from cutters every day, but had never really thought about what it meant to cut one's flesh with a steel blade. Now it seemed such a bizarre thing to do. *Yes, of course it's bad,* I wanted to write. *What a stupid question.* But it was too much effort, so I deleted the girl. I skimmed the next twenty messages and deleted them, too. I wondered what was happening to me. I had been like an athlete before, speeding through the messages no matter how trivial or annoying, but after being sidelined for a couple weeks, the Kitty part of my brain had atrophied. I had no idea what to say to these girls and I wished they would go away.

Carmen was the only part of the café I had missed, and I wanted her to visit with me. She finally stopped at my table, bringing with her a cranberry orange scone (480). She was always bringing me things I couldn't eat. *A saboteur,* Eulayla Baptist would have called her, but it wasn't intentional. I picked at the corner of the scone, not feeling any desire for it. One result of Y—— withdrawal was a loss of appetite — the only positive side effect.

As Carmen spoke about what had been happening in the café, I felt pulses of heat in my fingertips, which soon spread up my arms.

"Are you all right?"

"I'm still sick. Go on, tell me more." I listened to her words as if they were background music. In my mind all I could think about was the New Baptist Plan, about the two versions of me, Plum and Alicia, and about Verena and all the things we had discussed. This café life didn't fit me anymore. Being there was like hobbling around in too-tight shoes.

As she spoke, I wondered what Carmen thought of me. She was quick and light, even while pregnant. The boys on the corner wouldn't have laughed at her. She would never know what that was like. I was aware of the line that existed between us, the line that existed between me and most people. I had never liked to acknowledge the line, but there it was. Now I was too aware of it.

Carmen returned to work and I was alone at the table. With my fingernail, I dug a cranberry out of the scone and sucked it off my finger. As I did, I noticed that the woman at the next table was staring at me in a way I didn't like. Could I say something to her?

Just then I felt a stab of electricity in my left eye. I dropped my scone onto the table and squeezed my eyes shut, waiting for the sensation to pass. When I opened my eyes, the woman was still looking my way.

"What are you staring at?" My voice was deep and growl-like, not my own.

On the radio, Nola Larson King said: "I have a sister named Jennifer."

For days I didn't feel right, but I went to the café anyway. I skimmed hundreds of messages and deleted them. It wasn't clear to me why I attempted to read them if I was going to delete them. Maybe I was pretending to be God, receiving a prayer. Even with no intention of answering, I could send a comforting vibe into the universe: *I have heard you. Be at peace.*

When I was tired of staring at the computer screen, I stared at the people in the café. There was a steady stream of them throughout the day, since no one remained as long as me. I watched them order their coffees and teas, sandwiches and cakes, and felt the electric shocks move across my tongue and down my throat, like a trail of ants.

It was never quiet in the café and I heard snippets of conversation, the general chatter of life. Certain comments began to rise above the others, or maybe I was more attuned to them.

"If you don't eat lunch you're going to be hungry later. Why do you always do this?" At the next table, a young man was speaking to a skinny young woman, maybe his girlfriend. "I know you're hungry."

"I'm not." The girl, who had a beakish face, turned toward me. I returned to my laptop.

Dear Kitty, Last summer in Palm Beach I met this guy Ryan. See, Ryan knows my cousin Becky and well, this is a long story, so let me start at the begin—

Delete.

Dear Kitty, My friend Kelsie has a thigh gap and I was wondering how I can also get —

Delete.

Dear Kitty, I'm sending a photograph of me in a bikini. Do I look —

". . . fat?" A slim teenage girl two tables away stood up and turned around before the gaze of her mother. "Mom, pay attention. Do I look fat in these shorts?"

"You look fine," the mother reassured her. The mother was as fat as I was. When she saw me looking at her, she turned away.

In college, my roommates, four thin girls, all friends of mine, were fond of saying "Do I look fat?" just like that girl had said. Sometimes they would pose the question to me, not seeing or caring that when they said "Do I look fat?" they were really saying "Do I look like you?" It was assumed that no one wanted to look like me, not even me.

I turned again to steal a glance at the girl's mother, who was looking down at her hands, as if ashamed. If I were really going to confront someone, as Verena wanted, then I would confront that girl. I'd capture her and put her inside my laptop where she'd be trapped with thousands of Kitty's girls in a kind of hell and I'd force her to twirl around in her shorts forever saying, "Do I look fat? Do I look fat?

Do I look fat? Do I look fat?"

I was already fat. I was the worst that could happen.

I didn't return to the café again. Despite my initial fears, I didn't think Kitty would find out that I wasn't doing my work. She barely noticed me. Perhaps I could go on collecting paychecks for weeks or months, even years.

Instead of answering Kitty's email, I watched television. Stanley Austen appeared on *The Cheryl Crane-Murphy Report* to discuss what continued to unfold in London, but he refused to acknowledge that he had been threatened. "Even if I were threatened, I wouldn't worry in the slightest," he said, his sleek silver hair contrasting unpleasantly with his suntanned skin. "I'm used to crazy, bitter women making threats. They complain incessantly that my fashion magazines exploit women, then on the other hand they complain that the alleged exploitation isn't spread around equally among the fat ones and the ethnic ones. I gave up listening to them years ago."

"But what about all the metal detectors and barricades that have suddenly appeared outside the Austen Tower?" asked Cheryl Crane-Murphy.

"That was in the works well before all this Jennifer nonsense," he said. "Jennifer" was media shorthand for the violent events occurring on two continents and the group assumed to be committing them; even if Jennifer was a real person, she couldn't have been acting alone.

Cheryl Crane-Murphy moved on to discuss American HipHop, a cable channel that was headquartered near the Austen Tower in Times Square. Earlier in the week, the CEO admitted he had been threatened, but he wouldn't say how. In response to the threats, he announced that the twenty-four-hour music channel would no longer show videos that degraded women. Commentators wondered what the channel was going to show instead, since all day long it was *bitch this, bitch that* and there was an endless supply of booty moving through space like smooth brown planets. Cheryl Crane-Murphy and her roundtable of experts wondered if the station would go bankrupt. I turned the channel to American HipHop and saw they were broadcasting a test pattern with a message on the screen reading WE APOLOGIZE FOR THIS INTERRUPTION TO OUR REGULARLY SCHEDULED PRO-GRAMMING.

Verena called. I listened to her while staring into the void that was American Hip-Hop. She wanted to know about the second task. I decided not to lie and told her about the woman in the café and how I had responded to her: *What are you staring at?* I thought this would be enough of a confrontation — for Plum this was progress — but Verena wasn't satisfied. "It's a good start," she said, "but I want you to consider doing more than that." In response I moaned into the phone, experiencing a burst of shocks in my head. "You're not well at all," Verena said, as if she'd had nothing to do with it.

Although the first two tasks were ongoing, Verena wanted to discuss what was next. I demanded to know how many tasks were left in the New Baptist Plan. I was on the verge of quitting, but she said there were only three tasks left. I was nearly halfway to the $20,000.

"Now what do you want me to do?"

"For the next two tasks, I want you to live as Alicia."

"That's impossible."

"I know that Alicia is thin and Plum is fat, but I just want you to pretend to be Alicia. It's an exercise."

Verena explained that the third task was a makeover. "You've already started buying clothes and accessories, but let's go further.

I have a friend who is an expert at this sort of thing. She'll take you out for a few days and make you over from head to toe."

"What's the point? I don't *look* like Alicia. I can't even fit into the clothes I've bought."

"Trust in the process. Besides, it might be fun for Plum as well. You've imagined yourself as Alicia for so long that you don't give Plum a chance to be everything she can be."

"I've been Plum my whole life. She's had plenty of chances." I thought about the makeover. Shopping for cosmetics and new shoes, I supposed that's what she had in mind. I could handle that. "And the fourth task?"

"A week of blind dates."

An invisible hand punched me in the gut. "Verena —"

"My dentist, Gina, always tries to fix me up with men, which is annoying and offensive for a variety of reasons. She knows plenty of single men — they're in and out of her office all day long. So yesterday I called her and asked her to arrange a string of dates for a young friend of mine. She practically cackled with joy." I pictured Gina with a wart on her chin, clasping a broomstick.

"What did you tell her about me?"

"That you work for Kitty, that you're smart and pretty, that you live in Brooklyn."

"The men won't be expecting someone like me."

"These are blind dates. They won't know what to expect."

"Verena," I said in a tone that let her know I was tired of this game, "you know what I mean. I'm not a generic female. I cannot be set up on dates."

"Trust in the process, Plum. That's all I ask."

"I'll be humiliated," I said. "You know that. That's what you want to happen, isn't it?"

"You make me sound like a monster."

"I can't understand why you're doing this. I thought you wanted to change my mind about the surgery? So far you're not doing a very good job."

"I just want you to experience being Alicia. She wants to meet men. She wants to fall in love, get married, have babies, the whole predictable triumvirate. That's what you said you wanted."

"But I'm not Alicia yet."

"We're just going to pretend that you're Alicia. I want to move the present and the future closer together. It's an experiment."

"Okay, send the men over, I don't care. I

hope they do humiliate me. It'll confirm what I already know but what you can't accept: Plum shouldn't exist." Plum was moving into the past, like someone on the platform as the train pulled away, slipping from view. I wouldn't even bother to wave goodbye.

I didn't bother to ask about the fifth task. Verena said the makeover would begin the next morning. I was supposed to meet her friend Marlowe Buchanan at Café Rose in Union Square. The name Marlowe Buchanan was instantly familiar, but I couldn't recall why. I turned it over in my mind several times, and then it came to me. "Marlowe Buchanan . . . the actress?"

"Yes, I guess she was an actress. I don't think of her that way. She's just Marlowe to me."

I should have known it wouldn't be a normal kind of friend.

"Is there a problem?" Verena asked innocently.

The New Baptist Plan was becoming stranger by the day.

THE *NEW BAPTIST PLAN,* TASK THREE: MAKEOVER

When I was a girl living on Harper Lane, I watched Marlowe Buchanan in the sitcom *Ellie* every Thursday night. She played the title character, Ellie Waters, a young woman who had moved from Ohio to New York City to become a TV weathergirl. It was a fish-out-of-Midwest story, with beautiful small-town Ellie trying to make it in the big city.

The actress Marlowe Buchanan, and by extension her character Ellie, was most famous for her *Birth of Venus* hair, which was long and thick and honey colored. It was mesmerizing to watch her every week, her hair falling over her shoulders and down her back, swishing behind her like a hula skirt as she walked. Marlowe appeared in a series of shampoo commercials with a Rapunzel theme, and she posed for the cover of *Vanity Fair* naked, with only her hair to shield her. Her hair was her trademark. Before *Ellie,* she'd been a teenage model, appearing on the covers of *Daisy Chain* and *Seventeen.*

I watched *Ellie* for years, but when the show went off the air I became obsessed with something else and I hadn't thought of Marlowe again until Verena mentioned her. I couldn't recall ever seeing Marlowe on TV after *Ellie.* She seemed to have disappeared.

The night before I was supposed to meet Marlowe, I lay paralyzed on the sofa with electric shocks and nausea thanks to my continuing withdrawal from Y——. I found episodes of *Ellie* online, and while I went in and out of sleep, the show played in the background, a happy memory from my life on Harper Lane.

The next morning I was early to meet Marlowe at Café Rose. Before I left home, Verena had called and asked me to bring one of Alicia's dresses. I chose a white poplin shirtdress with purple trim, now folded in a bag at my feet. The opening credits of Marlowe's sitcom played in my head, with Marlowe in her raincoat, running around Manhattan in the drizzle, never mussing her glorious hair.

I expected her to look different in person, not only because she was older. Celebrities usually looked different in real life — I knew that from my days at Delia's restaurant, which sat at the edge of West Hollywood. Whenever a famous actress walked through the door it was usually a disappointment. I expected the women to radiate light like they did on the screen, where a tiny movement — the brush of lashes against a cheek — was exquisite and beautiful, a raven batting its wing. In person they were ghostlike, their normally bold features faint, as if their likenesses had been reproduced so many times that they were becoming faded.

This wasn't the case with Marlowe. When she arrived at the café, she didn't look like a dialed-down version of her former self, but like an entirely different person. I guessed that no one ever recognized her in public. She must have weighed around two hundred pounds, maybe more. Her long hair was gone, replaced by a short crop, which was still honey colored but threaded with gray. Wayward strands were pinned back with a tiny red barrette. She was wearing a white sundress, her skin tanned, the muscles in her arms and legs defined despite the roundness. There was a baby strapped to her chest, who was facing outward and smiling. He was a gyrating mass of bare arms and legs, a demi octopus.

"I feel like I know you already!" Marlowe said, settling into the chair across from me, having had no trouble picking me out of a crowd. "I'm Marlowe, this is Huck." I managed a startled hello.

She said she wanted to meet away from Calliope House so we could be alone and talk. As she settled in, disentangling her things and finding places for them on the empty chairs, I looked at her face, examining it for traces of Ellie, but I couldn't see any. The voice was the same, though, honeyed to match her hair, and it was funny to hear its tones directed at me in conversation rather than coming from a TV.

I went to the counter to fetch Marlowe a coffee and a cruller, which I offered to do to save her the trouble, given the baby. I couldn't imagine what kind of makeover she had in mind. Perhaps it was a reverse makeover, where she was going to make me look worse than I already did. I felt bad for thinking this, but beautiful Ellie was gone and in her place was this chunky, short-haired woman with a baby.

When I returned to the table, Marlowe had taken the baby out of his carrier and was bouncing him on her lap. While she ate the cruller she fixed her eyes through the massive plate-glass window next to our table and said, "You know, it's been about fifteen years since I left Hollywood, but sometimes those British tabloids send a pap to long-lens me eating a taco or something." With her mouth full of pastry, she held up her baby-free hand to the café window and extended her middle finger. "You never know if one of them is watching."

I decided to tell her about growing up in Myrna Jade's house, where I was watched. This was something I'd been unwilling to share with Verena, but Marlowe and I had more in common. I never thought I'd have anything in common with a TV star.

"I remember that little house on . . . what was it, Hanover Street?"

"Harper Lane."

"Harper Lane! I can't believe you lived there. I drove by that house once when my aunt visited me out in L.A. She was ancient and wanted to reminisce about the stars of old. When she spotted Myrna Jade's name on the star map we just *had* to go."

"Was that when you were playing Ellie?"

Marlowe nodded. When I was watching *Ellie* on TV, Marlowe was driving by my house, watching me.

"I loved Ellie," I said, cringing at the way

226

I sounded, but I couldn't help it. "I really wanted to look like you. I begged my mom to buy the shampoo."

"Sugar, the shampoo wouldn't have helped you look like me. I wasn't entirely au naturel back then. It took a committee to make me look the way I did. But those days are behind me." She cupped her breasts and gave them a squeeze. "I can assure you there's nothing inside this body with a serial number now."

Marlowe said that even her name hadn't been real. Her birth name was Marlowe Salazar, Marlowe being her mother's maiden name and Salazar her father's surname. Her management company thought Salazar sounded too brown, so they poked around in the family tree until they found the name Buchanan. "I was ethnically cleansed. I never changed the name back because it's my brand now."

On Marlowe's left bicep there was a message, black script on flesh, but I couldn't read it. As she fed the baby bits of pastry, I leaned closer: *women don't want to be me, men don't want to fuck me.*

"Is that a tattoo? A permanent one?"

She laughed. "Of course."

"But what does it mean?"

Marlowe said she would tell me the story

of the tattoo, but first I went to order her another coffee.

During the break between the fourth and fifth seasons of *Ellie,* Marlowe traveled to Italy for an extended vacation. Her handlers and her parents were pressuring her to accept a film role, but Marlowe wanted a break. She was exhausted from the pressures of carrying her own show and wanted to spend the summer out of the spotlight and on her own. "In L.A., so many people wanted a piece of me. I needed to get away."

Ellie was not broadcast in Italy and Marlowe could enjoy anonymity there, as much as was possible for any beautiful woman in Italy. She pinned her hair to her head and wore a ball cap and frumpy, loose-fitting clothes. Nobody on the plane recognized her. In Rome, she went sightseeing like every other tourist and ate whatever she wanted. The producers of *Ellie* had her on a strict diet, so Italy was like a giant all-you-can-eat buffet. "Breakfast at the hotel was bread smeared with chocolate. Did you know that's actually a thing in Italy? I went for gelato at Giolitti's, sampled pasta dishes at two different trattorias, ate pizza rustica while walking around the market at Campo de' Fiori and then I took a picnic to the Villa Borghese gardens, where I ate olives and cheese and drank wine while sitting under a tree. That was Day One." Marlowe said that the food combined with anonymity was like a narcotic.

I didn't know what it was like to be a celebrity, but the thought of walking the streets with no one watching me, and eating whatever I wanted, was exhilarating. When she said it felt as if her feet never touched the ground, I could practically feel it myself.

One afternoon she was walking through Trastevere taking photos when she passed a barbershop filled with old men. She peeked in the window, planning to take a photo. On the counters were jars filled with blue Barbicide and black combs; the men smoked and read newspapers; a dog slept in the doorway. She put her camera away and went inside. "I decided right then and there, on what was essentially a whim, to cut off my hair. *All of it.* I sat down in the chair and took off my cap. My hair tumbled out. I tried to explain to the barber what I wanted, but he didn't understand. He had probably never seen that much hair in his life." Marlowe braided her hair, from the nape of her neck down to the ends, and then she took the barber's scissors and cut the braid off. Her description of it was like a scene from a horror movie.

She said the men in the barbershop had gathered around to watch. She rolled the braid into a coil and put it in her backpack, then pointed to a teenage boy who was sweeping the floor. The barber understood that she wanted her hair like the boy's. The men were aghast at what this pretty young woman was doing to herself.

Marlowe paused the story to tend to her baby, who had become fussy. She looked in her bag for a bottle and slipped the rubber nipple into his mouth. "I was aware that my contract forbade me to alter my appearance in any way without permission from NBC. On some level I knew I was deliberately sabotaging myself and my career, but I wasn't really conscious of it at the time. I got up in the morning and didn't have to worry about washing and drying my hair — I just leapt out of bed and went on my way. I had a simple face buried under all that hair, pretty but more androgynous than I'd ever realized. I was almost unrecognizable, even to myself."

Marlowe left Rome to travel the hill towns of Tuscany and Umbria. While she was browsing an open-air market in San Gimignano, an American tourist somehow recognized her, pointed his camera at her, and snapped. Marlowe was startled by the clicking sound of the shutter opening and closing, as loud as a clap of thunder. She dropped the bunch of grapes she was holding and ran to her hotel, racing through the medieval streets. In her hotel room she shut the curtains and took deep, steady breaths. For the rest of the afternoon she remained in the darkened room.

In the late 1990s, before the Web ruled the world, the news cycle was slower — two weeks passed before the photo surfaced in the media. the *National Enquirer* ran it under the headline WHAT WAS SHE THINKING? In the photo, Marlowe was at the market in San Gimignano, standing in front of the fruit stand with her shorn hair and twenty-five extra pounds. *Entertainment Tonight* and the *New York Daily* made Marlowe's transformation their top story. The producers of *Ellie* called an urgent meeting in L.A., but Marlowe found out about what was happening only when she called her mother from a payphone to say hello.

"What have you done?" her mother shrieked, shattering the peace of an afternoon in Cortona. Birds in the Piazza della Repubblica took flight.

Marlowe knew she had to go home and face the consequences. On her last afternoon in Rome, she returned to her favorite church near the Pantheon, Santa Maria sopra Minerva. She sat there for an hour, mentally preparing for what was to come. Before she left the church she took the braid out of her backpack. There was a statue of Mary, surrounded by pots of flowers, with votive candles flickering at her feet. Marlowe nestled the braid among the candles that were the hopes and prayers of fellow travelers, and then she walked away, leaving a piece of herself behind.

The next day, Marlowe was greeted by paparazzi at LAX. The studio sent two bodyguards to meet her at the airport, as well as a dark car with tinted windows. Photos of her with her short hair were on the covers of celebrity magazines; Barbara Walters mentioned it on *20/20;* a late-night talk show host made jokes about it, holding up a picture and saying, "Who's this fat lesbian who's eaten Marlowe Buchanan?"

"The whole country thought I was ugly, which was a horrible feeling. It was a miracle no one found me hanging from a rope," Marlowe said. "You're probably too young to remember. When people I knew in L.A. saw me, they gasped. My family didn't want to speak to me. Even my agent wouldn't talk to me. 'My twins are starting Columbia in the fall. Do you have any fucking clue how much Columbia costs?' She was furious."

The head of NBC's entertainment division cut short a trip to Cape Cod and flew to L.A. Marlowe was put on a crash diet. Losing the twenty-five pounds was easy; she was under so much stress, she couldn't eat. But her hair was a different matter. The producers decided to tape a scene of the show with Marlowe wearing a wig, but test audiences gave it low ratings. They filmed new episodes without the wig, but the ratings sank and so did the show.

"I never knew why *Ellie* went off the air," I said. "I loved the show, but then you just —"

"Disappeared," she said.

NBC executives scheduled a meeting with Marlowe to tell her the show was canceled. "In the conference room I met with three balding men, all named Stu, and a woman named Sharlene. They laid out photos of me with my shorn hair. One of the Stus leaned across the table and said, 'We're sorry, Marlowe, but since you cut your hair, women don't want to *be* you, men don't want to *fuck* you. The show is canceled.' I can still see his face," Marlowe said, imitating the gravity of his expression. "I started laughing. How could I not? They probably thought I was having a nervous breakdown. Sharlene leaned forward and said, 'Unless you figure out a way to up your fuckability quotient, your career in Hollywood is finished.' Can you imagine? She was serious! She had an MBA! I just kept laughing. Suddenly it all seemed like such bullshit. I'd been paraded in front of the cameras since the age of six like a trained monkey whoring for attention and cash. That day was the end of it. I never wanted to forget it, hence the tattoo. It was the best day of my life." Marlowe slapped her arm where the writing was, then the baby copied her, slapping her in the same place.

"But how could . . ." I hesitated, afraid of offending her.

"How could that be the best day of my life? When a bunch of executives in a conference room told me I was unfuckable?"

I nodded. She drank the rest of her coffee and set the cup down on the table with a clatter.

"Stick with me, kid," she said, and winked.

When Marlowe's acting career ended, she earned a bachelor's degree and then a Ph.D. She wrote a book called *Fuckability Theory,* which took concepts from Hollywood and applied them to the rest of society. After

Verena read the book she invited Marlowe to Calliope House for lunch. That was four years ago. Since then, Verena had been funding Marlowe's projects, which included touring university campuses to give talks and workshops about fuckability, and also writing another book. Marlowe's office was on the third floor of Calliope House.

As we walked there, Marlowe holding her baby, me holding the bag with my dress in it, I realized I hadn't been registering the electric shocks and other unpleasant symptoms. Of all the women in Verena's orbit, I liked Marlowe the best so far, even though I knew she was part of the New Baptist Plan, the purpose of which was to change my mind about what I wanted so badly.

"What exactly *is* Calliope House?" I asked.

"If you want to be old school about it, you could call it a feminist collective. Verena has this massive house and more money than God, and she provides living space or office space for women who interest her for the work they do or the potential they have. Women come and go, as they need her. She's a good egg."

A collector of women.

I explained to Marlowe about the surgery. I wasn't sure what she knew already, but I explained about the thin woman living inside me. It seemed ridiculous when I said it out loud, but Marlowe had shared her story with me. She was fat too, though not as fat as I was. Maybe she would understand. "Verena wants me to practice being Alicia. She wants me to have this makeover and go on dates, since that's what Alicia would do."

"Let's not call it a makeover," said Marlowe. "We're going to up your fuckability quotient."

That didn't sound pleasant. A simple manicure and haircut was likely not what Marlowe had in mind.

We arrived at Calliope House, and as I walked through the door I felt a stab of electricity in my head. Even with my eyes closed I could sense that people were staring at me, but I needed to wait for the sensations to pass. When I opened my eyes, Julia was standing before me in the entryway, seemingly on her way out. She was wearing the beige trench coat, this time with the collar up.

"I dropped by to say hello. I trust that you are well," she said, nibbling the arm of her sunglasses.

"I've been better. How are you? How's Leeta?"

"Leeta doesn't work for me anymore. Don't ask about her."

"What happened?"

"I'd rather not talk about it. By the way, thank you for sending Kitty's list of upcoming articles. It's the usual sewage, but keep feeding me information. I like to know what's going on."

"I'm the last person on Kitty's staff to know what's going on," I said, not adding that I wasn't even doing my job anymore.

"Yes, but you're the only one I can trust, so I'll have to make do." She smiled primly and moved toward me, aiming for a kiss on the cheek but landing in the spot behind my ear, near my hairline. She lingered for a moment, her arm wrapped around my waist, her breath on my neck. She seemed to be inhaling me. When her head resurfaced, she said, "It was lovely bumping into you, as always," and walked out the door.

Marlowe, who had observed our interaction, said, "No comment." I was left to wonder what had happened to Leeta. Julia wanted information from me but rarely shared any herself.

I followed Marlowe into the living room. It was redder and brighter than I had remembered, like the inside of a cherry lozenge. She set a dozing Huck on the sofa, where he curled into a ball. In the middle of the room was an overturned plastic crate, and she asked me to stand on it.

"Let's see what you brought," she said, picking up the bag and pulling out the white poplin shirtdress. "This should be no problem. Do you mind if we measure you?"

A woman with a tape measure and a pad of paper appeared. "This is Rubí Ramirez," said Marlowe. I recalled the name Rubí from one of my conversations with Verena. She was the one who'd gone to Paris to get the diet drug she called Dabsitaf.

"Hello," Rubí said, and I returned the greeting. She began to wrap the tape around me, making me feel like a prize pig. She and I probably weighed the same, but she was short. Her black hair was nearly shaved on one side, shoulder length on the other, the tips of her spiky bangs bright blue. She wore shorts and a tank top, her olive limbs ringed with rolls of fat — an image of the Michelin Man came to mind. I would have never worn an outfit like that.

Rubí hadn't explained why she was measuring me, but if she was going to remake the white poplin shirtdress in my size, she'd be wasting her time. I had no intention of wearing any such dress in my size, but I didn't say so. I just needed to get through the makeover. It would be over soon and then the $20,000 would be mine.

"Rubí has made several dresses for me," Marlowe said. "DIY. Or what I like to call FFI — Fuck the Fashion Industry." I had never heard anyone say the word *fuck* in such a variety of ways. There was little doubt what Huck's first word would be. It couldn't be a coincidence that his name rhymed with it.

Rubí chatted as she measured me, explaining that she was campaigning against Dabsitaf with Verena. Before becoming an activist, she said she had been a headless plus-size model. Her modeling agency had made a fortune selling photos and film footage of Rubí to the major news organizations. From the neck down, Rubí appeared in magazines and especially on news programs, where she was featured walking down the street in slow motion, an ice cream cone or hot dog in her hand, while the voice of the reporter gave scary statistics about expanding waistlines and type 2 diabetes and said things like, "The obesity epidemic is America's looming holocaust." Rubí was filmed struggling to stand up from park benches and restaurant booths and airline seats. Dieting tips were flashed on the screen over a freeze-frame of her ass, which she said looked to be covered in acres of denim. Her head was never shown. Rubí was so successful as an "obesity epidemic" headless model that she earned a nickname in the industry: Marie Fatoinette.

"I gave up modeling to become an activist," she said. "We all do things we regret when we're young, right?" I supposed that question was directed at me, but I remained silent, my arms outstretched, waiting for the inventory of my body to be finished. A dark-haired woman poked her head into the living room, glancing at me in my scarecrow pose. She didn't say anything, but bit into a green apple. Half her face was scarred. It looked melted and pink. I turned away from her and from Rubí, looking up at the ceiling. Verena's house was some kind of freak show.

When the measuring was over, Marlowe asked Verena to take care of Huck until her husband could pick him up. Verena was wearing a top that looked like a remnant of an old prom dress.

Before the makeover began in earnest, I felt compelled to check with her one last time: "You're going to give me the twenty thousand at the end of this, right?"

"Of course. A Baptist never lies."

I looked at her skeptically.

"Correction. *This* Baptist never lies."

Marlowe and I left Calliope House to begin what she called "a few days of fabulous fuckability fun."

"Why don't you just call it attractiveness? I prefer that."

"*Attractive* is too benign. Quaint. In our mothers' day, it used to be enough to have a pretty face or a nice *figure,* which was bad enough, but now you must be the perfect fuck-doll too."

"What's a fuck-doll?"

Marlowe, oblivious to my question, spoke a language I didn't understand. She pulled a copy of *Fuckability Theory* from her bag and began to read from it: *"Page two: We all want to be attractive to our partner, but being fuckable is about more than that. It's about having a high fuckability quotient on the open market, as if we're stocks with a value that rises and falls."*

Our first stop was a salon with a pink awning. "My friend here has an appointment for a waxing," Marlowe said to the woman who greeted us at the door. The woman was wearing a coat like a doctor might wear, except hers was pink.

"What am I having waxed?" I whispered to Marlowe.

"Everything, including the downstairs area." When I began to protest, she said, "Fuckable women are hairless and smooth, like little girls." I felt shocks in my fingers and toes as I followed the pink-coated woman through the salon and down a flight of stairs at the back.

The esthetician spoke English with an unidentified Latin American accent. "I'm Liliana," she said, looking me over. "Take it all off, except the bra." She turned her back, as if privacy were going to be possible. I realized I hadn't shaved my legs or armpits in months. The hair was dark and baby fine. I didn't want Liliana to see, but there was nothing I could do. I lay down on the table. She waxed my legs and underarms, my upper lip and eyebrows, then took a pair of scissors from a drawer. "Don't move," she said as she began cutting the hair between my legs. She cut from the top all the way down to my ass. "You want a little Hitler?" she asked me. Had she said *Hitler?* "You want a little Hitler here?" she said again, putting her fingers on my mons. "Little strip, like Hitler mustache?" I said no.

Liliana dusted me with white powder, as if I were an enormous baby. She spread hot wax into every crevice and fold, all over my vulva and the sides of my legs, ripping off the wax with strips of cloth as she went. I gritted my teeth and held on to the table as what felt like a thousand ants bit me in the crotch at once. "Oh, sweet Jesus," I mumbled when I saw the silver cross flailing around Liliana's neck. She lifted my left leg up, bending it at the knee and pressing it back toward my chest. She asked me to hold it there while she grunted and smeared the wax around. "Hold it! Hold it!" This part of my body was a wild expanse of uncharted territory, unknown to man, but Liliana wasn't deterred, attacking the thicket with gusto. She wiped off the blood with cotton pads, then slathered me with antiseptic ointment. I rolled over onto my stomach and she continued her work, spreading my butt apart and smearing wax in the crease, ripping it off with the strips. She asked me to get up on my hands and knees so she could have a better view, and pulled stray hairs with a tweezer. I was so embarrassed, I nearly left my body and floated to the ceiling. I wondered what it was like for the tiny Latina immigrant to spend her days in this basement room, her face in women's vulvas and asses, making perfect Hitler mustaches. *The American dream,* I thought.

When I left the room, I felt like I'd just stepped off a roller coaster, winded and dizzy. I limped up the stairs, grasping the wooden rail. In the mirror I saw that my face was swollen and red, as if I'd been slapped around. I went to a drugstore to buy some ibuprofen. Marlowe trailed after me, but I didn't speak to her. "Are you all right?" she said when we were outside the drugstore and I was trying to remove the childproof cap from the bottle of painkillers with my teeth. She took the bottle from me and opened it. "I feel weird, like something is missing," I said, washing down the pills with Diet Coke (FREE FOOD).

"No cushioning," said Marlowe. "You're like an animal without her fur."

Next Marlowe took me to a department store, leading me to the plus-size area that was euphemistically labeled the "women's section," and Marlowe said, "Aren't we all women?" We were there to buy new bras and underpants. Marlowe read aloud from her book as we browsed the bikini briefs, boy shorts, and thongs, all of which were referred to as *panties,* as I had called my underwear when I was a little girl. Marlowe picked out a selection for me. When I tried on the bras in the dressing room, they actually gave me cleavage, like a busty wench in a pirate movie.

The salesgirl said I needed to buy Thinz.

"No offense. Even lingerie models have to suck it in." Thinz were the latest must-have item, like a girdle except they were sleek and almost invisible. Thinz were sold for the bottom to compress the hips, stomach, and thighs; for the top, there was a squeezy camisole. Putting on Thinz felt like crawling into a caterpillar's skin. Marlowe paid for the lot of it.

I left the department store wearing control-top tights and Thinz under my clothes. On my feet were the pair of impossibly high heels Marlowe had purchased on the way out. The heels thrust my bust forward and my butt up. Marlowe read from her book as we navigated the crowds in Herald Square. *"Page ninety-seven: The fuckable woman puts her secondary sex characteristics on display, like a baboon with a throbbing red ass."*

I hadn't worn heels since my college graduation and felt like a kid who'd raided her mother's closet. I hobbled down the street and held onto Marlowe for support. "I can't breathe," I said, and complained that I couldn't bend or sit either, thanks to Thinz. I was a sausage in casing. All of my rolls and layers were squeezed in, but where had they gone?

Marlowe said, "A fuckable woman doesn't

245

take up space. Fuckable women are controlled."

I said, "Control-top pantyhose."

"Fat women are not controlled. They are defiant, so they are unfuckable."

Once again I wondered about the logic of this makeover. How would telling me I'm unfuckable change my mind about the surgery?

Marlowe and I stopped at a coffeehouse for a break. I took the shoes off and instantly felt the symptoms of withdrawal, the zaps in my feet, the little pulses of heat. I stood next to the table and drank my iced coffee (183), since I couldn't sit down. "What is the point of Thinz?" I asked, hoping that my liver and kidneys and everything else that was in there hadn't become dislodged. "If you appear more fuckable because of Thinz, and then someone wants to . . . *fuck* you," I whispered, "then you go home and undress and everything just flops out. Won't that lead to shock and disappointment? Maybe even despair?"

Marlowe licked the whipped cream off her fruit drink. "Haven't you learned anything from your boss, Kitty? Being a woman means being a faker." Outside, a pigeon limped on the sidewalk, a torn piece of donut lodged in its beak.

The makeover continued for days. Marlowe took me to a dermatologist, who injected my forehead with a toxin and suggested a range of treatments to erase my blemishes and newly emerging fine lines. Marlowe said this was important, since the fuckable female body is factory fresh and new, as if the shrink-wrap has just been removed. The doctor said I was no longer allowed to go out in the sun. I had my makeup done by an expert named Kevyn. At his suggestion, Marlowe bought me a selection of high-end cosmetics that cost more than a thousand dollars. I thought of Julia and Leeta in the Beauty Closet, but they were no longer a team, as Julia had informed me.

At a hair salon on Fifth Avenue I refused a drastic change, so my short black bob was trimmed and buffed and I was sent on my way to the manicurist. I splayed my fingers on the manicure table while Marlowe selected the paint color for me, a Ryla Cosmetics shade called Show 'Em the Pink. Then Marlowe and I attended a class called Strippercise, but Marlowe's commentary didn't go over well and we were escorted out by a security guard. A woman on the Upper East Side taught me how to do kegels.

After the penultimate task we were in a taxi and I felt exhausted, resting my head against the window, letting it bang on the glass every time we hit a bump. I was used to life in Brooklyn, hidden away in my apartment on Swann Street, trekking to the café and letting myself go like an overgrown garden. The makeover had been days of mowing and pulling weeds, a whole landscaping experience that was painful and disheartening. I still didn't feel like Alicia. If anything, I had never felt more like Plum. It was her body I had seen in mirrors, her flesh that was painted and waxed and injected with toxin. If Alicia was buried under there, she was impossible to see.

"Next comes the dieting portion of the makeover," Marlowe said, "but you're having surgery instead. You're cutting right to the front of the line, you cheater." She took me to a plastic surgeon, Dr. Peter Ahmad, famous as the pioneer of the "mommy makeover," a package deal that included a breast lift, tummy tuck, and vaginal rejuvenation. He also specialized in post–weight loss surgery reconstruction, which is why Marlowe chose him. In the waiting room, a nurse came for me. Her nails were painted the same shade as mine. Marlowe stayed in the waiting room as I was led to the doctor.

Dr. Ahmad asked me to disrobe. We stood in front of a full-length mirror, him in his suit, me naked. I had never been completely naked in front of a man before. The humiliation would have been overwhelming before, but I was numb from days of being prodded and worked over. Even the sight of my crotch — sleek as a hairless cat — didn't inspire horror. As I stood before the mirror, beneath the bright lights, the shocks of Y—— withdrawal began to needle me again. I could feel them under my skin, but in the mirror I couldn't see them.

"As I'm sure you know, on a diet your body shrinks slowly," said Dr. Ahmad. "With the bypass you'll lose the weight quickly, so you'll be left with a lot of sagging skin. It will require a number of procedures, which I can do for you." He took the cap off the black marker he was holding. "First thing is a tummy tuck," he said. He lifted my stomach and pressed it in, as if it were clay. "You'll have a flat stomach when we're through. We'll cut here," he said, holding up my stomach with one hand and with the other drawing on me with the marker. He started on my left side and drew a dark, thick line all the way from left to right, showing me where the incisions would be and where he'd stitch me up. He let go of my stomach and let it flop back down.

"That'll be a long scar."

"It'll fade over time. You won't even notice it." He moved his hands to my breasts, pushing them up, cupping them in his hands. "You'll need your breasts lifted. I would also suggest implants to give you more fullness." He drew on my breasts with the marker, showing me where he'd cut and stitch me back up. He traced around my nipples; in the mirror they looked like eyes, the wide outer rim of my stomach at the bottom a smiling mouth. "You're not ever planning to breastfeed, are you? You probably won't be able to after this procedure." He showed me where my new nipples would be positioned, in a place higher than they'd ever been.

Next he asked me to hold my arms straight out. "Your batwings are pretty significant, so there will be a lot of hanging skin we'll need to remove." He drew on the flab hanging down from my upper arms. "We'll do an arm lift. The scar will be in your armpit, so no one will see it." I stood frozen with my arms outstretched as the doctor drew on me. He moved behind me and placed his hands on my butt. "The last big thing you'll need is a complete lower body lift.

We'll remove the sagging skin from your thighs and your behind and then lift everything, giving you a smoother, tighter appearance." He turned me around and gave me a handheld mirror so I could see my reflection in the larger mirror behind me. He bent over and continued to draw on my skin with the marker, long smooth lines and smaller dotted lines all over the back of me. I pictured him with a pair of scissors, cutting my flesh as if it were cloth.

He stood up and told me to put my arms down. He maneuvered me back slightly so my face was directly under the bright light above the mirror. "You're probably too young for a facelift, but we'll see how it goes with the surgery. Be prepared for the fact that you'll look older when you're thinner. Fat is like a natural collagen, so without it you'll wrinkle more." He turned my face to one side. "Your nose is a bit big. I could fix that." *Big compared to what?* I wanted to ask. Not compared to a Volkswagen.

Dr. Ahmad put the cap back on the marker and smiled at me. "That's it," he said. "You may need some lipo if you have small pockets of fat here and there, but we won't know that until you've had the bypass. You look worried. Don't worry. You're in good hands. I do this all the time. Several times a week, in fact. In about a year from now, you could be a whole new person."

He left me to get dressed and I looked at myself in the mirror, full on. There was Plum's body with black lines showing how Alicia would be carved out. I'd look like Frankenstein by the time it was over. I turned full circle, trying to take in all the black marks. No matter what I did, there was no escaping the body that trapped me. I could see that now.

In the taxi on the way back to Calliope House, I didn't say anything to Marlowe. She congratulated me on finishing the makeover and handed me a copy of *Fuckability Theory*, which she'd signed *For ~~Plum~~ Alicia, love Marlowe xo*. I noticed the book's dedication: *To the 3 Stus and Sharlene.*

"What's wrong?" Verena asked when we walked into Calliope House.

"Nothing, I'm just tired."

"Making yourself fuckable is a lot of work," said Marlowe.

"I'm not fuckable," I said. *I'm Frankenstein.*

Verena told me to go to her office at the top of the stairs, that there was a present for me. Hanging on the back of the door was a new version of the white poplin shirtdress with purple trim, along with a pair of purple tights. More than double the size of the original, this duplicate dress was like a cartoon. I set down my bag and Marlowe's book and held the dress in my hands. For some reason, I wanted to put it on.

I locked myself in the bathroom, where there was a pubic hair on the toilet seat, as black and spindly as a spider's leg. I took off my clothes and replaced the black control-top tights with the purple ones. There was a brief flash in my mind of Leeta, she of the colorful tights. I stepped into the dress and then stood before the mirror. Seeing Plum wearing Alicia's dress was like looking in a funhouse mirror. Alicia, blown up twice the size she should have been. The dress was sleeveless, so my upper arms were visible, with the pattern outlined by the doctor's black marker. The pattern of Alicia.

Thankfully I couldn't see my whole body in the bathroom mirror, but what I saw reminded me of Janine, the outcast from the Baptist clinic, with her bright and colorful wardrobe. What if it were my fate to look like Janine forever? *What if this is your real life? What if you're already living it?* Only a month earlier that had seemed impossible.

"Plum, are you all right?" Verena called up the stairs.

"Coming," I said. I turned away from the Plum-Alicia hybrid in the mirror and returned to Verena's office to collect my things. I didn't bother to change into my regular clothes — I wanted to leave the red-walled house as quickly as possible. As I was about to walk out of Verena's office, I saw the bottle of so-called Dabsitaf, the French diet pills, on her desk. I stuffed the bottle into my bra, in the space between my breasts. I was downstairs and out the door before Verena and Marlowe realized it, heading toward the subway in the dress, my legs bulbous and grapelike in the purple tights, which didn't press in my stomach.

In the subway station at Fourteenth Street, I waited on the platform for the train, conscious that people were staring at me in my costume. I concentrated on the blackness of the tunnel, but from the din of the station, a male voice cut through.

"Can you imagine doing *that*?" the man said, loudly enough for everyone in the vicinity to hear. He was about thirty, wearing a polished gray suit, standing between two other young men in suits. The trio was unshaven-on-purpose, wearing white shirts and ties in different colors, the only way to tell them apart. They laughed at the woman in the white and purple dress, knowing she could hear them, but not caring.

Not today, I thought. *Please don't do this today.*

I turned to face them. The shame and embarrassment I felt made me want to keep quiet, as always, but then I remembered:

A Baptist isn't afraid to take risks.

I looked at the man who'd made the comment and said, "I'm too much woman for you. From the looks of you, you probably like to diddle little boys." The two guys next to him, the friends, his white-guy posse, laughed.

They shouldn't have laughed.

The fist of the man who'd made the comment came flying at me. I saw it coming — the white paw, the hairy knuckles, the ring finger wrapped in a thin gold band. I opened my mouth as if to yell but his fist hit me before I could, the gold band smashing my lip into my incisor. I stumbled backwards, past the white line, near the edge of the subway platform. Someone screamed, but it sounded far away. I turned my head and saw the train approaching, the silver bullet, its white light heading toward me. My arms moved propeller-like as I fought for balance. Blood filled my mouth. I didn't want to die this way, not with these people watching, but the white light was moving closer. I

255

braced for impact, but then I felt hands pulling at me.

I fell to my knees on the platform as the train blew past. "He tried to push her onto the tracks. Did you see that? He tried to push her."

The doors of the train opened and the passengers stampeded out, knocking me from side to side. When the crowd thinned and the train closed its doors, a woman knelt down next to me. "Are you all right?" She helped me to my feet. Another woman handed me a wad of tissue from her purse, which I held to my lip. The man and his two friends were gone.

When the police came, they asked me to describe what had happened. "He said something rude to me," I told them, but I couldn't repeat what he'd said. "I confronted him and he punched me."

"He tried to push her," said the woman who'd offered me the tissue. "I saw the whole thing."

The officer said they would review the closed-circuit television and then contact me. I wrote my name and address on the form, as requested, and so did the witnesses.

The officer asked me, for the second time, if I needed the paramedics.

"I just want to go home."

A 2-train pulled into the station and I settled into one of the orange plastic seats. The man sitting across from me was shrunken and old, and I could see myself reflected in the glass above his head. I stared at myself, Plum in Alicia's dress, a bruise forming above her lip. The woman in the glass stared back.

Girls Will Be Girls

The 7:30 a.m. Metrolink to Los Angeles Union Station was due. The girl weaved between the waiting commuters. The women and men, staring into their newspapers and phones, took no notice of her. She should have been getting ready for school, this lone girl on the platform, a shawl wrapped tightly around her slender body. Her feet were bare, but she didn't feel anything; she couldn't. Her body didn't belong to her anymore, not after the attack, not after so many people had seen the photos online. Soon, she would leave her body behind.

When the women and men on the station platform looked at her with their morning eyes, they saw a girl, but not *that girl.* Her identity was a secret, but they had all read about her, even if they didn't know it. She'd been dissected before she was dead.

As the train approached the station, the girl

felt it in her feet before she could see it. "Stand behind the line," the man on the speaker said, but the girl didn't stand behind the line. She rushed forward, and leapt.

La luz se fue.

The girl liked to ride around in cars with boys, that's what they'd said. Did you see how she dressed? *Slutty-ass bitch.* She sure didn't look twelve.

Luz lived with her grandmother in a house on the outskirts of Santa Mariana, an hour north of Los Angeles. Her mother had been away from home for more than a year. If her mother had been around, Luz wouldn't have been riding around in cars with boys — she would have had to stay at home and do her homework every night and forget about sneaking out — but it was her grandmother who was in charge, half blind and hobbled by arthritis.

On television, a local resident said, "Where was this girl's mother? This is her fault."

With her mother serving as an army medic in Afghanistan, Luz was largely unsupervised and went where she pleased. This didn't go unnoticed around the neighborhood. She was a girl who had wandered away from the safety of the herd, a feral girl, easy prey. Did you see how that girl was dressed?

It happened in an abandoned apartment, on a dirty mattress in a bedroom with no curtains on the windows. A classmate's older brother, a man named Chris, had invited Luz to a party. Chris and his friend Lamar picked her up. They drove her to the apartment, but Luz could see there wasn't a party, just a group of men standing around, waiting. Chris told Luz to take off her clothes. Come on, Lamar said, we know you've done it before. He said if she didn't do it, he would cut her. He had a knife, so she undressed and lay down on the mattress in the middle of the room and that's how it began. Chris went first, then Lamar, then the other men, taking their turns one after the other. Luz stared at the ceiling, not wanting to see their faces, and waited for the hours it took to be finished.

On television, the mother of one of the accused men said, "That girl let them boys run a train on her."

When the men left, Luz was alone in the apartment. She crawled into the hallway and pulled herself up. She wasn't going to tell anyone about what had happened; they said if she told anyone they would kill her.

It was Chris's little sister who told. She saw pictures on her brother's phone of Luz naked on the mattress. There were photos of Chris on top of Luz, and photos of Lamar on top of her, and photos of other men she didn't recognize. The girl posted some of the photos online and shared them with her friends. She told the principal, hoping Luz would get into trouble. *Slutty-ass bitch.* The photos of Luz and the men circulated throughout the school and on social media.

The principal called the police. The faces of Chris Martinez and Lamar Wilson were the only recognizable ones in the photos, but the police counted at least four other men who'd been present. When questioned, Martinez, twenty-one, and Wilson, twenty-three, said the girl had consented to sex. They said she'd told them she was eighteen. She liked to ride around in cars with boys, they said. She wasn't a virgin.

In the newspaper, one of the mothers of the accused men said, "That little girl lured my son to the apartment."

After their arrest, Martinez and Wilson gave up the names of the four other men, who were also arrested. The local news media covered the case. A community leader said young men of color were being harassed by the police. Threats were made against Luz, the *slutty-ass bitch* who'd gotten the guys into trouble. Social Services was considering moving her to foster care in another part of the state until her mother returned home, but it never came to that. One morning, Luz made her way to the Santa Mariana train station, wrapped in a shawl.

On television, after Luz had jumped in front of the train, a pastor from the local church said, "Why wasn't this girl's mother supervising her? That's what I'd like to know."

Luz's mother returned home from Afghanistan to bury her daughter. Martinez and Wilson were released on bail, but the other men had been on probation and remained locked up, luckily for them. Soon after Martinez and Wilson returned home, they disappeared. No one had seen them in more than a month.

Every day for twelve days, the editors at the *Los Angeles Times* received a video via email. The videos, each titled "Death Porn," were shot in grainy black-and-white and featured a different man sitting in front of a concrete wall. There was a tiny shard of light to illuminate the scene, just enough to differentiate the man from the shadows. The men were unshaven, naked, and sweaty, their hands and feet bound with rope.

Twelve men, twelve videos.

The men in the first two videos were immediately recognizable to the newspaper's editors as Chris Martinez and Lamar Wilson. They both pleaded to be released, writhing and moaning against the concrete and restraints. A female voice, off camera, sexy, said, "Do you like pain?" Then the screen went black.

Each of the videos played out in a similar way. The men had been kidnapped over a period of a month, taken from their homes, offices, or hotel rooms, their disappearances reported by wives, mothers, coworkers. There was no trace of them, until the videos began to arrive.

The third video featured the star player for a Super Bowl championship team. He'd been accused of raping two women in two separate incidents, one in Miami, the other in Seattle. In both of the investigations, the police officers had asked for autographs and posed for photographs with the star athlete, who said the sex with the women had been consensual. No charges were ever brought, but he was suspended for three games by the NFL. On Super Bowl Sunday, millions of Americans ate potato chips and drank beer while watching the man throw a ball around a field. They clapped and cheered for him. On a visit to L.A., he went missing.

The next two videos featured two European soccer stars who'd been accused of paying an underage teenage girl for sex — a *prostitute,* the media had labeled her. The players denied the accusations, but the claims against them and media interviews with the girl had engulfed two of Europe's leading soccer clubs. Prosecutors eventually declined to press charges, but the scandal only grew wider in Europe, involving other athletes and even more underage girls. While in Los Angeles to play an off-season charity match, the two soccer stars went missing.

The star of the sixth video was a film director of Eastern European origin who was accused of raping a thirteen-year-old extra during the filming of a remake of *Lolita* a decade earlier. It was consensual sex, the film director had said; in his culture, standards were different. "The girl was a Lolita," the producer of *Lolita* had told the police, in defense of his director friend. Over the years, the acclaimed film director was dogged by protests and controversy, but no charges were ever brought, and he went on to win two Academy Awards. After a business lunch at the Chateau Marmont, he vanished.

Six other men with similar profiles were also targeted by the kidnappers, including a county attorney from Texas who'd refused to press charges against a teenage boy who'd molested a little girl because, as he told the girl's mother, "boys will be boys." Another target was Hal Jizz, the creator of the pornographic websites RevengeHer, where men retaliated by sharing intimate photos and videos of ex-wives and girlfriends, and VietCunt, which enabled Internet users in North America to access women and girls in Vietnam, who performed whatever actions the user requested via webcam. Someone in Ohio could pay to see a fourteen-year-old girl molested by an old man.

The media dubbed the twelve kidnapped men the "Dirty Dozen." The director of the FBI appeared on television to plead for their release: "We urge members of the public to come forward with any information that might lead to the rescue of these twelve men," he said, sounding official, but it was clear his heart wasn't in it.

The friends and family of the Dirty Dozen stayed mostly clear of the media. The mother of Hal Jizz, when confronted outside Saturday-night bingo at her local American Legion, said she had "no comment" on her son's kidnapping. When asked if she was proud of her son, the old woman, her hair wiry and gray like a scouring pad, took a drag on her cigarette and turned to the reporter, her black eyes penetrating the camera, "What do you think?" she said. In the parking lot of the Van Nuys accounting firm where he worked by day, employees ran from their cars to the building with file folders held over their faces, trying to outrun reporters.

The FBI director appeared on television again. "These twelve men have not been convicted of anything," he said, but many commentators thought that was the point. "Kidnapping is a serious crime. If you have any information, please come forward. It's not easy to transport and hide twelve grown men. Someone out there must know something."

But no one did, apparently. A week later a skydiving plane went missing from an airfield in Nevada. The twelve men were dropped from the plane into the desert. The coroner estimated that the men, alive and without parachutes, fell from an altitude of at least 10,000 feet. By the time anyone noticed the plane had been stolen, it had crashed into the Sierra Nevada and animals were feasting on the men's remains. There were no bodies in the plane. Investigators surmised that the kidnappers had parachuted out of it before the crash.

On her cable news show, Cheryl Crane-Murphy said, "As a committed Christian, it pains me to admit that I feel nothing but glee at the death of these pigs. God forgive me."

THE *NEW BAPTIST PLAN,* TASK FOUR: BLIND DATES

Nearly a week had passed since the make-over. The bruise on my lip had faded, but the black lines on my body hadn't. I wasn't bathing or dressing or eating. I reclined on the sofa, wrapped in a sheet, tortured by shocks and by nausea. The television news was filled with reports of the Dirty Dozen. I watched the scene unfold in the Nevada desert, where the police had erected tents around the bodies to keep the wild animals away.

"Is this the work of Jennifer?" Cheryl Crane-Murphy asked. She was on TV all day now, as if she were covering a war.

The FBI director said, "We have no evidence to suggest this crime is linked to the others, but all avenues of inquiry remain open."

The news coverage zigzagged across the

country. A high-ranking government official in Nevada, who was immersed in a scandal concerning his extramarital affair with a young female intern, spoke to the media: "This is the largest manhunt in Nevada state history," he said in front of the cameras, drinking from a glass of water every few seconds, his hands unsteady.

"Misbehaving men are feeling the heat," Cheryl Crane-Murphy commented to her viewers.

"If the perpetrators of this crime are still within the borders of the state, we will find them," the official said. "I realize these men were not particularly popular figures, but as my father always said, 'Hate the sin, love the sinner.' " If I hadn't been feeling so lethargic, I would have groaned.

The coverage then moved to the home of RevengeHer and VietCunt creator Hal Jizz, who had become a familiar face. There'd been a candlelight vigil outside his house. On the front lawn of the Jizz household in the Inland Empire, the votive candles in their glassy red holders had looked like fireflies. A woman named Monika T. was being interviewed. "I went to Hal's house last night to remind people of the values this country was founded upon," she said.

"Tying up a girl and [bleep]ing in her face

while screaming that she's a dirty [bleep]-ing whore?" Cheryl Crane-Murphy asked.

"It's called freedom of speech, Cheryl. It's in the Constitution," Monika T. said.

In Los Angeles, the mother of Luz Ayala, the girl who'd jumped in front of the train, was about to appear in a televised press conference. Soledad Ayala had been blamed for her daughter's rape, for being away in Afghanistan when it happened. She stepped forward to the podium now. Her head was ringed with a black braid, secured tightly in the way of military women, with no wayward strands, no hint of whimsy. She wore an ankle-length dark blue dress and no makeup or jewelry, her only adornment a badge on her chest that bore her daughter's smiling face.

"It's been a month since Luz's suicide," Soledad began. "I admit I've taken comfort in the deaths of two of my daughter's rapists, knowing they won't be able to attack anyone else. I'm not ashamed of this." She was looking down at a piece of paper, eyes hidden behind her lids, head tilted gently to the side, displaying the muted solemnity of a Madonna. "I've come here today at the request of the FBI. We don't know if you're a real person, Jennifer, but I would like to speak to you as if you are, woman to woman.

I served as a medic in Afghanistan and I saw death, too much death. When you take a life, you lose part of yourself. I don't want this to happen to you. Tell us, Jennifer: When will the violence end? You want change, we can all see that, but let's find a way to work together." Soledad's voice cracked at the end. With her statement finished, the insect sound of the clicking cameras intensified. She waved away reporters' questions and disappeared into a group of dark-suited federal agents.

"That woman is the epitome of bravery," said Cheryl Crane-Murphy, dabbing a tissue at her crusty lower lids. "She served her country honorably in Afghanistan, and while she was gone, a pack of wild animals ripped her daughter apart."

I switched off the television, having seen enough for one afternoon. Luz was even younger than most of Kitty's girls, the girls I had been deleting. I wondered if something so terrible had ever happened to one of them.

For a moment it was silent in my apartment, but then the phone began ringing. I knew it was Verena or Marlowe and didn't answer it. Since the makeover, they'd left many messages for me, but I had no intention of talking to them. I wished that I had never gone to Verena's house and had never gotten involved with her and the so-called New Baptist Plan. As with the original Baptist Plan, by the end of it I was fat and unhappy. I'd been replaying everything that'd happened during the makeover with Marlowe, and what happened after — the visit to the plastic surgeon, the man's fist coming at me. At night when I was trying to fall asleep I saw his fist.

The bottle of Dabsitaf I'd stolen from Verena was sitting on the coffee table. I reached for it and shook it, listening to the pills rattle like dead bugs in the amber plastic. If I decided against surgery, I could use the $20,000 to fly to Paris several times and stock up on the drug. Verena said there could be deadly side effects, but the same was true of the surgery. And besides, even crossing the street carried risks.

I considered taking one of the pills, but I didn't have an appetite so there was no point. No matter where my thoughts wandered, they kept returning to the man on the subway platform. Would he have hit Alicia? Maybe he would have flirted with her and she would have been flattered. The thought of it made me hate Alicia, and I didn't want to hate her.

There was a knock at the door, and

through the peephole I saw that it was a deliveryman with a brown parcel. I told him to set it outside the door, and when he was gone I took it inside, knowing what it was before I opened it — one of Alicia's new dresses, a pool of silky emerald fabric. Alicia didn't deserve such a nice dress, not after her flirtation with the nasty man on the subway platform, but then, Alicia didn't know he was nasty. Only Plum could see that side of him.

The telephone rang again but I didn't answer it. When I listened to the message, I expected to hear the voice of my mother or Verena, but it was a man named Preston, reminding me of our date.

The blind dates. Somehow I had forgotten it was time for the first one. Dates with four men awaited me, for which I had Verena's dentist, Gina, to thank.

"Well, hello there," Preston said when I called him back to cancel. I rested on the sofa, holding Alicia's new emerald dress. Preston told me that he had made a reservation at a restaurant called Christo's and asked if that was okay.

"About that, I don't think —"

"If you don't like Greek food, we can go somewhere else."

He chattered on. Gina via Verena had sent

me notes about each man. Preston was a financial analyst and Gina's cousin. I finally managed to say that I wasn't sure if the date was a good idea.

"I don't like blind dates either," he said, trying to sound casual, trying to win me over. "But let's just do it. No pressure. At the very least we'll have a nice dinner, right?" He was almost pleading, and I wanted to laugh. He thought he was speaking to a normal woman. He had no reason to assume otherwise; my voice sounded normal.

I had already fulfilled the first three tasks and there was no sense quitting now with only two tasks left, so I agreed to the date. I wanted to see the look on his face when he saw me. Plum would be humiliated, which is what she deserved.

There were several hours till the date, but I began to get ready, knowing it would take a while. My waxed body had begun to sprout hairs, so I lightly shaved my legs and underarms. The sink and the tile floor were littered with short black pieces of hair and drops of blood. I wiped up the blood with a piece of toilet tissue. I didn't shave often and realized I should have done this in the tub. In the mirror I saw that my vulva was still mostly hairless and sleek. I didn't like looking at it. Even the place from where I pissed and bled had needed beautification and improvement.

I bathed and washed my hair, then put on my underpants and Thinz and control-top tights and my push-up bra. The white and purple dress that Rubí had made for me was black at the knees from the subway platform, so I wore one of my usual black dresses. I was like a horse all saddled up. Sitting down at dinner would be difficult, never mind eating, but girls didn't eat on dates. At least I didn't think they did. I'd never really been on a date, so I didn't know what I was supposed to do. I tried to remember what characters in movies did. Deception was part of it. Pretending to be prettier, slimmer, and less hungry. *Being a woman means being a faker.* That's what Marlowe had said.

I fixed my hair in the bathroom mirror, straightening and smoothing the black bob. Next I applied the makeup as the makeover expert had shown me: primer, foundation, concealer. This erased much of my natural face. Then I began to paint with my brushes, applying the blusher and bronzer first, but then wiping them off because I looked burned from the sun, not sun kissed; I was aiming for sun kissed. Next, my eyes. I curled my lashes, what there were of them; I lined my eyes and then daubed a light shadow over my lids and applied mascara. Then I penciled in my brows, saving my lips for last. After looking through my collection of liners and lipsticks, I settled on a pink shade called Statutory.

I stood back to observe. According to Marlowe, the makeup was meant to enhance my fuck-me look, but the face in the mirror didn't say *fuck me,* it said *punch me,* as it had said to the man on the subway platform. The bruise had faded, but I didn't want it to fade. I wanted everyone to see it. I turned away from the mirror and tried to resist what I felt like doing, but I couldn't. I balled my right hand into a fist and then punched myself on the lip, on the spot with the faded bruise. I hit myself once and then again so it would hurt more. Hurt is what I wanted. *It hurts, but it feels good too.*

PRESTON

I heard the street door downstairs open and braced myself for the knock at my apartment door, and then for *the stare.* Preston would be expecting a thin person — people always expect a thin person — and so I knew when he laid eyes on me for the first time, he would react as everyone reacts, by trying to hide his surprise and disappointment, even revulsion. From the inside I felt small and insignificant, but that's not what people saw when they looked at me.

It took a few moments for me to overcome my reluctance to open the door. Once I opened it, I saw standing before me Preston, a generic white guy with brown hair, around thirty years old. And there it was: *the stare.* "Hello. You're . . . uh. Is Plum at home?"

"I'm Plum," I said, hating the sound of my name.

"No you're not." Preston laughed.

The door was obscuring half my face, the bruise hidden. Preston reached for my arm. "Oh, I'm sorry, I didn't . . . I mean, sometimes Gina plays these practical jokes on me and I —" He ran his finger around his shirt collar. "Let's have dinner," he said.

I went inside to get my handbag, letting the door close slowly behind me as Preston stood in the hallway. He made no move to open it or come inside. I collected my bag from the kitchen counter, but when I went back to the door, instead of opening it, I locked it — the double bolt and the chain.

"Plum?" Preston called from the other side.

"Go away."

He didn't argue with me. I heard him walk down the stairs and open the door to the street.

JACK

My next date was with Jack. According to Gina's notes, he was an assistant professor of literature at NYU. I readied myself in the same way as I had for my first date, putting on makeup and compression garments, though this time I covered up the bruise on my lip with a bit of concealer. My face was finished, my *fuck me* look complete — except I didn't think Jack would want to fuck me. He would be like Preston.

My wands and brushes were scattered over the shelf in the bathroom, but I didn't put them away. I decided to continue. I applied powder to my face, the lightest powder that I could find in my bag of tricks, covering up the foundation and blusher I had just applied. *Your skin is white as a rose,* Julia had said when we first met, but now it was whiter than that, a shimmery corpse-white. I reached for a lacquered compact with a cake of black powder meant to be wetted and used to line the eyes in a sexy Cleopatra way, but I smeared it over my lids instead, all the way up to my brows and under my eyes as well. I added layers until my eyes were sunken into dark black holes, like the hollow pits in a skull. My lips were already painted with Juicy Plum, the shade that Julia had given to me, but I added some of the black powder so they were purplish and dark, the lips of someone deprived of oxygen. When I stood back to observe, Jack was already knocking.

"Just a minute," I called, slipping on the white and purple dress with the stained knees.

When I opened the door I saw another generic white guy, this time with blond hair. "Are you . . ."

"Plum, that's me."

I couldn't be sure, but he didn't seem to notice the makeup. He didn't seem to know where to put his eyes; they jutted every which way but at me, to the door frame, to his watch, to his feet. Finally he scanned my body, trying to take me all in. He swallowed a lot. We made it as far as the bottom of the stairs before he said, "I heard you work at a fashion magazine."

"Yeah, I do."

"No offense or anything, but you're not really my type. I'm attracted to a different sort of woman. It's nothing against you personally or anything. I don't like redheads either, not that you're a redhead, but you

278

know what I mean."

We stood at the bottom of the stairs, on the inside of the street door. He didn't want to be seen with me in public. "Let's forget dinner. Go home," I said. Then I added, "You're not my type either. You look like a girl."

He wiped a curl back from his forehead. I walked up the stairs and knew he was watching me from behind, my ass cheeks moving, my hand grasping the rail as I huffed my way to the top. "Fat bitch," he called after me.

I reached the landing and turned to face him, out of breath. "I'm afraid you'll have to try harder than that to insult me, sweetheart. I'm bulletproof." Thanks to the New Baptist Plan, my sensitive side was growing a callus.

Once in the apartment, I locked the door and held my breath until I heard the downstairs door shut. I took off my tights and the Thinz and my bra and my dress. I washed off all the Halloween makeup and then rummaged in the cupboards. I didn't have my appetite back, but I pulled out a graham cracker, broke off a corner (15), and popped it in my mouth.

"Fat bitch," I said.

ALEXANDER

I was going to meet Alexander at a BBQ restaurant in Brooklyn Heights. Once again I was wearing the white and purple dress, which I had washed out in the sink, leaving the knees not black but a dishwater gray. For this date I wore only light makeup and no Thinz. There was no need to go to extremes. Alexander was blind.

When I read Gina's notes I was intrigued. I had often wondered what it would be like to have a blind boyfriend. I thought it might feel nice for a blind person to run his hands over so many soft layers, without the hardness of bones getting in the way.

In the taxi on the way to the restaurant, a wave of nausea hit me. The never-ending symptoms of Y——— withdrawal. I nearly fell over onto the back seat.

"We're here," the driver said, and I picked up my head.

Inside the restaurant, the hostess, wearing a denim skirt, led me to the middle of the crowded room, forcing me to squeeze between the tables. When I arrived at Alexander's table, there was no *stare.* What a relief, I thought. He took my hand in his, but I pulled it back quickly, worried that my fleshy fingers might give me away. I was playing Alicia tonight.

Alexander's brown eyes were vacant and slightly shrunken, but he looked in my direction when he spoke, as if he could see me. I didn't know if this was for his benefit or mine. I took my seat and looked at the menu. Alexander ordered a platter of ribs, but I wasn't hungry and ordered a salad. He probably thought I was one of those girls who didn't eat.

When the waiter left, Alexander began to talk without pause. I could tell he didn't like silence in conversation. I wondered how many dates he went on and how he could decide whether he liked a woman. He must have been sizing me up for my potential as a sexual partner, but there wasn't a hint in his questions to let me know what he was looking for. He told me about himself and his work as a session musician. He asked me about my job with Kitty. His blindness didn't seem to imbue him with any special qualities. Nothing about Alexander interested me, but I played my part. I was sitting across from a man on a date in a restaurant, just as Alicia would do. Alexander didn't know I was an impostor. He talked about musicians I had never heard of and I was glad I didn't have to hide the bored expression on my face.

When our food came, Alexander navigated

his plate, the ribs and sauces and side dishes, with remarkable skill. He cleaned each bone of meat and then dropped it onto his plate. My salad was modest and I picked my way through the tangle of lettuce leaves, radish slices, and tomato wedges. The sight of Alexander feasting on the bones, with the red sauce on his lips, was unpleasant. His eyebrows jutted out from his forehead as if on a ledge, almost prehistoric; he had the profile of a Neanderthal.

"Are you enjoying your salad, Alice? Are you sure you don't want something more?"

"It's Alicia," I said. "And no thanks, I don't have much of an appetite."

"You're not on a diet, are you?" he said, somewhat playfully.

"I like to watch my figure. It's not easy maintaining a size two." It was difficult to say this without laughing. I nearly choked on a lettuce leaf.

"Don't want to get fat?" he said, and smiled.

I laughed, a deep-bellied guffaw, too big for my imaginary thin self. He continued eating, cleaning one bone and dropping it onto his plate, then doing the same with another. There was a growing pile of bones in front of him, stripped clean of meat, the sauce sucked off.

"I used to be fat," I said. "*Enormously* fat. Morbidly obese, in fact. On the insurance company weight charts, there's only one level after morbidly obese and that's death. It goes *underweight, average, overweight, obese, morbidly obese,* and then *certain death.* When you reach certain death, they ask you to write your will and special-order your coffin. I was nearly at *certain death,* Alexander. I was browsing the coffin brochures."

"Jesus, how fat were you?"

"Over three hundred pounds. I was a real blimp."

"*Really?* How did you lose the weight?" He held a bone in midair.

"I tried dieting, but that didn't work. Then I had surgery. My stomach is now the size of a walnut, hence the salad."

"Does your body look, uh, *normal?*"

I saw the black marker, the arrows, the dotted lines. "With clothes on, yes. Naked it's another matter. I have scars all over my body. I've been reconstructed, you see. Imagine Frankenstein."

Alexander set down his bone and looked as if he was fighting off a belch.

"It's not a pretty sight, Alexander, but what does it matter to you?"

He wiped his mouth with his napkin. "The

thought of it is unappealing, I must admit, but I appreciate your honesty, Alice."

"Alicia," I said. *I am Alicia. I am Alicia.* I repeated it to myself, but that didn't make it true. I was not Alicia and I feared I never would be.

"I'm not feeling well," I said, setting down my fork and scooting my chair back. The Y—— -related symptoms returned. It felt as though there was a sparkler inside my mouth. "I think I should leave."

"Don't let me keep you. I'll just stay here and order dessert."

I left him alone at the table. Alicia's first date was over and it hadn't gone well.

AIDAN

It was Sunday night, my last date. Aidan had been described to me as a human rights lawyer and drinker of fair-trade coffee. I put on my dress and the Thinz and the makeup. Aidan knocked on the door, and a few moments later a generic white guy with brown hair stood before me.

"You're my date?" he asked.

"That's me."

"You've got to be kidding."

"Screw you," I said, and slammed the door.

■ ■ ■ ■

After Aidan left, I washed my face while still wearing my dress; the front of it was splashed with water and stained with makeup. I took off the control-top tights and the Thinz so I could breathe, then crawled into bed on my stomach, still wearing the dress. I had completed four tasks of the New Baptist Plan, with only one left to go, and then the money would be mine. The date of my surgery was still a couple of months away. Before meeting Verena I'd been moving toward it in a straight line, but now there was movement in another direction, a subtle drift.

I thought back to the winter, when I'd decided to have the surgery. I'd undergone my annual physical exam, and though everything appeared normal, the doctor wanted me to have an ultrasound done, to make sure everything was "okay inside." I had never had an ultrasound and was nervous. That afternoon I reported to the hospital and a young technician named Pooja placed a condom on a probe and stuck it inside me. She flicked a switch and a screen on the wall revealed an ultrasound image of my reproductive organs.

"There are your ovaries," she said, and I squinted to see them. They were a whitish blur against a gray background, slightly alien-looking. "And that's the entrance to your womb."

It was such an odd word, *womb.* I had never thought of myself as having one. A uterus, yes, but not a womb. A womb was a place for something small to curl up in and sleep. For the first time, I realized such a place existed inside me. It didn't look like anything nice on the screen, just a dusty balloon waiting to be inflated.

"I have a womb," I said.

"Of course you do. You're a woman." The technician stared at me as if she thought I wasn't quite right in the head. "Are you okay?"

I didn't answer, but stared at my womb until I couldn't anymore. I closed my eyes so I didn't have to look at it. Why did she have to call it that? *Womb.*

"You'll be ovulating from your left ovary next month," she said. "See that follicle?"

"Yes, I see it," I said, still with my eyes closed.

Pooja spoke to me as she spoke to her other patients, the women who had things going in and out of them, like trains in a station. On the screen I was like them, the

286

sum of my parts. Underneath my bulky exterior I was like every other woman, even if I had never been allowed to feel that way.

After my appointment, I walked home in a daze. I had never liked to call myself a woman. I knew I was one, but the word never sounded right when applied to me. For days I thought of nothing but the womb on the screen. It haunted me.

Over the years I had considered weight-loss surgery, but the thought of knives and incisions and complications had always scared me, so I had never done anything more than think about it. But in the days after seeing my womb, I finally made an appointment with a doctor and scheduled the surgery, knowing it was time to act. Verena had said the surgery was about becoming *smaller,* but it was about more than that. That's what I hadn't been able to tell her.

Now in the wake of the New Baptist Plan, the dream of the surgery had been tarnished. I could still have it, and the $20,000 would help, but there would always be scars, not just on the outside, but on the inside too. Verena had been intent on reminding me just how much everyone hates me. Alicia would never be able to forget the horrible things that had happened to Plum. The surgeon's knife couldn't cut that away.

Alicia would always be marked.

My bottle of Y—— was on the nightstand. I'd been taking the half tablets for a month; there was only one left and I worried about what would happen when I ran out completely. Maybe Y—— was the glue holding my life together — not a life so much as pieces of cracked china that had been fit together haphazardly. I took the last half tablet and then opened my nightstand drawer to find the bottle of Dabsitaf. I swallowed one, then another, then a few more.

I wanted to hear another person's voice, a kind voice. I considered calling my mother, but she would have been able to tell something was wrong. She was alert to even the slightest shift in my tone of voice, the length of silence between words. I didn't want to worry her, so I called my father. It was eight o'clock in New York, but it was only six where my father lived, in a place where life was slower and everything lagged.

His wife answered the phone. She told me he was mowing the lawn and set the phone down to get him. I thought of my father as I always thought of him, in the chair on the deck where he liked to sit after work, listening to birdsong. Through the phone I heard the lawn-mower stop and imagined the smell of fresh grass clippings, a whiff of the heartland.

When my father picked up the phone, out of breath, I didn't tell him about the dates or Verena or the other women at Calliope House. He didn't know much about my daily life, so we talked about what he was doing in the yard, that after he cut the grass he would read the newspaper. On his end of the phone, unlike mine, it was quiet. In the suburbs there was an absence of noise.

"Are you all right?" he asked.

"Maybe I'm not having such a good day."

"Do you want to talk about it?"

"No."

He said nothing else, giving me time, allowing the silence. My mother would have asked questions and demanded to know what was wrong. I liked that my father was quiet on the other end of the phone, simply breathing, letting his yard work wait until I no longer needed him.

I listened to his breathing and wished that I could touch him. I wished that he could see the bruise on my lip, but he couldn't.

"Are you there?" Dad said.

"Plum, are you there?"

Verena called to explain about a series of blind dates. She said there would be four men: Preston, Jack, Alexander, Aidan. These names sounded familiar. Hadn't we done this before?

After six months on Dabsitaf, perhaps I was ready to date. Dr. Ahmad had been wrong about my body. After such rapid weight loss there was no sagging skin, no need to cut and stitch. I had simply shrunk, my flesh vacuumed in, with no evidence of a void left by my fat. I was Alicia. That's who people saw when they looked at me.

On Dabsitaf I wasn't hungry. I didn't starve and binge. I simply had no appetite. Many people skipped breakfast, but I skipped lunch and dinner, too. Eating a slice of bread would have made as much sense as eating a book or a shoe. I didn't want food. I didn't want water. I didn't want to get out of bed or go outside. I didn't want to talk to anyone. I didn't want to think. I didn't want to buy anything, not even clothes or shoes. I didn't want love or friendship or sex. I didn't want to listen to music or read or watch TV.

I didn't want.

Without food, I didn't have energy or mental focus. I didn't want to work, but I needed the money. Kitty had forgiven me for deleting her messages, and when she saw how I'd been transformed she invited me to work in the Austen Tower in the office next to her. Reading and forming sentences was beyond my ability, given the lack of nutrients, so I sat at my computer and typed gibberish words that looked vaguely Norwegian — lsjfslkf jslkfjsl kfjalkjfla kjdflsk jflasjflsakjf — until it was time to go home. No one seemed to notice.

In my natural state, after my factory settings had been restored thanks to Dabsitaf, I was lovely. On the way home from work, men whistled at me. I couldn't walk by a construction site without causing a commotion. On the subway men pinched my ass, they followed me, they asked for my phone number and gyrated their pelvises as if they were pronging me. I was supposed to find this charming, so I acted flattered. I was supposed to want this kind of attention, but I didn't want anything. Not anymore. Thank you, I said when they gave me flowers, but I didn't feel thankful. The inside of my head was blank.

Before long I weighed one hundred pounds. I hadn't weighed that little since elementary school. One day when I came home from work there was a note taped to my back that said, FEED ME! Women came up to me in the street and asked me what my secret was. "I don't eat anything, ever," I said, but this wasn't entirely true. I swallowed my Dabsitaf tablet once a day. I could see the oblong pill descend through my body, down my neck, between my breasts, heading toward my bellybutton. It looked like a bug inching along beneath my skin.

When I reached ninety pounds, chunks of my hair began to fall out, my fingernails became brittle, my cheeks sunken and hollow. "What's your secret?" a woman in the park asked me.

I was a size zero, but only for a few weeks, and then I was less than zero. At the department store, the saleswoman said, "We don't have clothes in your size," and I seemed to remember that people said things like that to me in my previous life, but they would laugh and snicker. Now they were jealous. "Bitch," a woman whispered to her friend. I was sent to the children's section, but even that was difficult. I was taller than most children, and whereas children were round, I was as slender and pointy as a garden rake.

On the night of my first blind date, I had taken to wearing pink gingham overalls that I cinched around my waist with an extra-large rubber band. Preston asked if I'd like to go to dinner at Christo's, but I said I didn't eat anything, ever, so we sat on my sofa and talked. Well, Preston talked. The inside of my head was blank.

By the end of the evening, predictably, Preston was thrusting on top of me, filling me with his juices, injecting me with calories, nothing by mouth. I didn't try to stop him. I didn't want to. When he finished, I thought I felt one of my bones crack.

"I'll call you," he said on his way out.

"If that's what you want."

The next night, a man named Jack was at my door. "Are you Plum?" he asked.

"Plum? She doesn't exist." *Burst!* "I prefer to be called Alicia."

Jack said he was a professor of literature and asked me what kinds of books I liked to read. I told him I had thrown my books away, that I no longer wanted them. "You're not one for conversation," he said, so he took me dancing. During the slow dances, he nibbled my ear. Later on, in the ladies' room, I saw that one of my earlobes was perforated. Now I was even lighter.

Back at the bar, I stirred Jack's martini with

my finger. He licked my finger clean and then bit off the top, chewing the tip and the nail along with his olive. "You taste so good," he said.

My next blind date was with Alexander, who was a blind date, literally. He was fond of ribs and slathered my torso with BBQ sauce. There wasn't much meat on my bones, but he contented himself with the gristle, and by the time he left I weighed fifty pounds. *This is too low,* I thought. *At some point I'll disappear.*

It wasn't Aidan who came next, as I had expected, but the man who had punched me in the subway. "No, not you!" I screamed, but he chewed my tongue and took a bite out of my neck. When the others came back for seconds, I couldn't object. They were all in my bed at once, devouring my pieces. This had gone too far. I wanted to scream but no sound came out. I wanted to hit them with my arms but I didn't have any. I wanted to cry, but they'd taken my eyes. Soon they finished me off.

I was the flame of a candle, blown out.

The telephone rang. It sounded as loud as a church bell in my quiet apartment. I opened my eyes and began to reach for it, but then I saw my hand in a strip of gray light coming in through the window.

My hand. It was pudgy and white.

I tossed back the covers and looked down at my body, patting my breasts and my thighs through the white and purple dress. At the end of the bed I saw my ten toes. *This little piggy.*

I was still me.

There was the bottle of Dabsitaf on my nightstand and the aftertaste of medication on my tongue. I wasn't sure what was real, besides the ringing telephone. I picked it up.

"Plum?" a woman said.

I tried to place the voice. "Is this Kitty?"

"Plum, I need to see you right away."

I rubbed my eyes. "Did I forget about our meeting?"

"This isn't about our meeting. I'm at home right now but leaving for the office soon. Come see me as soon as you can." She hung up the phone without saying goodbye.

Kitty rarely called me. Something was wrong. My bladder ached, so I rushed to the bathroom. As I sat on the toilet, I looked at the rippled white of my inner thighs. In the dream I'd had perfect thighs and breasts and legs.

Thighs, breasts, legs — an order of fried chicken.

As I brushed my teeth, I stared in the mirror at my bloated face, at my chin and the chin beneath that. In my dream the men had taken bites of me, crunching my eyeballs and fingers like crudités. The memory of it made me wretch in the sink. I hadn't eaten anything substantial in days, and there was nothing in my throat but the lingering taste of Dabsitaf.

After drinking some coffee, I dressed quickly and left my apartment, not knowing that I wouldn't return for a long time.

It was raining. I was awake, not dreaming, I was sure of it. Men didn't look at me. A woman in a business suit was doing butt clenches at a bus stop and eyed me warily as I passed. I was wearing a clear raincoat printed with colorful flower buds that in my size looked like a bedspread.

Storm clouds grew darker overhead and I decided to skip the subway and take a taxi instead. I didn't want to see other people. I didn't want them to see me.

As we drove through the rain, it occurred to me that Kitty was going to fire me. She must have found out I'd been deleting her email, or maybe she knew I'd given the addresses to Julia. No matter what the reason, I knew it was over.

The taxi driver was eating sunflower seeds. The sight of his stubbled jaw moving up and down, his Adam's apple jutting outward when he swallowed, was disgusting. The sight of a man eating anything was something I couldn't bear. I wanted to roll down the window, but it was raining too hard, so I wiped the fog from the glass and peered outside. We were crossing the Williamsburg Bridge, heading into Manhattan.

The driver turned up the radio. "We know Jennifer cannot be a single person. She has to be a group," said Nola Larson King.

He dropped me off near Times Square, as close as he could get to the Austen Tower given the barricades. As I walked toward the building, my feet plunging into deep puddles, I heard someone call my name from behind. It was Kitty.

I turned to face her, but I wasn't prepared for what I saw. She'd been caught in the downpour. Her hair was wet and flat, the ends of it resting against her white blouse in sharp points, like snakes' tongues. I had only ever seen her with her red curls in their trademark formation, the carefully formed ringlets like a great strawberry bush.

"Kitty?" She was barely recognizable, a superhero without her cape.

"Let's go down the street," she said,

motioning to a coffeehouse. She didn't want me in the office in case I made a scene when I was fired. I followed behind her and noticed she wasn't carrying an umbrella. She was glum and I wondered if her mood, and her indifference to the rain, and most of all her hair, were because of me. She must have felt betrayed. I didn't know what I would say when she confronted me about the deleted messages. I looked at the sidewalk. Julia was down there beneath the wet concrete of Times Square, which now reflected a pretty pattern of neon light.

Kitty was far ahead of me down the sidewalk, and I considered turning around and running away. I hadn't committed a crime, after all, and maybe it was better to go home and send her a letter of resignation in the mail. Then I wouldn't have to face her. I slowed my pace, about to change direction and blend into the crowd, when I saw something ahead that made me stop and suck in my breath.

Leeta's face was on the side of a building.

I lifted the hood of my raincoat and wiped the wet hair from my face. The rain continued to splatter, but even through the water and the fog I could see Leeta's face.

Kitty noticed I wasn't beside her and started walking back toward me. "Hurry up, it's pouring," she said, but I was frozen in place. It was really Leeta.

"Plum?" Kitty said. "What's wrong with you?"

I pointed to Leeta on the screen. "Do you see that?"

There was her face, then the faces of the Dirty Dozen, then the faces of Stella Cross and her husband, then the other faces associated with Jennifer, all flashing on the jumbo screen in Times Square. Leeta, with her thick black eyeliner and long dark hair, was staring out at the New York masses the way she'd stared at me in the café. It was her face on the screen, and now everyone was looking at it.

"Plum?" Kitty said again, but I was walking back to the Austen Tower and into the lobby. I went through the metal detectors and asked the guard to call Julia Cole in the Beauty Closet, but he said there was no answer. I could have used my employee ID to go past the guard and find Julia myself, but Kitty was behind me. "I've had enough," she said. "You're fired." Her words echoed around the marble lobby. *Fired, fired.* People turned to look.

"I allowed you to write in my voice. I trusted you to pretend to be *me*," she said, "and you threw my girls in the trash. Thousands of them."

There were things I could have said to Kitty, but without the hair she had lost her power. I pushed past her, heading out into the street to find a taxi.

"Did you hear me?" Kitty shouted, but I had already left her behind.

When I arrived at Calliope House, I was in a state of near panic. I opened the door without knocking and was enveloped by the comforting red walls. Verena came from the back of the house, her pale hair and skin a light moving toward me through the long, dark hallway.

"I've been trying to get in touch with you," she said.

"Leeta." That's all I could say.

"You've seen the news."

"This can't be happening. Is this real? I don't know what's real anymore." I went into the ruby red living room and sank into a chair, wetting the fabric.

"No one knows what's happening," Verena said, with Marlowe at her side. "Leeta's wanted for questioning, but she's disappeared. The police are looking for her. I'm sure she hasn't done anything wrong."

"Then why are the police looking for her?"

"It must be some sort of mix-up," Marlowe said.

I was vaguely aware of the news playing on television or radio, a monotone recitation of events. "My life is unraveling and now this, now *Leeta*. It's too much."

Verena knelt down next to my chair and pushed the strands of wet hair from my eyes. "I think you're ready for the last task of the New Baptist Plan."

"I've had enough of your stupid plan. Before I met you I had some semblance of a life. I had a job and now that's gone. I had plans for surgery and now I'm confused about that. Everything is slipping away from me."

"I never said the New Baptist Plan would be easy."

"No calorie counting and no weighing, right? If I don't become thin, what's going to happen to me?" I saw a calendar reaching years into the future and every page was blank.

"Let's finish the New Baptist Plan," Verena said. "You can do it right here at Calliope House. We'll take care of you." Being taken care of is what I needed.

Marlowe said, "Please stay here with us, Plum."

And I did.

I followed Verena and Marlowe outside

into the rain, down the front steps of Calliope House. To the right of the steps, unseen by passersby, there was another series of steps leading down to a red door, its frame overgrown with ivy. This was the door to the basement.

I followed them down the steps. Down we went, down to the very bottom.

■ ■ ■ ■

UNDERGROUND

■ ■ ■ ■

THE *NEW BAPTIST PLAN,* TASK FIVE: DISCONNECTING AND REFLECTING

The underground apartment was nestled into the earth beneath Calliope House, deep in the place where roots grow. The walls vibrated faintly whenever a subway train passed by. This dark, cool space was where I landed after weeks of falling. It was Leeta's appearance in the café more than two months ago that had caused me to lose my balance. I tripped into a hole, where strange things happened and even stranger women dwelled. Spinning and falling, trying desperately to steady myself, I kept reaching for something to cling to on my way down.

In the underground apartment, darkness wrapped itself around me. I didn't resist. I'd taken my last half-tablet of Y—— and a handful of Dabsitaf the night before I went underground. I slept deeply, but I was also restless at times, rolling around in the twin-size bed, sweating into the sheets. My body was screaming for Y—— in those moments, but it wasn't going to get it. I was finished with drugs.

When I finally opened my eyes after many hours, I swung out of bed and placed my feet on the floor. There was a lamp on the nightstand and I switched it on, surveying the bedroom, only vaguely remembering my arrival hours — days? — earlier. I was dressed in a baggy beige shift and black leggings, which Verena and Marlowe had given me after I'd followed them down the stairs. The clothes were my size, so they'd prepared for my arrival. Verena had given me her phone and told me to call anyone who would notice I was missing. I called my mother and Carmen. There was no one else. I made up a story about going on a retreat with Kitty and her staff. I explained that it was a last-minute trip because Kitty had forgotten to invite me, which is something that could have been true.

Then Verena and Marlowe left me alone. In the bed, on the edge of sleep, I recalled Leeta's face on the screens in Times Square and hoped I'd been hallucinating.

My bedroom in the underground apartment contained only the starkest, most minimalist furnishings. The furniture and walls were white, the linens were white, everything was white — I was living inside an aspirin. In the dresser, more beige shifts and black leggings, plus pajamas and underthings. I didn't know what had happened to the backpack I'd brought to Calliope House. My laptop and wallet and everything else must have been aboveground, in that world I'd left behind.

On top of the desk was a stack of books, including *Adventures in Dietland* and *Fuckabilty Theory,* a cup full of pens in different colors, and a notepad with a message on top:

Plum, I'll see you tomorrow afternoon. Rest until then.

Love, V.

Tomorrow afternoon meant nothing to me. I had no idea what time it was or even what day it was. There were no windows or clocks in my bedroom. I opened the door and peeked into the hallway, then stepped out in my bare feet. It was quiet and the overhead lights were dimmed. The underground apartment was a maze of underlit hallways. I ran my hands along the walls as I walked, feeling my way.

There were three other bedrooms along the narrow corridor outside my room, all of them unoccupied. At the end of the corridor was a bathroom, with the usual toilet, sink, and tub, but there was no mirror on the wall. Around the corner, down another narrow passage, there was a cramped kitchenette, with a refrigerator and microwave, a sink and cupboards, a table and chairs. Like the rest of the apartment, it was pill-white, but in the semidarkness looked dullish gray. In the cupboards I spotted boxes of cereal and crackers; in the refrigerator a jar of pink yogurt and a sandwich on a plate, wheat bread with a ruffle of green lettuce sticking out. I assumed the sandwich was for me, but I still didn't feel like eating. Before going underground, I'd been weaning off Y—— for more than a month and experienced loss of appetite; before that I'd been following Waist Watchers obsessively. For as long as I could remember, I'd been coasting on a near-empty belly. I guessed I had lost at least thirty pounds, maybe more.

Leaving the kitchenette, I continued my tour, turning a corner and heading down another dark corridor, lined with cabinets. I opened one of them and glimpsed stacks of white towels and sheets, plus cakes of white soap. I was about to snoop in another cabinet when I heard a noise, something in the distance. I had assumed I was alone. Closing the cabinet lightly, I strained to listen. What I heard was moaning, muted cries, wounded-animal sounds.

In a tiptoe, I moved to the end of the hall and poked my head around the corner, afraid of what I might see. I was faced with another dark corridor, this one entirely black except for the light emanating from the end of it. The light was shifting and crinkling, like an electrical storm viewed from afar. I walked through the darkness toward the light. The sound grew louder, the light grew brighter — I held up my hands to shield my eyes as I stepped through an archway.

The room was circular, larger than my bedroom and the other bedrooms combined. The walls were banks of screens, all of them synchronized with the same scenes. I rotated in the middle of the room, disoriented, the space dark except for the light from the screens. There were two folding chairs in the center and I sat in one of them.

On the screens were a naked woman and three naked men on a bed. The men's penises were inserted into the woman's vagina and anus and mouth. After a minute, the men removed their penises and reinserted them in different places. There were always three penises inside the woman. The men twisted themselves and contorted the woman so that what they were doing was visible to the camera. As the scene went on, the woman became haggard, her black eye makeup smeared with semen and sweat. She was the underside of a piece of Lego, her bodily orifices nothing more than slots for the men's penises.

I stood up from my chair and backed away. In my haste to escape the room, I tripped over the second chair and fell to the floor, wincing as I landed on my right arm. Squeezing it in pain, I rolled over onto my back and looked up at the ceiling. There were screens there too. In the basement I couldn't see the sun or the moon or the stars, but these screens were there in abundance, showering me with moving light. The Lego woman was looking down at me, as if imprisoned behind the glass, as if she could see me. She wasn't beautiful, but I supposed she had the necessary parts. Brass-colored clumps of hair fell to her bony shoulders; on the top of her head was a ring of thick black roots, like a dark halo. I tried to picture her getting off the bed and drying herself, putting on her clothes and leaving the windowless bedroom, but I couldn't.

She didn't exist outside that room, not without the men's penises filling up her empty spaces.

Rushing down the hallway, I wound my way back toward my bedroom, my eyes still blotchy from the screens. In only a short time, I had become accustomed to darkness.

I didn't know why that room existed or whether I'd been meant to see what was playing on those screens. What did that room have to do with the last task of the New Baptist Plan? I had thought the worst of the plan was behind me, but now I wasn't sure.

Passing my bedroom, I proceeded to the front door, the entrance to the underground apartment. Perhaps it would be easier to leave than to find out what Verena had in mind. The door was heavy steel, gray and mottled. I didn't know whether it was locked, but I reached for the handle and felt the shock of cold metal.

I paused, then let go of the handle and backed away. I knew what was on the other side of that door. If I went outside and walked up the steep flight of stairs, it would be like emerging from a cellar after a storm. I would be forced to survey the wreckage of the life I didn't recognize anymore, not in the wake of the New Baptist Plan. Above ground, I no longer had a job. I was confused about the surgery. I was upset about the treatment I'd received in recent weeks — the humiliation, even violence. On top of it all, I no longer had the protection of Y——.

My life was like a handbag that had tipped over, the coins and keys and tubes of lipstick scattering on the floor. I couldn't bring myself to bend over and pick up the pieces, not yet. Despite the darkness of the apartment and the room with the screens, it was easier to stay underground than to face it.

The front door hinges shrieked, announcing an arrival.

"How are you feeling?" Verena stood in the doorway of my bedroom. I was sitting on my bed, doodling on the notepad. She handed me an iced coffee in a tall plastic cup. The green straw was a shoot of plastic grass, a reminder of the summer that was playing out above my head.

"I've been resting," I said, setting the cup on my belly, using it as a shelf. Verena sat at the desk, the chair turned toward me, and crossed her legs. Her skirt looked like an old petticoat, the white linen yellowing, the eyelet at the bottom frayed.

"Glad to hear it. That's what the last task of the New Baptist Plan is about. Disconnecting and reflecting."

I sucked up a mouthful of coffee through the straw. "I found that creepy room. What's that about?"

From her bag Verena pulled out her notepad and opened it in her lap, taking one of the pens from the cup on the desk. "Let's not talk about that today," she said. "For now I don't want you think about that room. I want you to spend a bit of time in there and *feel* it."

At this point I knew Verena let things unfold in her own time no matter how hard I pushed, so I moved on to the more important topic. "Can we talk about Leeta? I keep hoping I hallucinated her face on the screen in Times Square," I said, recalling my drug-induced haze.

"Yes, I noticed you stole my bottle of Dabsitaf. I hope you're not planning to take that? It's unsafe."

My dream of being devoured came back to me and I shook my head. "I did take it, but it gave me nightmares."

"If nightmares is all it gives you, consider yourself lucky."

Verena confirmed that my vision of Leeta

wasn't a hallucination. Leeta's roommate had contacted the police and told them Leeta had confessed that she knew the identity of "Jennifer" without providing specifics. The roommate said Leeta claimed she was "haunted" by something "bad" she'd done, but she wouldn't say what it was. The next day, Leeta had vanished and the roommate was worried. The police were anxious to speak with Leeta, but no one had been able to find her, so they made a public appeal.

"I'm hoping this is all a misunderstanding. Try not to let it upset you. I know it's a terrible shock," Verena said.

"How could it be a misunderstanding?"

"Julia came by the house yesterday. She said Leeta had a habit of disappearing, so there's nothing unusual about that. Julia thinks Leeta was joking around about knowing Jennifer. She said Leeta is, um, what was the word Julia used?" Verena looked up at the ceiling. "*Kooky.* Julia said Leeta just needs to return home and clear this up."

I knew from my own experience that Leeta was "kooky," but this behavior seemed beyond that. "If she's innocent, why hasn't she come home?"

Verena didn't have an answer. "Maybe she's scared? I don't know, but Julia said the idea that Leeta is involved in criminal activity is ludicrous."

I knew very little about Leeta, but what I did know for certain was that Julia wasn't a reliable source.

"I don't think Julia is lying about Leeta," Verena said, noticing my skepticism. Then she added, more quietly: "At least I hope not."

The last time I'd seen Julia, she hadn't explained why Leeta stopped working for her so abruptly; she had simply refused to discuss Leeta at all. In any interaction with Julia, what she didn't say was more important than what she did say. I asked Verena if she would bring me copies of the news stories so I could read them myself. It was still too difficult to believe that Leeta had been dragged into this, even by accident.

"All right, I'll bring them next time," she said, "but I've told you the whole story, which is nothing much. Leeta is important to you, isn't she?"

It seemed silly to say yes, since I didn't really know Leeta. She knew me better than I knew her. Leeta was as mysterious to me as she was to the people seeing her face in the news, and yet as I reclined on the bed in the underground apartment, I knew that she had led me to this place. I explained this to Verena.

"I had planned to talk about the surgery today and whether you'd made any decisions about it," Verena said. The surgery. It seemed as if my plans for it existed in the distant past, in a lifetime belonging to another woman. "But rather than us talking about that today, I think you should read this." Verena picked up her bag from the floor and dug through it. She pulled out a red spiral-bound notebook. At first I didn't recognize it. She handed it to me and I opened it to the first page and began to read:

may 18th: louise b. at café, typing on laptop. i think she's doing her work for the kitty-cat. she's been here for hours — so boring. two teen boys say something to her (what?) & laugh but she ignores them. i wish i could punch them in the face.

(she seems friendly with the owner of the café)

question: louise b. went to church this morning. why??

"Louise B.?" I asked Verena, confused.

"That was the name Leeta gave you in her notebook. Your black bob reminded her of

316

Louise Brooks."

Charmed by the nickname, I ran my hand over the notebook as if it were a priceless object. "Where did you get this?"

"When Julia came over yesterday, she gave it to me. She didn't want any trace of Leeta in her office, just in case."

"In case of what?"

"You know how paranoid Julia is. She thinks the police suspect her of having secret information about Leeta. She already thinks everyone at Austen is after her, and now this." Whatever the reason, I was glad Julia had given Verena the notebook.

Verena left me alone to read, saying she'd return again soon for another session. Only about ten pages of the notebook contained writing, a loopy scrawl in blue ballpoint. I had often seen Leeta holding the blue pen. Now I'd get to find out what she'd written with it.

may 21st: success!! today i figured out why louise b. and so many women visit that church during the week. they're not religious fanatics — even worse, they're waist watchers. (!!) the church rents out the meeting room in the basement. now we know louise b. is dieting (not surprising)

(jules, are you actually reading this?)

may 22nd: wondering how louise b. can afford to live in a brownstone in this section of brooklyn. (??) lots of really asshole-ish and pretentious people around here. louise b. would be better off elsewhere (in my opinion). but how does she afford it?? austen media pays shit. i don't think she has a roommate (her name is the only one on the mailbox). she's too square to be a drug dealer. family money? hmmm, doesn't seem like it.

may 23rd: i've never seen anyone from austen media visit louise b. i don't think you have to worry about her being friends with any of them, jules. i never see her with anyone outside the café, not ever ever ever. she's always alone.

it's so hot today but louise b. wears a long skirt and long-sleeved top. she never shows any skin except her hands, neck, and face. her clothes are black. she stares at the sidewalk as she walks. poor louise b. always looks like she's on her way to a funeral.

at the café all day. boring boring. (the coffee is good though)

may 24th: she spent all day at that café. went to supermarket on the way home & i saw some of the stuff she put in her basket:
— waist watchers frozen fettucine alfredo dinner/shanghai-style chicken & rice/fish & chips
— apples
— cans of tuna
— fat-free blueberry yogurt (!)
— fat-free mayo (!)
— licorice whips (huh?)
two skinny white guys (mid-20s, facial hair) browsing in the frozen food section took a photo of louise b. from behind with their phones. they were laughing at her. she had no idea. motherfuckers.

on the way home, louise b. asked if i was following her. OOPS! better work on my technique. (i played dumb) may 25th: ho hum ho hum. same old everything. louise b. goes to café, works on laptop, goes home. why's she so dedicated to the kitty-cat? (the patron saint of girls, our lady of teenage sorrows, the queen of austen media!) louise b. should aim higher.

(jules, did i tell you the rumor that's rampant on the 4th floor? apparently, the kitty-cat is a secret lesbian & the b-friend is just an accessory. heh. makes me think twice about her new column — "why are boys so baffling?" hardy har har.)

7:00 p.m. i'm outside louise b.'s place now. lights are on, curtains drawn. she's not gonna budge. she never does. i'm outta here.

may 26th–28th: memorial day weekend. i sat outside for **hours** this weekend. you're lucky i brought some good music but i'm getting tired of this jules. there's nothing to see here. she went out for a while on saturday but that's it. it's such a pretty day & her curtains are drawn. if i lived this life, i would slit my wrists. louise b. is making me seriously depressed.

i know you've forbidden me from speaking to her but i'm going to give her a copy of your friend verena's book. hear me out: louise b. needs a kick in the ass. watching her is like watching a caged animal at the zoo, except she doesn't know she's in a cage, she doesn't see the bars. i really think i could come back here in 30 years

& she would still be living this same existence — still dieting, living alone, working
at a job that's beneath her. she deserves
more than this. i like her, jules. she de-
presses me but i like her. don't be angry
at me for giving her the book, k?

my verdict: i think you can trust her to help
you spy on kitty. she might not agree to do
it but ask her anyway. push her. maybe
this is what she needs??

p.s. i wish she could meet your friend verena. can you make this happen, jules?
pretty please?

I read through the notebook greedily, my
eyes moving swiftly across each line. Leeta's
observations about me would have stung
much more if I'd read them back then, but
since I'd met Verena and the others, un-
flinching commentary about my life had
become the norm.

As an observer, Leeta had gleaned a lot
about me, but not the whole story. She
didn't know about the surgery, my plan for
escape so that I wouldn't be in the same
place thirty years later, filled with regrets,
having only lived half a life. I knew this
wasn't the kind of escape she'd envisioned

for me: surgery and weight loss, the ability to blend in with the crowd. She wasn't the blending-in type.

The margins of the notebook were decorated with doodles of butterflies and daisies and a stick figure hanging from a rope. I thought again of Leeta's face on the screen in Times Square. It wasn't real — it couldn't be. I didn't know where she was or what she'd done, but she had led me to Verena. Her notebook read like a story about me, but the next chapters were missing. She'd started the story in motion but hadn't stuck around to record the rest of it. I turned to a blank page. I started to write about the New Baptist Plan and the underground apartment, telling my own story. I realized I had no idea how it was going to end.

In the morning, or what I pretended was morning, I showered in the mirrorless bathroom and dressed in a fresh set of clothes from my closet. I'd never gone so long without seeing myself in a mirror. I patted down my hair, wondering what it looked like.

I went to the kitchen for a glass of water and saw that someone had been there. On the table was a plate with a cinnamon roll and a cherry Danish; next to that, a bottle of orange juice, a granola bar, a banana. The room smelled pleasantly of butter and icing, but I still didn't feel like eating. Also on the table was a file folder. I opened it to discover a cache of articles about Leeta.

LEETA ALBRIDGE LINKED TO "JENNIFER"?

NEW YORK: . . . After a tip from her roommate, whose identity is being protected, the authorities have sought Ms. Albridge for questioning . . . FBI Agent Lopez explained that Albridge's roommate said she confessed to knowing the identify of "Jennifer." Albridge also claimed to have done something wrong, but provided no details . . . With no one else linked to this baffling series of crimes, Ms. Albridge is quickly becoming the face of the mysterious group referred to in the media as "Jennifer," even though there is no evidence that she is involved . . .

WHEREABOUTS OF LEETA ALBRIDGE UNKNOWN

AMHERST, MA: The family of Amherst native Leeta Albridge, 23, held a press conference last night . . . "Leeta, please come forward. We know you're not a criminal," said her father, Richard Albridge . . . "There's not a violent bone in her body," said Albridge's mother, Ruth . . . Ms. Albridge's older half brother, Jakob Albridge, a Hampshire County police sharpshooter, said he taught his sister how to fire a gun, but "she was never any good at it" . . . Ms. Albridge graduated from the University of Southern California last summer and moved to New York City afterward . . . As a student in Los Angeles, she had volunteered as a rape crisis counselor and was considering graduate study in her home state of Massachusetts this fall . . .

AUSTEN SHOCK! WORRY SPREADS OVER "JENNIFER" INTERN

NEW YORK: . . . Albridge quit her internship at Austen Media before her disappearance . . . Editors liked the dark-haired young woman, though one recalled she had a penchant for snooping. A *Glamour Bride* editorial assistant claims she spotted Albridge photocopying a list of staff home addresses and telephone numbers . . . Austen Media chairman Stanley Austen has paid tribute to the company's nearly 300 unpaid interns, who he said are not violent or political . . . counseling offered for Austen staff . . . Julia Cole, Albridge's former supervisor in the cosmetics department, insists that Albridge has not done anything wrong . . . "I am simply shocked that her name has been connected to Jennifer," Cole said. "Leeta has a bright future ahead of her in cosmetics management. I know she'll be vindicated."

Julia. She'd been forced out of hiding into the spotlight. I wondered how she would fare.

I read through the articles several times, trying to reconcile the Leeta from the news with the woman who'd written about me in her notebook. The notebook, despite its incisive observations, was also girlish and in some ways reminded me of the Dear Kitty letters. It seemed absurd that she could know anything about the mysterious "Jennifer," but I had to admit that her behavior, at least according to the articles, was suspicious.

I left the kitchen with the articles, and once again the noises from yesterday filled the hall. This time they were louder. Could the person who'd left the articles and the food still be in the apartment? My stomach tensed at the thought of that room.

I moved down the dark corridor, approaching the light, and stepped through the archway into the circular room. Stella

Cross appeared on the screens, undead, animated and full of life. I had never seen her in action before. She writhed around naked on a bed before the camera moved to a close-up of her bare vulva, framed by the insides of her white thighs. This image, repeated on every screen, appeared like a flock of white birds with their wings spread open.

Into Stella's vagina went various objects: a penis, a dildo, and then other things — a Coke bottle, a string of rosary beads, a man's fist. I closed my eyes, wanting to erase the images from my mind, but Stella's vagina remained on the backs of my eyelids, as if imprinted there. She had nothing more than a sanitized slit between her legs, like the coin slot on a vending machine. All the women I'd seen on the screens looked that way. That's not the way I looked.

I recalled another screen: my womb on the ultrasound monitor.

With my eyes still closed, I turned around in the direction of the door and crashed into someone. "Don't close your eyes," a woman's voice said. "This room is about keeping your eyes wide open."

The woman with the burned face was standing before me, smiling calmly. I had seen her in Calliope House the day I began the makeover with Marlowe. She'd been eating an apple. I'd thought of her as a freak.

"Sorry I scared you. I'm Sana," she said. She pronounced Sana as sa-*naw,* the emphasis on the second part. She pushed a button on a control panel near the archway and the sound was muted, but the images continued to play. Without the sound for context, some of the scenes on the screens could have been from a horror movie, the women's faces twisted in what looked to be terror.

"Can't you turn off this porn?" I asked her.

"It doesn't turn off," she said. "It stays on all the time."

Apparently, the pornography was like wallpaper.

Sana explained that she worked upstairs with Verena and had brought down my breakfast and the news articles. She looked Middle Eastern and spoke with an accent that was pleasing but faint. Only one side of her face was scarred, I assumed from a fire. The flesh below her right cheekbone looked as if it had caved in, like clay on a potter's spinning wheel that had lost its shape and sunk. The scarring went from her face and down her neck and crept underneath her clothes. The left side of her face was unblemished, giving her two distinct profiles.

I didn't know where to look. I was so uncomfortable that I almost turned to the screens, just to have something else to focus on. To stare at the burned flesh would have been rude, but to avoid staring might have also been rude.

"I'm worried you're not eating," Sana said. "The food we've left for you hasn't been touched."

She was worried about me, even though she didn't know me. "I don't have an appetite."

"You're going to get sick if you don't eat. I'll bring you something tasty for dinner. How about a burrito?"

"I don't feel like eating."

"Vietnamese? Thai? I'll continue this tour of Southeast Asia until you tell me what you want."

"What I want is to leave this room."

"Don't leave," Sana said. "I know this room is crazy and sick, but it's also necessary. It's Marlowe's creation."

With the mention of Marlowe's name, the room instantly made sense. "I should have known," I said, feeling foolish for not seeing the connection sooner.

"She wrote *Fuckability Theory* in this room and she spends time down here working on the companion volume now. She says that if you're going to write a book about the sexual objectification of women, you need to face it. She says too many women look away. They close their eyes, like you did."

My eyes were open now. On the screens, Stella Cross was replaced by another woman. A man shoved his enormous penis so far down her throat that her face turned red. She gagged and choked. He went through a string of women this way. They lined up like baby birds with their mouths open, accepting whatever was shoved in.

"Does wanting to make yourself fuckable mean turning yourself into that?" I pointed to the open mouth on the screen. Not a face, not a body, just a mouth belonging to an anonymous woman.

"You're thinking about it too literally," Sana said. "Think of this room as the curtain pulled back."

I would have preferred that the curtain remain closed. I moved away from Sana and took refuge under the archway.

"You're lucky to experience this," she said. I glanced at her skeptically. "Women come to this room from all over the world. Two Egyptian activists left the day before you arrived. They'd been down here for two weeks, living in this room practically day and night. They'll never be the same again."

"I don't doubt that."

"No, it's a good thing," said Sana. "They're going to change the world. That's the power of this room. You do have to be careful, though." Sana explained that a young Ph.D. student from Toronto stayed in the room for a week. One night, everyone in Calliope House was awakened by her screams. They found her in the middle of Thirteenth Street, ripping out chunks of her hair. An ambulance transported her to Bellevue. "The mother called Marlowe a few days later to say that her daughter had completely cracked up," Sana said. "Of course Marlowe paid for her hospital bills. The point is, it's important to experience this room, but don't overdo it."

There was little danger of that. After only minutes in the room, I was feeling dizzy. Even without looking directly at the screens, I saw the pornography in my peripheral vision — the blur of rhythmic movements, pelvic thrusts, and forced entries. The repetition gave the sensation of rocking back and forth, as if I were on a ship, floating at sea. I leaned against the archway for support.

Stella Cross appeared on the screens again. "Why is Marlowe playing so much

Stella?" I asked, breathing deeply in an attempt to quell my nausea.

"Marlowe doesn't control what plays. Everything on the screens is streaming from Porn Hub U.S.A. Right now there are countless men and boys around the world with their pants around their ankles, masturbating to a dead woman," Sana said. "In a different age, a great poet would have written a ballad about that."

Standing in the middle of the room, Sana, with her brown skin and burned face, was incongruous among the cookie-cutter white body parts surrounding her. Her presence had filled the apartment with a different kind of energy. She was chatty and friendly and seemed too vibrant for this dim, underground place. I would have preferred to have met her aboveground.

"Do you come down here often?" I asked.

"When I need to. All the Calliope House women spend time down here."

The sight of Stella Cross on the screens again made me think of "Jennifer," which made me think of Leeta, who was never far from my mind. Had Leeta ever been in Marlowe's room?

"No," Sana said when I asked. "Access to this room is strictly controlled. Marlowe never met Leeta and she doesn't allow anyone down here unless she assesses them first and feels confident they can handle it. She made a mistake once, but I think she was right about you."

"What do you mean?"

"She said that you're strong. She described you as a survivor."

It was difficult to understand how those words could apply to me. "I don't see it that way," I said.

"It's not easy to live in that body, is it? Not in this culture, with so many shitty, hateful people everywhere. You haven't had an easy time of it. Anyone who can survive that is strong."

I turned from Sana and the screens and stared for a moment in the opposite direction, down the dark corridor, into the comforting black. I had always thought of myself as merely existing, but Marlowe thought I was strong. Leeta, Verena, Marlowe — since I'd met them, the eyes with which I interpreted the world around me were new.

Another day and night passed, or at least that's how it seemed. I lived by my body's rhythms, sleeping when I was tired, drinking when I was thirsty, and experiencing the stirrings of hunger. Since I hadn't been eating, I was weak from lack of nutrients and I had to drag myself from my bedroom to the bathroom. Without a mirror I couldn't see myself, but I knew my hair was straggly and matted in places. I had only the essentials — toothpaste and soap, a hairbrush. I didn't have deodorant or a blow dryer or a razor or tweezers or makeup. Running my tongue over my upper lip, I could feel the prickly hairs there. I was slowly reverting to nature.

I spent most of my time writing in Leeta's notebook, which I was making my own. The New Baptist Plan replayed in my mind: the doctor and his black marker, the man in the subway station, the blind dates, my Dabsitaf-induced dream. I felt humiliation and sadness, but also something else, an emotion I couldn't yet describe.

When Verena finally arrived, I had been writing in the journal for most of the day. "Are you ready to talk?" she asked, sitting in the desk chair.

I was ready. Verena asked if I had read Leeta's journal and I told her that I had. *poor louise b. always looks like she's on her way to a funeral.* There were lines that I'd never forget.

"What did Leeta see when she looked at you?" Verena asked.

"She saw a woman in pain."

"That's what I see too. You carry a great deal of pain around with you, Plum. Can you envision ever letting it go?"

"You can't let go of pain. It's not a balloon that can float into the sky."

"Okay, but imagine for a minute that it is. You put your pain into a balloon and you let go of it. It floats away. How do you feel?"

If I let go of my pain, there would be a hole inside me that was so vast I would cease to exist. I would be the balloon floating into the sky, not the other way around. There would be nothing pulling me down, nothing keeping my feet on the ground. My pain was my gravity.

"Without my pain, I wouldn't be me anymore."

"Pain takes up a lot of space," Verena said. "You could fill that space with other things. Love, perhaps? In our first session together, you said you wanted to be loved."

"I can't imagine anyone loving me while I look like this."

"That's only because you've never *allowed* yourself to imagine it. How can anyone love you if you hate yourself?"

"I know what you want, Verena. You want me to cancel the surgery, to stay like this." I ran my hands down the front of my body. "You're asking me to live a life that I don't know how to live."

"Calliope House is full of women who've chosen another path. It's possible."

"So I would have to live at Calliope House for the rest of my life?"

"Of course not. Think of Calliope House as a way station."

I picked up the notebook from where I'd set it on the bed next to me and skimmed the pages of Leeta's observations, the men taking photos of me in the grocery store and laughing, the teenage boys taunting me.

"I think there might be something good about being fat," I said. It felt good to say the word *fat*. I had always avoided it, but it had the same thrust as *fuck* and the same power — an illicit f-word, the top teeth digging into the bottom lip, spewing the single syllable: *fat*.

"Because I'm fat, I know how horrible everyone is. If I looked like a normal woman, if I looked like *you,* then I'd never know how cruel and shallow people are. I see a different side of humanity. Those guys I went on the blind dates with treated me like I was subhuman. If I were thin and pretty, they would have shown me a different side, a fake one, but since I look like this, I know what they're truly like."

"Explain why this is a good thing."

"It's a special power. I see past the mask to the real person underneath. I'm not living a lie like so many other women. I'm not a fool."

"Is Alicia a fool?"

"Alicia wants the approval of all the horrid people in the world."

"What does Plum want?"

"Don't talk about me in the third person anymore. This is my real life. I'm already living it, remember?"

"Okay, what do *you* want?"

"I don't want their approval."

"You wanted their approval before."

"Well, I don't want it now. Fuck them."

"You sound very angry."

"I am angry." That was the word that was missing from my journal. "But wasn't the purpose of the New Baptist Plan to make me angry? That's what the confrontations and the blind dates were all about."

"I didn't know how you were going to react to the New Baptist Plan. It might have strengthened your resolve to have surgery."

"It didn't."

"You've always been angry, Plum. I just want you to direct that anger where it belongs, not at yourself."

Verena was trying to help me, even more than she already had, and I was grateful, but I couldn't help feeling annoyed at her sometimes. She didn't know what it was like to be me, no matter how empathetic she was. There was a line between us, the line that existed between me and most people.

"I'd like to be alone now," I said. I moved from my sitting position onto my side, resting my head on the pillow, curling up under the sheets.

Verena didn't argue. She stood up and collected her belongings. On her way out, she placed a slip of paper on the nightstand in front of my nose. It was a check for $20,000.

"Why are you giving this to me now?"

"It's time," she said. "You made it to the final task of the New Baptist Plan. No matter what you decide to do with your life, we had a deal. A Baptist always keeps her word."

I picked up the check, noting all those zeroes. "If I don't have the surgery, I'll have to say goodbye to Alicia. I'll miss her. Is that silly?"

"You'll grieve for her," Verena said, "and then you'll move on."

When she left, I pulled the sheet over my head and began to cry, welcoming the release. Crying existed beyond thinking, beyond words. It felt good. When I couldn't cry anymore, I thought about what Verena had said. In my mind the balloon was red, like the walls of Calliope House. I thought about the painful things I might put into it. I imagined letting go.

"Knock, knock." Sana entered my bedroom, a white box in her hands. I had fallen asleep, but now lifted my head from the pillow. "What time is it?"

"About four o'clock in the afternoon." She came into the room and set the box on the desk. I struggled to sit up, worried that my face was red from crying. My eyes still felt swollen.

Sana was wearing loose gray slacks and a white T-shirt, with Keds on her feet. Her body wasn't thin or fat, but a slightly curvy place in between, and solid as well, as if she had strength. She smelled like the outside, like fresh air and sunshine.

"You need to eat," she said, not as a suggestion. From the box she removed a platter of small pastries and cakes, as well as a dish of what she said was saffron-infused cream. To make room, she pushed aside the books, including Verena's *Adventures in Dietland.* "If you don't eat you're going to get sick."

"Did you make all that?"

"You're kidding, right?" She placed a knife, a fork, and a tiny spoon on top of a napkin. "There's a Persian bakery on Seventh Avenue that I like. I thought I'd buy you a treat."

I appreciated her kindness, but I also felt exposed. "I need to wash my face. I feel like a mess."

"Take your time."

In the bathroom, I felt the urgent need to shower, wanting to wash from head to toes. Under the stream of water, in the steam and heat, I stood for much longer than was necessary. I didn't have access to the summer sunshine, so this was the next best thing.

When I returned to my room, the pastries and cakes, the dish of cream, were all spread on my desk, but Sana wasn't there. I picked up a slice of cake with my fingers — white sponge with icing and a sprinkling of crushed pistachio nuts on top. Once I bit into it, I tasted cardamom and rosewater. The bliss inside my mouth soon reached my stomach, filling the empty space, and I finished the cake in three rapid bites. I was so close to heaven, there were angels all around me.

I ate and ate. I thought of the baby birds and how their mouths were filled, but this wasn't the same. I didn't bother to count calories. There was no time for math. I had always hated math. Into my mouth I placed the leaves of phyllo, honey, and nuts, the deep-fried pastry sweetened with syrup, the soft cookies flavored with coconut and almond, dipped into the saffron cream. Vibrations of pleasure ran through me. My lethargy ebbed with every bite and I began to feel human again.

When I was finished, I placed my hand on my belly, unable to stop smiling. After several minutes I was thirsty, so I went to the kitchenette and drank two glasses of water. On my way out, I heard the sounds from Marlowe's room growing louder, then stopping suddenly.

"Sana, are you still here?" I called out.

"Yes!"

For the last time, I walked down the dark corridors to the circular room, feeling full and satisfied. Sana was there, sitting in one of the chairs in the center of the screens.

"I don't know how you can stand this place," I said.

"Sometimes I think of it as my church."

"You've lost me." I found that this often happened when I was talking to the women of Calliope House.

"You know how Christians believe Jesus

died for their sins? And they go like this?"
She made the sign of the cross. "For me
this room is like that. It reminds me of a
central truth about my life. Sometimes you
need to be reminded of that."

I didn't reply, but looked at her quizzi-
cally, letting her know I needed assistance.
She rose from the chair and came toward
me. "You and I can never look the way
women are supposed to look." *You and I.*
Only weeks before, such a comparison
would have plunged me into despair, but
now I could see her point.

"Do you think we're the same?"

"In the ways that matter, yes. We're different in a way that everyone can see. We can't
hide it or fake it. We'll never fit society's
idea for how women should look and be-
have, but why is that a tragedy? We're free
to live how we want. It's liberating, if you
choose to see it that way."

The line that existed between me and
most people didn't exist with her. I wanted
to touch her face. I didn't ask if it was all
right, I just placed my hands on either side,
touching the burned place, feeling the
smooth, pearly flesh. My hands were filled
with the warmth from her skin. In her pupils
were tiny reflections of the screens, like
white flecks.

She blinked them away.

"Thank you for feeding me."

"You're welcome, Sugar Plum. Do you mind if I call you that?"

"I don't mind."

"I hope to see you aboveground soon," she said. She left me alone with the screens. My impulse was to turn away, but she had warned me not to do that. The sanitized slits, these entrances to the world, filled the room.

The slits disappeared, making way for a naked young woman kneeling in a patch of grass. She was outside in a yard or a park, surrounded by a pack of men. The men were only visible from the waist down, their voices muffled like the adults in a Charlie Brown cartoon. They took turns shoving their penises into the young woman's mouth. They grabbed at her body, pulling her hair and jerking her head back. She was soaked with their fluids, but still she smiled, this causer of mass erections, her naked body beamed around the world to subscribers of Porn Hub U.S.A. The scene went on and on, until the men were spent, and when it was finished, the young woman wiped the semen from her eyes.

Sana would have been pleased that I didn't look away. What I'd seen was a surprise. I couldn't recoil from the young woman on her knees in the grass, even though I wanted to, because we had something in common. If there was a spectrum, the young woman was on it and I was on it and so was every other woman I knew. Eulayla Baptist was there, bursting through her jeans. *In nine months, you'll be looking foxy!* That's what Gladys had said at my first Baptist Weight Loss meeting. *Foxy, hot, fuckable.* Whatever it was called, that's what I'd wanted — to be hot, to elicit desire in men and envy in women. But I realized I didn't want that anymore. That required living in Dietland, which meant control, constriction — paralysis, even — but above all it meant obedience. I was tired of being obedient.

I left the circular room, passing through the archway, walking briskly through the dark corridors to the front door of the underground apartment. I turned the handle and there was a click — the door swung open, revealing a tiny vestibule and the red door that led to the outside. I tried the handle of the red door and it opened. For the first time in days I felt sunshine and fresh air on my face. I snapped off the head of a rose that was dangling from a vine near the door and rubbed its petals against my cheek.

Shutting the door behind me, I walked up the steep concrete steps, which were warm beneath my bare feet. Outside there was no thrusting, no back-and-forth rhythm, and I steadied myself as I climbed. At the top I was awash in sunlight. The brightness of the sun burned through everything before me, and I saw nothing but shadows and shapes at first.

"Here she is," said a voice. It took me a moment to recognize that it was Marlowe's.

"She made it." That was Sana.

"What took you so long?" asked Verena.

Through the sunlight they appeared before me, swathed in light. "I'm here now," I said.

I had made my escape.

■ ■ ■ ■

Eat Me

■ ■ ■ ■

I'd been living aboveground in Calliope House for more than a week, sleeping peacefully every night. Then the bomb threat came. I was awakened by pounding on the doors, which began with the front door downstairs and then spread throughout the house, far away at first but moving closer — an outbreak of thunder, an approaching storm.

My bedroom door opened and Sana's face appeared through a strip of light. "Bomb threat," she said, as if I knew what this meant. Before I could ask a question she was gone. I heard scurrying on the floors above and below me and rolled out of bed, then changed from my pajamas into my clothes. If there was a bomb, it might have exploded while I was wasting time putting on my bra and shoes.

The young policeman standing on the stoop as we trailed outside was probably wondering why so many women were living together in the same house, without any men. He held the door open and, once Verena was out, asked, "Is that it?"

We were cordoned at the end of the block with the rest of the neighbors. The clusters of red and blue police lights made our genteel street look like a disco, but we shuffled along slowly, barely awake. On Sixth Avenue, Verena claimed two benches. There were eight of us: Verena, me, Sana, Rubí, and four women who were staying as guests. We looked like we had fled a slumber party. There wasn't much traffic at three a.m., but the cars that did pass slowed down to stare at us.

Sana yawned and set her head on my shoulder, resting her arm across my back. "Are you wearing a *bra*?" she asked.

"I put it on before coming outside."

"In the face of possible death by explosion, you put on a bra?" Rubí said.

"That's not proper bomb threat etiquette," Verena said.

"Ha ha." I let them tease me. No one bothered to tell me what was happening and I assumed someone wanted to blow up Verena — an old disgruntled Baptist, perhaps, or someone else she'd angered with her rants against the diet industry. As I sat on a bench in the black hours of night, it made sense. But then a man in pajamas and leather slippers walked toward us. The pajamas were patterned with tiny cowboys lassoing tiny steers. He stepped over a passed-out homeless man, whom I hadn't noticed. "We've got to do something about this," the man said. "Do you like being woken up in the middle of the night?"

Verena looked up at the man. "I'm not going to help you throw out the Jews," she said. She was marmoreal under the street-light, in her white gown, with her light hair.

"This has nothing to do with the fact that they're *Jews,*" the man said. "Don't say it that way."

"If they weren't Jews, terrorists wouldn't be terrorizing them," Verena replied.

The man waved his hand at her in disgust. "We're going to act with or without you," he said. "Don't forget — if they go down, you go down."

As the man stalked away, Verena explained that the Jews in question were our next-door neighbors, the Bessie Cantor Foundation for Peace and Understanding, a nonprofit organization that occupied the townhouse next to Calliope House, which was in fact attached to it. *If they go down, you go down.* For years the foundation had been the target of frequent bomb threats by unknown terrorists, who claimed that Bessie Cantor was a front for the Mossad. The businesses and residential neighbors wanted to evict the foundation from the block for all the trouble the bomb threats caused, for the evacuations and police presence and potential for mass casualties. Verena refused to take part in the growing campaign. "First the Jews, then us," she said.

The man in the cowboy pajamas approached another group of neighbors, and it was clear they were talking about us. They stared and pointed at us, the women on the benches, as if on an island.

We were the outcasts.

At dawn, we were allowed back into the house. The other women returned to their beds, hoping to sleep for an hour or two, but I went directly to the kitchen. Since leaving the underground apartment and moving upstairs, I had spent most of my time in the red kitchen. Verena maintained a well-stocked pantry and in a frenzied few days I had worked my way through it, cooking and eating under the shadow of Eulayla Baptist's fat jeans. I couldn't remember when I'd spent such a happy, carefree time. I loved to bake most of all, making cakes and breads and fruit pies from scratch. Baking was restorative. I was soothed by the jeweled berries, the yellow of an egg yolk punctured with my fork, and I liked the texture, too, placing my hands in the soft flour, cutting into the white flesh of a bright green apple and feeling its juices on my fingers. After being underground, I now found an apple to be wholesome and pure.

I shared what I made with the other women but always kept enough back for myself. I could eat half a dozen cupcakes at once, followed by great gulps of cold milk. I could eat a peach pie in the afternoon with a pot of coffee and a can of whipped cream. No matter how much I ate, I didn't feel full. In the past, after I binged, I'd rein myself in. I'd been doing that for years — diet-binge, diet-binge, the old two-step — but this was different. I never felt full, no matter how much I ate. It was as if the hunger from a decade of dieting was stored up inside me and the chains that had been wrapped around it were beginning to break.

That morning, while the other women slept, I made breakfast in the blue light at the back of the house. I put quiches in the oven and warmed the waffle iron. I hadn't known about the bomb threats, but even with this new information, and the realization that we could all be blown to smithereens at any moment, I had never felt safer. Calliope House was filled with the scarred and the wounded, like me. Some scars were visible, some not.

Only a few of us actually lived in Calliope House. Each morning around nine a.m., the other women who worked with Verena arrived, filling the house with hivelike noise and energy. With me in the house, the kitchen became a gathering place, my homemade food devoured instead of the usual takeout and deliveries. The morning of the bomb threat was no different. I set out the quiches and piles of waffles, pitchers of orange juice. The smells filled the house like warm, fragrant breath. Soon I had company.

Rubí was the first to fill her plate. I had admitted to her that I'd ruined the poplin shirtdress she'd made for me during Marlowe's makeover, but she said she still had the pattern and some of the fabric, if I decided I wanted another one. Sana was next in the breakfast line. When we first met, I didn't know how to look at her, but I no longer saw a *scarred* face, just a face. This allowed me to notice her beauty, especially her eyes. They'd been spared any damage and were deep brown with a touch of gold, like two polished stones.

As the women took their places around the table, Marlowe arrived with baby Huck. "Ooh, is Plum cooking again?" She rubbed her hands together in delight.

"Plum is always cooking," I said, sliding a platter of bacon onto the table and catching sight of her tattoo: *women don't want to be me, men don't want to fuck me.* I finally understood what it meant.

"You all look tired," Marlowe said. "Let me guess — bomb threat?"

The answer was confirmed by groans, and I put on another pot of coffee. We ate and talked about the bomb threat, then moved on to the far more interesting topic: Jennifer. We talked about Jennifer every day. The morning papers were scattered around the kitchen. The television in the corner was switched on. Leeta remained missing, which heightened suspicion that what she'd told her roommate was true: She knew who Jennifer was and had done something wrong. The news of the day was that Leeta had been spotted in Alaska. The day before she'd been sighted in El Salvador, and before that it was Kentucky. Whenever I saw her face, flattened in newsprint or flashing on the television screen, I felt a jolt. It didn't seem possible — and yet it was true.

"These people seem convinced they've spotted her," Sana said, digging into the quiche. "It's a mass delusion."

"She gets into your head and she haunts you," I said. She had done that to me, and now she was doing it to everybody. The women at Calliope House knew about my history with Leeta, but I had never shown them the red spiral-bound notebook. Only Verena and Julia had seen that.

"I tried to call Julia again last night," I said, buttering a waffle. Since leaving the underground apartment, I'd been trying to contact her. "She's incommunicado."

"Not surprising," Rubí said. "Look at this." She held up one of the newspapers, smeared with greasy bacon fingerprints. The headline read: DOES JULIA COLE KNOW LEETA'S SECRETS? Julia's job working for Austen Media made her an irresistible target for the New York tabloids, which were already obsessed with Stanley Austen and his editors.

"Julia's feeling the heat," said Marlowe. "I wouldn't be surprised if she and her loony sisters *do* know something."

Verena drank her coffee, her normal brightness dimmed by lack of sleep. "If she does have more information, I don't want to know about it. I don't want to risk a connection to this tawdry business, no matter how tenuous." Verena motioned in the direction of the television, where footage of some of Jennifer's greatest hits was playing: the Harbor Freeway interchange, the bodies in the Nevada desert, Stella Cross and her husband. "It's not Julia's fault that her former intern got mixed up in this, but I'm not upset that she's avoiding us. I'd prefer that she keep away. Is that awful?"

Murmurs of agreement spread around the table. Everyone assured Verena that they agreed with her point of view, that they all worked so hard on their various projects at Calliope House and it wouldn't be fair for Julia's connection to Leeta to taint their good work. Julia wasn't part of Calliope House anyway, only an occasional visitor.

"I can see the headlines," Verena said. "BAPTIST HEIRESS CONNECTED TO JULIA COLE, LEETA ALBRIDGE'S FORMER BOSS. You can imagine the kinds of stories they'd make up about me."

"And me," said Marlowe.

I listened to the women try to distance themselves from Julia, and I didn't blame them. With her paranoia and secret projects, and her inability to be forthcoming about anything, it wasn't surprising that Julia hadn't endeared herself to the women of

Calliope House. She irritated me as well, but I wasn't so willing to throw her aside. She and I shared a connection to Leeta, which is something the other women couldn't appreciate. They'd never even met Leeta.

As more women arrived, I replenished the table with fresh slices of toast and pots of jam, which were eagerly received. In Verena's house there was never any mention of calories, there was no *I shouldn't eat this, I shouldn't eat that.* Plates were scraped clean, *oooh*s and *ahhh*s were abundant, women asked for more. No prayers were offered up to the diet gods: *I'll go to the gym later; I didn't eat dinner last night.* There was pleasure that didn't have to be bargained for.

"Did I tell you I talked to my dad in Shiraz yesterday?" Sana said. "He told me that what Jennifer is doing reminds him of the American Westerns he likes to watch — the Wild West."

"People in Iran are talking about Jennifer?" Rubí said.

"*Everybody* is talking about Jennifer. She's the most famous woman in the world," Sana said.

Like everyone else, we spoke about Jennifer as if she were a single person, even though we knew that if Jennifer existed, she had a lot of help. For some she was a hero, for others a bogeywoman.

"Did you see the column in the *New York Daily* this morning?" Marlowe asked. "The columnist argued that Jennifer just needs to get laid, and guys in the comments section were writing things like, *I bet Jennifer is fat* and *Jennifer is a ball-busting bitch* and *Who'd want to fuck her.*"

"I love that their only defense against Jennifer is to label her unfuckable," Rubí said.

"That's how dudes always try to bring us down," Sana said.

"Jennifer will give herself up and do a nude spread in *Playboy* to make amends," Marlowe said.

"Maybe she'll do a Waist Watchers commercial," I said. "She'll say, 'I was on a killing spree until these guys on the Internet called me fat. That was just the wake-up call I needed. Now I've taken control of my life by losing thirty pounds!' "

"Burst!" said Verena.

Laughter erupted. Sana and Rubí beat their fists on the table. Even Huck was giggling.

"I don't think anything is going to stop her," said Verena. "She's an avenger, a Fury. She's in our midst, but at the same time, I think she's left this world behind."

"After I'm finished with the companion volume to *Fuckability Theory,* I'm going to have to write a whole book about this," Marlowe said. "Did I tell you that a journalist called me yesterday and asked, *off the record,* if I'd masterminded the whole thing?"

"Did you?" asked Verena, eyebrow arched.

I turned to Marlowe: "Are you Jennifer?"

"I thought you were Jennifer," she said to me.

"Maybe I'm Jennifer and I don't know it," said Sana.

"Jennifer could be anybody," Rubí said.

On the television in the corner, a yellow banner appeared at the bottom of the screen: LEETA ALBRIDGE SPOTTED? I scrambled to pick up the remote control and turn up the volume. A news reporter was speaking from the parking lot of a Dairy Queen in El Paso, place of another alleged sighting. A swarm of police officers circled the darkened fast food restaurant, many of them carrying automatic rifles. German shepherds on leashes scoured the area; a helicopter hovered overhead.

"What are they going to do if they find her?" I said, feeling sick and scared for Leeta.

"She wouldn't be stupid enough to flee to

Texas," said Sana. "That's the last place I'd go if the Man was looking for me."

"True. And besides, Leeta wouldn't do something as prosaic as hide out in a Dairy Queen," Marlowe said.

I appreciated that they were trying to make me feel better, but the sight of men with guns hunting Leeta was a reminder that the Jennifer phenomenon wasn't a joke. Like everyone else, we talked about what was happening as if it were a Western, as Sana had said, or a comic book or a super-hero movie, since there were no comparisons that could be drawn from real life. But it wasn't fantasy. Sometimes it was difficult to comprehend that.

"Such a show of force to find Leeta is ridiculous," I said. "She was an intern at Austen Media. She's not an outlaw."

"But she *is* an outlaw now, that's the problem," Verena said. "And since there's no other link to Jennifer, they're going after her hard."

Sana took the remote control from me and switched off the TV. "That's enough for now," she said, patting me on the head. "You Americans are supposed to start the day with Cheerios, right? Or is it Wheaties? Whatever it is, Sugar Plum, it's not footage of men with guns."

She was right. I picked up my plate and carried it to the sink. It was time to begin the day.

In my new routine, I spent the most time with Sana. We'd forged a connection in the underground apartment that had only grown stronger in the light of day. She knew about Alicia, the thin woman who had lived inside of me, the New Baptist Plan, and Y—— withdrawal. I knew that her face had been burned in a house fire when she was thirteen, a fire that had killed her mother. She'd come to New York to study for her master's degree in social work ten years ago and had been here ever since, having lived at Calliope House for a year. She had recently turned thirty-three and called this her "Jesus year." She and Verena were working together to create a clinic for at-risk adolescent girls. They hoped to open within six months, with Sana as the director.

Sana's project was one of many ongoing at Calliope House. A lawyer was working on a class-action lawsuit against an American cosmetics company that had poisoned people with skin-lightening creams in Africa and Asia; there was a justice fund for immigrant women and children from Mexico and Central America; there was a whole team of women, in New York and in Washington, who were focused on reproductive rights, at home and abroad. Then there were the projects I was more familiar with. Marlowe was busy writing. Verena spent some of her time working with former Baptists and helping them heal, but the New Baptist Plan was the deluxe service, she'd said, and just for me. She also worked closely with Rubí on other projects related to the weight-loss industry, the campaign against Dabsitaf their current focus. I wondered if Dabsitaf would have worked on me now. My appetite seemed impossible to suppress or control. I was hungry for everything, for food and for life. It was odd to think that a pill could take that away, or that I had ever wanted it to.

Besides cooking, I didn't have a project like Sana and the other women, but Verena didn't mind. She gave me space. "The Plum project needs tending to," she said, and she even gave me a salary, double what Kitty had paid me, drawn from her vast supply of dieting dollars.

In the afternoons, after the lunch rush but before afternoon snacks and dinner, I spent time in my red-walled bedroom. It was on the second floor and overlooked the street. There was a glossy white mantel framing a sealed-up fireplace and a selection of tattered flea market furniture: a wrought-iron day bed, a red wing-back chair, a desk, a chest of drawers. From the chandelier a severed Barbie head dangled — a "welcome" present from Rubí and Sana.

During my first visit to Calliope House, Verena had told me about the Catholic charity that had owned the house. In my bedroom closet, one of the teenage mothers had scratched a message into the paint: *calliope was born in this room / january 1973.*

Calliope House. Verena thought it was a fitting name, in honor of the young woman and the daughter she would never see again. I was glad Calliope's room had become my room.

Most afternoons, at my desk in front of the window, I wrote in the red spiral-bound notebook. Sometimes I called my mother to talk about my new life. I had sent her a copy of Verena's book and she was in the middle of reading it. I'd look online for news about Leeta and send emails to Carmen, to let her know how I was doing. I enjoyed this quiet time. While I loved the activity in the house, and the companionship after so many years alone, I also needed some moments to myself.

After the discussion of Julia at breakfast, I

decided to email her. To my surprise, a response appeared several minutes later:

From: JuliaCole
To: PlumK
Subject: Re: Where are you???

Dear Plum,

I did not know that you called. I threw my phone in the garbage and with any luck it is in a landfill by now. Good riddance. I am sick of reporters bothering me about Leeta and so I am living "off the grid" as much as possible. I will tell you what I have told everyone else: When Leeta and I worked together, I never knew much about her personal life. I do not know where she is now.

For what it's worth, I do not believe she is involved in criminal activity. You might not know that Leeta is quite flighty. I don't like to speak ill of her, but this facet of her personality always exasperated me. I do not know any terrorists myself, but I imagine being a terrorist requires discipline and focus.

I am afraid I have nothing more to say

about the matter. Must dash. These lipsticks will not sort themselves.

J.

P.S. I am coming to Calliope House soon. I need to ask you for a favor . . .

Those three dots at the end might as well have been written in flashing neon. The email was typical of Julia, focused as usual on what I could do for her, leaving out the most important details. Verena wouldn't be happy to see her at Calliope House, but I was curious to know what she wanted. The last time she'd asked for a favor I'd given her 50,000 email addresses, and I still didn't know what she'd done with them. I would resist agreeing to another favor unless she offered up more information about Leeta, which I thought she probably had. Julia owed me more.

She was the one who'd dropped Leeta into my life.

I returned to writing in my red notebook, Leeta's notebook. I had clipped a photo of her from the newspaper and pinned it to my wall. She was watching me as I wrote. *Where did you go, Leeta?* I scribbled in the margin. *What have you done?* I filled several pages with notes about my days of cooking and eating in Calliope House. When I was finished, I put the notebook in the bottom drawer of my dresser.

There was an oval mirror above the dresser. After I had been without mirrors underground, my reflection was still a novelty. I noticed the weight loss I'd experienced during the New Baptist Plan, but at the rate I was eating, the weight wouldn't be lost for long. It would find me again, as it had always done. Despite everything I had been through, I looked about the same as I had before, but I was different in a way that couldn't be seen. Made over.

. . . you can lick my nuts, bitch, and then get the fuck out . . .

Rise and shine.

In Calliope House, from Monday through Friday, no one slept in. At 7:30 a.m., misogynist music blasted throughout the house. The music played for exactly one minute. Verena said it was intended to remind us of our purpose at the beginning of each day.

My stomach rumbled, so I showered and dressed quickly, then went downstairs to the kitchen, intending to make French toast. I tied my apron around my waist and flicked on the television to keep me company while I worked. As I turned on the coffeepot and removed the eggs and milk from the refrigerator, I was only barely cognizant of the news report. I should have known this wasn't an ordinary day, given that Cheryl Crane-Murphy was working the early shift.

"At least now we have a clear connection between Leeta Albridge and one of Jennifer's crimes."

I dropped the carton of eggs on the counter and hurried to the television. Cheryl was discussing the twelve-year-old girl, Luz, who'd been raped and then jumped in front of the train. I saw the familiar photos of the Dirty Dozen, including two of Luz's rapists, and the crime scene in the desert. Then there was Luz's mother, Soledad, and her subsequent press conference: "When will the violence end, Jennifer?" she asked before the world.

With all the drama her voice could muster, Cheryl announced the big news again: As a college student in Los Angeles, Leeta had known Soledad and Luz. She had traveled to L.A. at the time of Luz's funeral and was there when two of the rapists, Lamar Wilson and Chris Martinez, were kidnapped.

I sat in a chair, deflated. I'd been holding on to hope that Leeta had been mixed up in this by mistake. Now that seemed unlikely.

Sana walked into the kitchen, her hair damp from the shower. "No breakfast?"

"There's big news. Leeta knew Luz and her mother." Sana joined me in front of the television. After all the violence and bloodshed linked to Jennifer, we had returned to one of the saddest stories: the little girl who'd been raped.

"I'm wondering if the answer to the Jennifer mystery lies here," Cheryl said, "but maybe we're just not seeing it yet."

Cheryl turned to the Los Angeles correspondent, who explained further that while Leeta was a student at the University of Southern California, she'd volunteered at a local women's clinic as a rape crisis counselor. Luz's mother, Soledad, worked there part-time as a trainer.

"And this is just coming to light *now*?" said Cheryl.

"Apparently, the clinic didn't keep records of volunteers from more than two years ago," said the correspondent. "A witness now recalls that Leeta and Soledad not only worked there at the same time, but might have spent time together outside the clinic."

Cheryl Crane-Murphy was irritated. I had seen her face so many times in recent weeks that I could read her expressions. "This revelation is certainly important, but what *exactly* does it mean for the investigation?"

"We simply don't know," the correspondent told Cheryl, "but chronologically, the kidnap of Wilson and Martinez was the first Jennifer-related event, although we didn't know it at the time. They were kidnapped, and the rest of the Dirty Dozen were kidnapped, and they were all held somewhere for a month before being dropped from the plane into the desert. During that time, the other Jennifer attacks began." On the screen, there was footage of the Harbor Freeway interchange and the brown canvas bags containing Simmons and Green, which at the time had seemed like the first Jennifer attack. I felt queasy as I recalled the slips of paper that'd been stuffed down the men's throats — Jennifer's calling card, the way she'd announced herself to the world.

The correspondent explained that Luz's mother, Soledad, had recently traveled to Mexico City to visit her sick aunt, so the FBI was working with the Mexican police to locate her for further questioning. "I should remind our viewers that Soledad Ayala served as an army medic in Afghanistan with distinction," the correspondent said. "Nevertheless, according to my sources, she was investigated after Lamar Wilson and Chris Martinez, two of her daughter's rapists, went missing and were later killed, but she had an alibi and the police have never considered her a suspect."

"So what are we supposed to think?" Cheryl asked the correspondent. "That Jennifer decided to avenge this woman's daughter? And that Leeta Albridge helped out because she knew the family?"

"That's one theory," said the correspondent.

"Did Soledad help out too?"

"Anything is possible," said the correspondent.

Sana stood up from her chair and sighed. "In other words, they have no idea what any of this means. You can just tell that Cheryl wants to scream, *Who the hell is Jennifer?* at the top of her lungs. Look at those bags under her eyes. She probably hasn't slept for weeks."

Sana went to the cupboard and took a box of corn flakes from the shelf. "I assume I have to eat this crap since you're not going to feed me?"

I told her I was sorry, but the news had derailed my morning.

"Are you okay, Sugar Plum?"

I told her I didn't know how to feel about Leeta being connected to Luz and Soledad, people we had seen in the news, characters in a national drama. I was thinking about Leeta and those days only months earlier when she followed me around the neighborhood. I wished she could go back in time and become that carefree young woman again, but that Leeta was gone, perhaps forever. I thought of the police officers with their guns drawn, searching for her.

Cheryl Crane-Murphy went to a commercial break, so I joined Sana, pouring myself a bowl of corn flakes too. We still didn't know anything about Leeta's actions, but I feared she was destined for capture and prison. If she hadn't done anything wrong, she wouldn't have run away. The authorities called this *consciousness of guilt.*

"I've never known an outlaw," I said, packing my mouth with cereal, not even tasting it.

"Me neither," Sana said.

The other women began trickling into the kitchen and Sana shared the news. I must have looked visibly shaken, because everyone tiptoed around me, grabbing cereal and yogurt, making toast, not engaging me in conversation. When the breakfast rush ended, Sana and I were alone in the kitchen again. She asked if she could make a suggestion.

"Have you been out of Calliope House at all since you left the underground apartment?"

"Just for the bomb threat."

"I think it'd be a good idea for you to go out. Maybe you could go back to your place in Brooklyn and pack some clothes?"

I was wearing the beige shift and black leggings from the underground apartment. I had nothing else. "No, I don't want to go back there." I pictured myself opening the door to my old apartment, a lobster about to be dropped into a boiling pot of water. If I left the door closed, my unhappiness would remain sealed there, trapped inside.

"Then go out and do something else. Fresh air will do you some good," she said. "You should listen to me, okay? I'm a licensed social worker. I'm also very wise."

Perhaps Sana was right. Since moving upstairs into Calliope House, I had stayed within its womb, or in its bosom — Verena's house always brought to mind female metaphors — but there was a whole world out there, lapping at the door. I couldn't avoid it forever.

I squeezed my feet into my tattered black flats and opened the front door of Calliope House. Outside there was fresh air and sunshine and people who stared at me. Outside hadn't changed — but I had changed.

On the side of a bus, a pair of breasts whizzed by.

I might have needed fresh air, but I also

needed clothes. On Sixth Avenue a taxi approached and I flagged it down. A handful of chain stores in Manhattan sold clothes for women of my size, and I directed the driver to the nearest one. Inside the boxy store, most of the fat women looked resigned, having been exiled to this outpost of the fashion world. I didn't want to let their negative energy suck me in. I steered myself away from the long black dresses, the enveloping shrouds I'd always worn as a cloak of invisibility. I wouldn't buy much. I had lost weight in the basement but had been eating nonstop since then; I wasn't sure where I'd end up. Rubí was handy with a sewing machine, but she couldn't work miracles.

A saleswoman was walking around the store, a chunky woman with hair in a thin layer that barely covered her scalp. She wore yellow-framed glasses and a short avocado-colored dress that revealed her muscular brown legs, the backs of which were lined with stretch marks, as if fingernails had run down her flesh, leaving a trace. She hadn't tried to hide the marks with tights. Her sandals were decorated with tiny beads. She was comfortable with herself, I could tell.

"Can you help me?" I asked her. "I don't know where to start." Having sworn off long black shrouds, I was lost. Until Marlowe and Rubí, I had never had fat friends, no role models for how to dress. The only fat women I had ever known were at Baptist Weight Loss and Waist Watchers, but they were sad and none of them invested in clothes. They didn't view their fatness as a permanent state, no matter how long they'd been fat. They were just passing through Fat Town on their way to Slim City. I knew how they thought. I had been one of them.

The saleswoman, named Desiree, seemed eager to help. "What have you got at home to work with?"

"Nothing. I'm a blank slate. *Tabula rasa.*"

Desiree installed me in a dressing room and brought me outfits to try on. The first was a knee-length red-and-white dress, belted at the waist. I would never have noticed such an outfit on my own. I put it on and instantly thought of Janine. I had spent perhaps twenty minutes in Janine's presence, yet after more than a decade, that brightly dressed outcast from Baptist Weight Loss was seared into my memory, a flame burned into celluloid.

I invited Desiree into the dressing room and she stood next to me, both of us looking at my body in the mirror.

"That dress is amazing," she said.

I wasn't so sure. I saw my white legs, my bulbous knees, the slabs of my calves. I never put them on display. The only time they were exposed was when I wore my nightgown, and no one saw me in that. I could wear tights with the dresses, but they wouldn't make much difference. The legs were still there, enormous and unavoidable. "I'll think about it," I told Desiree.

Next she brought me a selection of trousers in different colors. There wasn't an elastic band in sight. I had never worn fabric that didn't stretch, and it felt different against my skin. It made me feel that my body had borders. I would have liked to pair the trousers with baggy sweaters that could be pulled down over my stomach, but Desiree brought me fitted blouses, a coral-colored one with wooden buttons and another in turquoise that came with a sash. They were the same bright colors that I had bought for Alicia, only now they were for Plum.

Desiree left me alone and I looked at myself in the three-way mirror, dressed in the khaki trousers and coral blouse, observing my body from every angle. The only time I had ever dressed this way was in those few delirious days during and after the makeover. I tried to decide if I liked the clothes without thinking about what other people would see when they looked at me. Alicia wanted their approval, but Plum didn't.

There was a phantom woman in my mind that I was comparing myself to, and I had to force her from the dressing room. When she was gone, I looked at my body, the body that had kept me alive for nearly thirty years, without any serious health problems, the body that had taken me where I needed to go and protected me. I had never appreciated or loved the body that had done so much for me. I had thought of it as my enemy, as nothing more than a shell that enclosed my real self, but it wasn't a shell. The body was me. *This is your real life. You're already living it.* I removed the clothes and stood naked before the mirrors, turning this way and that. I was round and cute in a way I'd never seen before.

I told Desiree I would take the red-and-white dress and the trousers and the blouses. On the racks I found a scratchy oatmeal skirt that I adored and I took that, too, along with three more knee-length dresses, one that was dark brown and printed with violet stars, another in emerald, and one that was white with colorful poppies sewn into the neckline and hem. I bought the basic necessities, too — tights and underwear, track bottoms and T-shirts to wear around the house. I also treated myself to a new satchel.

Desiree rang up my purchases and I realized that I was buying more than I'd intended, given my ballooning body, but I decided it didn't matter. Alicia had a wardrobe of fashionable clothes, and Plum deserved one too. Still, as I watched Desiree fold the colorful items, I worried that I might lose my courage once I left the store and not wear what I'd bought. After I paid I went to the dressing room and put on the red and white dress and red tights. I slipped the beige shift and black leggings that I had been wearing into the trash can.

At first, when I walked outside with my shopping bags, it was like one of those naked-in-public nightmares. I felt exposed and visible, with nowhere to hide. People stared at me, but then they always stared. I realized it didn't matter what I wore.

On the side of a bus, a pair of breasts whizzed by.

As I walked I steadied myself, raising my chin confidently, daring someone to say something. People had always insulted me by calling me fat, but they couldn't hurt me that way, not anymore. I *was* fat, and if I no longer saw it as a bad thing, then the weapon they had used against me lost its power.

I was wearing bright colors, refusing to apologize for my size. The dress made me feel defiant. For the first time, I didn't mind taking up space.

After all that walking and shopping, I was hungry. I stopped at a diner on Twenty-Third Street and ordered a Denver omelet with hash browns. When I was finished with that I wanted more, so I ordered a grilled cheese with extra fries. Two teen girls in the booth across from mine stole glances, whispering to each other and laughing. I knew they were laughing at me, at the way I barely fit into the booth, at my red and white dress and my pudgy fingers holding the sandwich. I'd been feeling exhilarated by my triumph with the clothes, but they were trying to ruin it. How dare they. My anger snapped like a rubber band pulled too tight. I wanted to reach over and rip off both their heads.

"What the hell are you staring at?" I said loudly, my lips slick with oil. My vehemence surprised me. The words slipped out of my mouth, bypassing the filter that had always been there.

The girls didn't reply, but looked away. Other diners turned in my direction. A waiter came and stood between my booth and the girls' booth. "We got a problem here?" he said in a dad voice.

"No problem," I said. "Bring me a slice of lemon meringue pie, please."

While I waited for the pie, I turned my body in the direction of the girls, fixing my gaze on them. I watched everything they did, sometimes chuckling to myself. For several minutes I kept my eyes on them. They did everything they could to avoid looking in my direction and they pretended they were unaffected, but unlike me, they didn't know how to react while under constant surveillance. Finally, they fumbled with their wallets, gathered up their shopping bags and purses, and left the diner.

My pie arrived and I savored it, my anger deflating. When the waiter brought the bill I opened my backpack to get my wallet and noticed a paper slipping out of an internal pocket. It was the check for $20,000. I had placed it in the pocket for safekeeping and forgotten about it.

I took note of the Baptist name at the top of the check. I could have deposited it, but something stopped me. I was entitled to the money, having completed every task of the

New Baptist Plan, but Verena had said that her plan would leave me completely transformed. She had guaranteed it. But after the ups and downs of the day, I couldn't be sure — was I completely transformed?

I wandered for a few blocks. Glancing at the window display of a boutique, I caught sight of myself in a window and at first I didn't recognize the woman in the colorful dress as me.

On the side of a bus, a pair of breasts whizzed by.

I spotted a shoe store and decided to replace my black flats. I browsed the pumps and heels, the slip-ons and sneakers. There was nothing I wanted to try on, but then at the back of the store I noticed boots, furry ones and rubbery white ones with stiletto heels. Tucked into a corner was a pair of black combat boots. The salesman leaned lazily against the wall nearby; I told him I wanted to try the boots on.

"Those are the men's boots," he said. Without moving, he pointed out the female equivalent, slim and black with a curvy silhouette and narrow heel. Those boots weren't wide enough for my calves and I wasn't interested in them anyway.

"No thanks, I'll take the men's boots."

He reluctantly brought me different sizes, and I found the ideal fit. I laced up the boots, tying them in a knot rather than a bow.

"So?" the salesman said.

In front of the mirror, I stood at different angles, still not accustomed to the sight of my legs on display, but the combination of colorful tights and black combat boots was something I couldn't resist. "This is exactly the look I want."

"It's certainly a look."

I handed him my black flats and asked him to throw them in the garbage. Out on the sidewalk, I clomped with purpose, feeling almost gleeful. The boots changed the way I walked, demanding a more confident stride. Though I was unlikely to stomp anyone, I knew that I could.

After several blocks, I found a bench, empty and beckoning, and sat down, grateful for the chance to set down my shopping bags. I stretched my legs out in front of me, still admiring my boots, and while doing so I considered dinner possibilities, thinking of perhaps stopping at the market on the way home. A bus stopped in front of me, idling at the red light like an impatient animal. I saw the breasts again, the ones that had been unavoidable all day. The breasts were on the side of the bus, part of an ad for V— S—, the lingerie chain. Marlowe had dedicated an entire chapter to V— S— in *Fuckability Theory.* She referred to it as Bonerville. In the ad, a model lay on her side in a sheer lilac-colored negligee, her breasts slipping out, each one as large as my head.

The bus pulled away, taking the breasts with it. After the cars passed, I saw a young man in the middle of the street, heading in my direction. He was perhaps eighteen or nineteen and remarkably slim, wearing jeans and a black bowler hat. The hat is what first attracted my attention, but as he came closer I was able to make out what was printed on his lavender T-shirt: an illustration of a woman's face — dark hair, black eyeliner.

I knew that face.

The boy saw me staring at his shirt. "You like?" he said, pinching the shirt where his nipples were.

"But how . . . why is she on your shirt?"

"They're selling them in the East Village. Get yourself one." He continued on down the sidewalk. "Later, sister," he called over his shoulder.

I watched him walk away in his lavender shirt, wondering how it could be that the girl who used to stalk me at the café was now emblazoned on T-shirts like Che Guevara. In a few weeks, Leeta had become both a symbol of rebellion and a fashion statement. She was the face of a movement.

Soon, there would be other faces.

Airman Tompkins

During her deployments in Afghanistan, United States Air Force captain Missy Tompkins had eliminated more than two hundred enemy combatants. She returned home from active duty to live with her mother in Reno, but wouldn't speak about her experiences in the war or the men she had killed. Missy kept her feelings about that to herself.

The daughter who returned home from the war wasn't the daughter that Mrs. Tompkins remembered. The new Missy was withdrawn. She rarely spoke, slept most of the day, and sat at the kitchen table at night, smoking roll-up cigarettes and drinking Jack Daniel's. She didn't bother with her appearance, her dark blond hair limp with oil, her skin blooming with blemishes she didn't attempt to hide. Sometimes she made late-night phone calls in the parking lot of their apartment complex, sitting in the grass near the dumpsters so her mother wouldn't hear what she was saying. Missy disappeared for days at a time without a word. Whenever Mrs. Tompkins tried to talk to her, Missy told her she wouldn't understand.

One day Missy went out to buy tobacco and never came back. For days, Mrs. Tompkins returned home from her shift at the Silver Dollar Steakhouse hoping to find her daughter sitting at the kitchen table, which for once would have been a welcome sight. After a week passed, Mrs. Tompkins considered calling the police, but Missy was a grown woman who could go where she pleased without having to report to her mother. Instead of calling the police, Mrs. Tompkins searched her daughter's bedroom, where she found a note. Missy had left it inside the jewelry box she'd had since she was a little girl. She wrote that she loved her mother and her country, and then confessed that she'd flown the plane that had dropped the Dirty Dozen into the desert.

Missy's mother didn't follow current events, but news of the killings had trickled down to the tabloids she browsed at the drugstore during her breaks from work. In the note, Missy wrote that she wanted her mother to come to terms with the news and then, once she was ready, send the note to the editor of the *Los Angeles Times* so it would be published.

Mrs. Tompkins didn't know where her daughter was, but she knew she would never see her again. She decided to burn the note, had started to burn it — the corner was jagged and singed — but then she pulled the sheet of paper back from the flame. She read Missy's words again and decided they didn't belong to her. She didn't understand what Missy meant, exactly, but her daughter had been in the war and people would respect what she had to say. Mrs. Tompkins sent the note to the newspaper, where soon after it was printed on the front page.

"Jennifer asked me to help her and I don't regret what I did," Missy had written. "This is a different war, not an official one, but who decides which wars are legitimate?"

The Jennifer Effect
Jennifer was already a national obsession, but after the publication of Missy Tompkins's note, she became a national *frenzy.*

MISSING AIRMAN SAYS "THIS IS WAR"

Federal law enforcement swooped down on Mrs. Tompkins's Reno apartment complex. She was questioned about her daughter for days with barely any food or sleep. Along with Missy's brother, she appeared in a nationally televised press conference with FBI agents, military officials, and members of Congress, urging Missy to turn herself in.

Immediately after the press conference, Cheryl Crane-Murphy turned to her guest, a retired military general, and asked him if he wondered why Missy Tompkins had written a note and wanted it published. "Why broadcast her guilt? Excuse my language here, general, but that note is really just a big *eff you* to the military, isn't it?"

The general, tightly gripping the armrests of his chair as if to restrain himself from lunging at the camera, responded without answering the question. "We do not train American women for combat so they can come home and use those skills on us."

"Might Jennifer also be in the military?" Cheryl Crane-Murphy asked. Missy's reference to "Jennifer" in her note bolstered the idea that there was a real person named Jennifer who was commanding others.

The general became so enraged at the thought that he turned to the camera and said: "We don't know who you are, Jennifer, but we're going to find you and kick your ass."

Every aspect of Missy Tompkins's life was examined, from her childhood in Reno to her enrollment in the Air Force Academy to her years of military service as a fighter pilot. It didn't take long for investigators to discover that Missy Tompkins had spent her high school years in Southern California, where she lived with her father, and that during this time she had a classmate named Soledad Ayala.

"The plot thickens," said Cheryl Crane-Murphy. "Leeta Albridge is connected to Soledad Ayala, the mother of tragic Luz, and now

Missy Tompkins is connected to Soledad too."

Soledad was supposedly in Mexico City visiting her sick aunt, but the police discovered that she didn't have a sick aunt. They were searching for Soledad so they could question her about the events unfolding in the United States, but she seemed to have disappeared.

The FBI director appeared on television for what the media dubbed his daily "Jennifer" briefing. "We have issued an arrest warrant for air force captain Tompkins and a material witness warrant for army specialist Ayala," he said. "We are actively seeking the identity of the person known as Jennifer — if such a person exists. If so, she is working as part of a large criminal network, one that appears to involve at least one female member of the U.S. Armed Forces, but possibly more."

On *The Nola and Nedra Show,* Nola Larson King said: "Clearly we have some kinda lady terrorist group here with someone named Jennifer as their leader."

"I'm not comfortable referring to members of our armed forces as *terrorists,*" said Nedra Feldstein-Delaney.

"Then what would you call them?" countered Nola Larson King.

Three days later, the editors at the *Los Angeles Times* received something new: a letter containing a "Penis Blacklist," signed by

Jennifer. There was a postmark from Phoenix and nothing more.

The Penis Blacklist comprised the names of one hundred men, whose penises, the letter said, "must not be given shelter inside any woman." The editors didn't know if it was legitimate or a hoax, but they published the list of names anyway. Anything Jennifer related was big news.

One of the names on the list was Senator Craig Bellamy (R-Miss.), an antiabortion advocate who was under investigation for reports that he forced his secret girlfriend to have an abortion and then blackmailed her to cover it up. Upon being told by a reporter that her husband's name was on the Penis Blacklist, Mrs. Bellamy panicked and agreed to appear on *Good Morning America.* "Craig and I don't have sex," she said, looking directly into the camera. "The last time was when I conceived our son, Craig Junior. He's thirty now."

Another name on the list was Todd Wright, the producer of a series of popular videos in which girls on spring break were urged to bare their breasts and take off their underpants and make out with other girls when they were drunk. When confronted by a camera crew for CNN, Todd Wright's girlfriend said, "I'm not going to stop having sex with Todd just because some [bleeping] bitch named Jennifer says so. [Bleep] her." The next morning she started her car and it blew up.

In response, Todd Wright, who did not seem devastated, said, "Jennifer can suck my dick." His strangled body was found three days later under the Santa Monica Pier, his severed dick shoved in his mouth.

After the murders of Todd Wright and his girlfriend, the FBI director appeared on television again. He went through a PowerPoint presentation with ninety-nine slides, one for each of the living men on the Penis Blacklist. Each slide featured the man's photo, his occupation, and where he lived. Among the names: professional athletes, CEOs, world leaders, Stanley Austen, and members of the U.S. Congress who'd voted against women's reproductive rights.

"We take this threat very seriously," the FBI director said. "While we do not condone giving in to terrorist threats, I strongly urge women not to have sex with any of the men on this list. Do not date them, do not even be seen with them, for your own protection."

Senator Bellamy's daughter chose to have her mother walk her down the aisle at her wedding, just to be safe.

As the search for Jennifer intensified, many women named Jennifer complained that they were under attack. The owner of Jennifer's

Bridal Boutique in Idaho Falls appeared on Cheryl Crane-Murphy's show, saying: "Somebody threw a rock through my window yesterday with a note that said 'You're a man-hating lez.'" Likewise, a police officer named Jennifer Leoni from tiny Caldwell, Delaware, said someone had spray-painted LESBO on her garage door.

"I'm noticing a trend with the *lesbian* insults," said Cheryl Crane-Murphy, shaking her head. "If I were a young thug, I would have gone with *terrorist,* but perhaps *lesbian* is more abhorrent."

The FBI director appeared on television yet again. "It's unlikely that there is a terrorist mastermind named Jennifer. I urge people to remain calm and rational and not let women named Jennifer fall under suspicion. Between 1970 and 1984, Jennifer was the single most popular name for baby girls in this country. There are well over a million women named Jennifer in the United States. It's as close to a generic woman's name as you can get. Jennifers are our daughters, sisters, wives, and mothers. Jennifers are everywhere among us."

"If there are Jennifers everywhere among us," asked Cheryl Crane-Murphy, "then how are we supposed to remain calm?"

Soon, what the news media described as the "Jennifer effect" began to spread.

At a prestigious Connecticut university, fraternity pledges marched outside the women's dormitories chanting, "No means yes, yes means anal!" In previous years, this type of misbehavior would have been handled by a tweedy disciplinary committee in a conference room with tea and coffee, but this time the female students took matters into their own hands. They left their dorms en masse and destroyed the fraternity house, breaking all the windows and setting it on fire. By morning there was nothing left but charred remains.

On Cheryl Crane-Murphy's show, one of the women involved in the attack said: "When I heard the frat guys chanting, I thought, *What would Jennifer do?* That's when I grabbed my lacrosse stick and just went for it." Cheryl explained that the female students added the names of the fraternity members to their own Penis Blacklist, a practice that was quickly adopted by women's groups at other campuses.

The Jennifer effect showed no sign of slowing down. Women engaged in violence and civil disobedience. Men took precautionary measures. The bad-boy lead singer of America's most popular rock band famously sported a topless mermaid tattoo on his bicep, her cartoonish breasts like round cupcakes with bright red cherries on top. Before his cover shoot with *Rolling Stone,* the makeup artist painted over the breasts, dressing the mermaid in a demure long-sleeved top that wouldn't have looked out of place in a J. Crew catalog. The rock star didn't protest or throw a tantrum. He had no interest in being dropped out of a plane.

On *The Nola and Nedra Show,* Nola Larson King said: "I've been thinking about what you said earlier, Nedra, and I agree with you. I don't think this is *terrorism* or *lady terrorism.* Do you know what I think it is?"

"I'm dying to know," said Nedra Feldstein-Delaney.

"I think it's a response *to* terrorism. From the time we're little girls, we're taught to fear the *bad man* who might get us. We're terrified of being raped, abused, even killed by the *bad man,* but the problem is, you can't tell the good ones from the bad ones, so you have to be wary of them all. We're told not to go out by ourselves late at night, not to dress a certain way, not to talk to male strangers, not to lead men on. We take self-defense classes, keep our doors locked, carry pepper spray and rape whistles. The fear of men is ingrained in us from girlhood. Isn't that a form of terrorism?"

"For God's sake, Nola. You're going to get us both fired," said Nedra Feldstein-Delaney.

The search for Jennifer and her cohorts continued. By September, sales of *Fuckability Theory* had increased dramatically and Marlowe was in demand by news organizations as an analyst on Jennifer-related topics. Verena had been asked for analysis too, particularly by Japanese news outlets, as Eulayla's documentary, *Born Again,* had been a cult hit there, but Verena refused. She said that Jennifer was a distraction from real work.

In between media interviews, Marlowe had begun writing a new book called *The Jennifer Effect.* The sound of her furious typing filled the kitchen as I finished my baking for the morning. I wrapped up the pastries and cakes, then sorted through the piles of newspapers and magazines that were scattered all over the table. "Leeta Albridge in Montana?" read one of the familiar tabloid headlines. I barely noticed these stories anymore. Wherever Leeta was, I was sure it wasn't at the fast food restaurants and shopping malls where she was routinely spotted.

With Marlowe and the other women busy with their projects, I began to crave one of my own, something beyond cooking and eating, writing in my journal, and obsessing about Jennifer. Marlowe was so engrossed in her work that she didn't respond when I tried to start a conversation, so I washed the dishes and prepared to go out for the afternoon.

I forced myself to go out for a while each day. When I did, I often had run-ins with people who stared at me in a way I didn't like or who were somehow rude. I'd perfected the evil eye, and my favorite response: *What the hell are you staring at?*, which I sometimes upgraded to *What the fuck are you staring at?*. I had begun to look forward to these encounters. The people I confronted seemed shocked that I responded and didn't give me a fight. Sometimes I wondered if a fight was what I wanted. After years of not fighting back, I was coiled like a snake.

I took a few freshly baked ladyfingers from the kitchen and ate them as I headed to the bus stop, the front of my dress speckled with powdered sugar. "Look at that big lady," said a little girl as she walked by, holding the hand of her mother or nanny. The woman blushed and was about to say something, but I spoke first.

"Yeah, look at me," I said, popping the last ladyfinger into my mouth and brushing the crumbs from my hands. "Aren't I fabulous?"

I rode the bus to Midtown, then got off and walked for a few blocks. Through the forest of buildings, I looked up and saw part of the Austen Tower's chrome trunk. Kitty was up at the top and Julia was down in the depths.

Back at street level, another familiar sight: a poster of the lilac negligee woman, whose breasts I'd seen sailing around town on the sides of buses. Outside one of the flagship branches of V— S—, the poster was more than two stories high, the woman's breasts tire-size. If I'd had Jennifer's powers, I would have demanded the posters be taken down. They were everywhere, like leaflets dropped on a population during a war. Propaganda.

When the hordes of pedestrians thinned out, I could see myself reflected in the plate-glass window of the store, superimposed over the lilac negligee woman's knees. I was wearing my knee-length brown and violet dress, with violet tights, the black boots on my feet. I smiled at my reflection, which then disappeared behind a group of people streaming by. No matter how big the crowd became, the woman on the poster loomed large, her breasts conquering Manhattan. I'd first seen her the day I saw Leeta on the T-shirt: two women, two different messages. I could never be like the negligee woman — I no longer wanted to — but I wondered if I could be like Leeta.

A Baptist isn't afraid to become an outlaw.

I headed to the drugstore to buy supplies and gather my courage. Then I breezed into V— S—, doing my best to appear nonchalant. The sizes at Bonerville didn't reach the outer limits, so the sight of me entering the store raised some eyebrows. *One of these things is not like the others!* A bouncy-haired salesgirl bodychecked me at the entrance.

"Can I help you with something?" she said.

"I'm shopping for a normal-size person. I hope you don't mind that I've come in here."

"Not at all. I'm here to help," she said, expertly deflecting all sarcasm.

I was left alone to roam the store, the walls

lined with life-size posters of the Swedes and Brazilians who modeled the lingerie. As I pretended to browse, I discreetly slipped things into my satchel, using my bulky body as a shield. That part was unexpectedly easy. The difficult part was removing the security tags. I needed to be in the dressing room to do that, but I had no reason to go in there. Even the robes weren't likely to fit me, the unfuckable female.

Though I'd said I was shopping for some-one else, I spotted a display of scarves, necklaces, and other size-free items in the middle of the store that I could pretend were for me. I selected a few accessories that would go with my dress and asked the salesgirl if I could try them on in the dress-ing room, to see how they looked. She wasn't suspicious of me; people rarely were.

In the dressing room, I used the scissors I'd bought at the drugstore to cut the saucer-shaped security tags off the under-wear. The scissors weren't quite sharp enough and I gnawed at the fabric and ruined the items, which wasn't something the average thief would have done, but then I had no intention of wearing the under-wear. I didn't know what I was going to do with it, but stealing it felt good.

I was prepared for the alarm to sound as I

walked out the door or for the bored security guard to tackle me, but nothing happened. This was one of the most reckless things I'd ever done, and though I wasn't likely to see my face printed on T-shirts anytime soon, it gave me a thrill.

At home, I dumped the lilac negligee and the rest of the contraband in my closet. *calliope was born in this room / january 1973.*

"What are you going to do with all that underwear?" Sana asked when she came upstairs to visit me in my room, looking at the tangled, frayed, colorful heap on the closet floor. I confessed to her that I'd stolen it. She clearly disapproved, but didn't berate me.

"I'm saving it for a special occasion," I said.

"Waiting for Mr. Right?"

"I already met Mr. Right, didn't I tell you? I encountered him in the subway station. He punched me in the face."

For the rest of the week, I settled into a routine. In the morning I was up at the sound of the music and made breakfast for everyone. After the women cleared out of the kitchen, I'd spend a few hours baking, still in my nightgown, listening to the radio for any news of Leeta. While I stuffed myself with cupcakes and popovers and whatever else I'd made, I'd call my mother. She wanted to talk about Verena's book and was full of questions about my new life and where I was living, relieved that I was away from Brooklyn and surrounded by new friends. When I finished baking and eating, I'd put the rest of the baked goods onto platters and trays for the other women and then I'd shower, dress in my new clothes (which were becoming snug), and visit a branch of V— S—.

On the fourth day, when I went down the stairs, ready to go out, I paused in the red-walled entryway to make sure I had put my scissors in my satchel. Then there was the shattering of glass followed by screeching tires. I feared that a bomb was finally blowing up the Bessie Cantor Foundation next door and I was experiencing the blast in slow motion. I stood frozen in place until I felt certain that a fireball wasn't about to rip through the walls.

I walked into the living room and bent over to pick up what turned out to be a brick with a piece of paper rubber-banded around it. One side of the paper, in block lettering, read: DIE BITCH. On the other side: EULAYLA 4-EVER.

"What's going on?" Verena said, coming

into the living room and taking the brick from me. She read the messages and frowned, seeming resigned rather than surprised. "This happens sometimes," she said. "Former Baptists. So many of them hate me." She handed me the brick and asked me to unwrap the rubber band and save the piece of paper.

"If they'd added a T, it could have said DIET BITCH," I said. "That would have been far more clever."

Verena didn't laugh. She collected the broom and dustpan and began to sweep up the broken glass. I unwrapped the paper and flattened it on the coffee table. I figured I'd leave the brick out back, but when Verena wasn't looking, I slipped it into my satchel, enjoying the heft of it.

I headed out of the house, a bit shaken but determined to carry on with my plan for the day. I was working my way through the many V— S— stores in the city, returning home with the frilly stolen goods. This afternoon, I decided to venture farther afield to a shopping mall in Queens. I visited the bathroom in the food court first — it seemed sensible to pee now, in case I was arrested — but I wasn't arrested, and as I left the mall, lingerie hidden in my satchel, the phone in my purse vibrated. The number looked familiar, but I couldn't immediately place it.

"Ms. Kettle? This is Deborah from Dr. Shearer's office. We haven't heard from you in months. Your surgery is approaching — can we expect to see you at your appointment?"

I stopped between a set of double doors. Other shoppers bumped into me from both directions, but I didn't move.

"Hello, Ms. Kettle?" I turned off my phone. The call was an unwelcome interruption to an otherwise perfect trip to the mall, a hand reaching out from my past, trying to knock me over.

I should have told the doctor's secretary that I no longer wanted surgery, but instead I'd said nothing. For a good part of the next day, I tried to write through the confusion in my notebook. Killing the thin woman inside me, the perfect woman, my shadow self — but how could I know if she was truly gone?

I decided to get out of the house, to go to a café and write, like old times. I visited Sana downstairs and asked if she wanted to join me. "I'll need a caffeine break soon," she said, sitting on the edge of her desk. She wore jeans and a billowy sleeveless top in midnight blue, her hair in the usual ponytail. She'd be free in half an hour, so I went ahead of her. Since I had nearly filled up my notebook, I brought my laptop along as well.

At Night & Day Café, I settled at a table near the window and ordered a lemonade and a mocha brownie. I reviewed the pages I'd written in my notebook during the previous weeks, Leeta's messy blue ballpoint giving way to my careful black printing. I was glad I'd brought my laptop — it was time to impose some kind of order on my writing. Maybe, like some of the other women at Calliope House, I would write a book one day. When I was working for Kitty, spending all those days in front of my laptop at Carmen's café, I'd wanted to write articles and essays, but maybe now I could write something longer. I had something more to say, despite the confusion I currently felt.

The Dear Kitty mailbox was positioned at the bottom of my screen. I'd never bothered to delete it, so I clicked it, intending to drag it to the trash can. Somehow it popped open, so suddenly and unexpectedly that I held my right hand in front of my eyes, as if a flash of light had blinded me. When I dared to look, I saw that fifteen new messages had trickled in before it was severed from the Austen mothership months ago. They'd languished in my inbox, their cries ignored. For fun, I opened one of them: *Dear Kitty, My boyfriend says I have a fupa. How can I —*

I was interrupted by a familiar voice.

"Hey, lady!" Sana was coming in my direction, in time to rescue me. Her shout elicited stares from all corners of the café, but she wasn't afraid to call attention to herself, knowing that people were going to stare at her burned face anyway. I pushed my laptop aside. I'd already finished the brownie and sucked up the last of my lemonade, so Sana went to the counter for more, returning a few minutes later with Cokes and a plate of soft macaroons crisscrossed with chocolate stripes.

"What's Sugar Plum been up to today?" she said, popping open her Coke, her silver bangles sliding down her arms. "More underwear?"

"Not today."

"Good. One of these days I'm going to have to bail you out of jail. You know that, don't you?"

"They'll never catch me. I'm as quick as a cat."

She smiled but said, "Seriously, do I need to worry about you? As your friend and as a social worker, I'm required by law to ask."

"I like doing it," I said, shrugging. She backed off. I didn't tell her about the other things I'd done recently, such as swearing at the yoga mat–carrying woman in the supermarket who'd scoffed loudly upon seeing the contents of my shopping basket, and hiding a brick in my satchel.

"I'd like to ask you about something," I said, "if you're willing to play social worker for a moment?" I told her that the doctor's office had called and that I hadn't canceled the surgery. "I'm wondering how I can be sure that Alicia, the thin woman inside me, is truly gone. What if she comes back to life?"

"Do you mean like a zombie? To kill a zombie you have to shoot it in the head."

I played along. "That won't work. She lived *inside* me, remember? If I shoot her, I'll have to shoot myself." In a serious tone, I tried to explain that I was worried my new life could be a novelty, one that might lose its appeal. This seemed impossible while sitting at the café with Sana, but I couldn't predict the future.

"It's a lifelong process and it's never going to be easy, Plum," Sana said, "but there comes a moment when you realize you've changed in some irrevocable way and you'll never go back to the way you were before. Think of it as crossing over to a new place."

I liked the idea of crossing over. "But how will I know for sure that it's happened?"

"If you're not sure, then it hasn't happened yet. You're still in flux."

In flux — that's how I felt. She had helped me understand what I was feeling, as I knew she would.

She noticed my laptop and I explained that I was going to type up what I'd written in my notebook, but I didn't mention the possibility of writing a book. That idea was too new to be shared. She told me about her day raising funds for her clinic. She planned to run the New York clinic for a few years, then return to Iran to open one there. I hated the prospect of her leaving.

Sana talked about the teen girls she was going to help at the clinic. Much of what she was saying about the girls sounded familiar to me.

"I feel a kinship with girls, don't you?" she said.

I hadn't thought about my job like that. I'd seen my girls as a burden. Sometimes I had resented them, perhaps because I had been in a state of suspended adolescence myself.

"I was burned at thirteen, around the time that puberty set in," Sana said. "I had always been a *tomboy* — is that what you call it? My friends and I were starting our periods and growing breasts — you know the awkwardness of that age — and here this horrible thing happened to me at the same time. I've always connected the two in my mind: being scarred and becoming a woman, both traumatic processes in their own way. An attack on my sense of self."

The trauma of becoming a woman — that's what all those Dear Kitty letters had been about at their core. I had responded to the girls' fears and tried to soothe them, but I had never felt like a woman myself.

Sana returned to Calliope House for a meeting, but I chose to stay behind. Thanks to our conversation, I decided to read through the Dear Kitty messages that remained in my inbox before deleting them. I ordered a sandwich and soup, and opened one at random:

From: dolcevita95
To: DaisyChain
Subject: **confidential**

Dear Kitty,

I have really small breasts. They aren't even really breasts. I mean, I have nipples, two pink buds, but there is virtually nothing underneath them. I might as well be a boy. My grandmother is giving me $5,000 when I graduate from high school in June. I want to study art history at Stanwyck College next year, so I plan to take the $5,000 and go to Italy in the summer to look at art. But maybe with the money I could get breast implants instead. What do you think? I know I seem shallow, but even though I'm smart, I think having bigger breasts would make me feel more normal.

Love,
Alexis J. in L.A.

How had I done this job for three whole years? If I'd printed out all my responses, they would have been as thick as a pile of books — books that I had written, but not in my own voice.

I stared at Alexis's message on my screen, my finger hovering over the delete key, but obliterating her didn't seem like the right thing to do. I knew how I would have responded to her if I'd still been working for Kitty: "You don't need breast implants, Alexis! You're beautiful the way you are!" Kitty insisted that I use that last line as much as possible. I told her it wouldn't ring true, since she had never seen the girls who were writing, but Kitty had said that was irrelevant. *All girls are beautiful,* she liked to say, but she only featured the usual models in the magazine. I decided to respond to Alexis from my personal email account:

From: PlumK
To: dolcevita95
Subject: Re: **confidential**

Dear Alexis J.,

Kitty never bothers to reply to these messages herself, but maybe I can help you. You're at a fork in the road, and for argument's sake, we'll imagine you taking the path that begins with two silicone pouches being inserted into your chest. You've obtained the breasts of your dreams. You max out two credit cards buying revealing clothes, because hey, what's the point of having huge breasts if you can't show them to people? The attention you receive from men is exhilarating, and as such, during your first semester at Stanwyck College, you spend more time at parties than you do studying Frida Kahlo. You meet men at parties who rarely look you in the eye because they're too enamored with your graduation present. You sleep with a lot of them. You repeatedly turn up late for class, hung over, without having done your homework, and before you know it your grades plummet and you're kicked out of college. You move out of your dorm and into a Torrance apartment complex called Pacific Gardens with two other women and take a job managing a dental practice. Your boss, Irwin Michaelson, D.D.S., a fifty-one-year-old widower, compliments you when you wear low-cut blouses. In between drilling holes in people's teeth, Dr. Michaelson likes to drill you in the supply closet. Pretty soon you become Mrs. Irwin Michaelson, D.D.S. You move into his condo in Santa Monica and quit your job because Irwin says that no wife of his needs to work. You learn to have a gourmet dinner ready for Irwin when he gets home from work each night; otherwise, he goes berserk. You begin to wonder whether his first wife died in a scubadiving accident, as he claims. Your Internet searches for "Gloria Michaelson, scuba death" don't return any hits. You consider leaving Irwin and returning to school, but he knocks you up and the two of you buy a house in Redondo Beach. Before you know it you're thirty years old, with a son named Irwin Jr.

and twin daughters named Maddison and Maddalyn, driving a Kia Sedona, the inside of which smells like stale french fries and baby shit. Irwin, you suspect, is having an affair. You start to drink. A lot. Irwin says you look a bit baggy, so you get a tummy tuck and lipo, but it doesn't help. He announces the day before your tenth wedding anniversary that he's divorcing you to marry Angie, a new dental hygienist in his office. You offer to supersize your breasts and he accuses you of implying that he's a superficial prick. You threaten to take him to the cleaners in divorce court and he laughs. *Ha ha ha!* You threaten to accuse him of being a wife beater and he throws the tiki statue you bought on your honeymoon to Oahu; it ricochets off your eye and shatters on the fireplace mantel and you have to wear an eye patch, like a pirate. You don't say anything else, because you fear you might end up at the bottom of the sea like the first Mrs. Michaelson. Irwin leaves and doesn't come back for three days. When he returns, the police arrest him for domestic abuse. As they cuff him in the driveway, he screams, "What have I ever done to you, you ugly cow?" The whole neighborhood pretends not to hear. Maddalyn cries. Or is it Maddison? You hire a private detective to take incriminating photographs of Irwin and Angie in flagrante delicto, since it's the only way you can ensure that after your divorce you can continue living the life of an upper-middle-class mother of three in Southern California. Without half of Irwin's bank account, you're screwed.

Not a pretty picture, is it, Alexis? Do you really want to end up a lonely, bitter housewife with a drinking problem? Be grateful for your A-cup. Go to Italy next summer. Eat lots of gelato.

Love,
Plum

P.S. If you give me your address, I'll send you a signed copy of *Fuckability Theory*.

I stayed at the coffeehouse until it closed, responding to the rest of the girls in my inbox, offering them each a signed copy of Marlowe's book or Verena's, whichever they preferred. Then I clicked open the spreadsheet of 50,000 email addresses that I had sent to Julia, which was still on my desktop. I would email the girls in batches, offering to send them books, which we could discuss if they were interested. Even if only a handful of them agreed, it would be worth it.

I had wanted a project of my own. Perhaps this was a better use of my time than stealing underwear. I'd write to Kitty's girls illicitly, becoming a different type of outlaw.

Within only a few days of starting my new project, I had numerous requests for copies of *Fuckability Theory* and *Adventures in Dietland.* I spent hours each day addressing envelopes and lugging packages to the post office, which left less time for roaming around the city, getting into trouble.

Returning from the post office one afternoon, I turned the corner onto Thirteenth Street and saw Julia teetering down the sidewalk ahead of me, pulling a small suitcase. She was wearing her trench coat, as usual, and when she turned around — paranoid as ever — she noticed me following her. Having been discussed but not seen for so long, Julia had taken on a mythic quality. Seeing her was like spotting a nearly extinct creature; I had the urge to take a photograph or maybe look at her through binoculars.

"I've come for the night," she said when I

caught up to her, black streaks on her cheeks.

"What happened to your face?"

"We had a spill at work. Mascara," she said, trying to wipe it off. "It has not been a good day, if you must know. We were unpacking a shipment. One of the interns — Abigail or Anastasia or something — actually crawled into a crate and was nearly crushed to death by several thousand eyebrow pencils. Now she's limping. They are completely useless, those girls. Little Kittys, all of them."

"Kittens."

She asked me to walk ahead of her and she would follow. I was relieved that Verena and Rubí had gone to Washington, D.C., for the day to attend meetings about Dabsitaf; Verena would not have welcomed Julia's presence.

Marlowe was startled at the sight of the two of us coming through the door of Calliope House. "She's alive!" said Marlowe, giving Julia a quick peck on the cheek. Julia's expression remained blank. She entered the living room, removing a plastic bag from the front pouch of her suitcase. It was filled with cosmetics.

"For the scholarship fund," Julia said. She handed the bag to Marlowe, who explained that Julia stole high-end products from work and they sold them online, using the money to send working-class women to college.

Julia flung her trench coat over a chair and reclined on the sofa, not bothering to say anything else to Marlowe and me. "Don't go near her," Marlowe whispered before heading out the door. "It'll take a while."

"What will?"

"The transformation. Watch and see."

Julia took off her heels and massaged her red and swollen feet, wincing as she did. She removed her silver jewelry — earrings, necklace, bracelet, and rings — and set the items on the coffee table. Then she reached into her blouse and removed her breasts. They were pink jellylike mounds that she placed on the table next to her jewelry. She slipped her arms into her blouse and contorted this way and that, removing her bra, a pink V— S— number.

After taking off her shoes, jewelry, breasts, and bra, Julia disappeared upstairs to remove her figure-hugging clothes and the Thinz that compressed her curvy body into a boyish pillar, as well as the rest of her stripper underwear. She washed her face of makeup, then showered. When she came downstairs thirty minutes later in leggings and a tank top, a ball cap on her head, she was someone else.

"It's me, Julia," she said when she saw my surprise, but only her voice was the same. Her face had changed from wide-eyed cartoon princess to tired thirty-something.

In the kitchen, she rummaged through the fridge and pulled out a turkey leg and mashed potatoes, as well as the pistachio ice cream and buttery shortbread I'd made earlier in the day. She spread the dishes all over the table and worked her way through them. I had wanted the turkey leg but didn't say anything. Julia was sucking on the bones.

Normally I would have joined her by eating something myself, but I was too enthralled to do anything but watch her stuff her mouth under Eulayla Baptist's fat jeans. She was normally so controlled. She finished the mashed potatoes and moved on to the ice cream and shortbread. "How many calories in this?" she asked, holding up a piece of shortbread, globs of grease in the corners of her mouth.

"I'd say a couple hundred each."

"Oh no." Julia set it down on her plate, half eaten. No one at Calliope House ever discussed calories, but Julia's undercover work required it. In order to fit in at Austen, she had to diet.

"I've been binge eating lately," she said.

"That's what dieting does to you."

"I can't do this anymore. The women in my family are not *lithe*. This is a losing battle. You know why the women at Austen are such bitches? It's because they're hungry."

"Then why don't you stop dieting?"

"I can't. I've gained weight recently. Thinz can only hold in so much. If they see that I've gained, they'll know I'm not one of them. They won't confide in me." Everything about Julia was different here, even the way she talked.

"I've never been part of their club, so I don't know what it's like," I said.

"You think I'm part of their club? I'm *passing.* Passing for thin. Passing for white, too. You know my mother was black, right?"

Julia took off her ball cap to reveal a head of silky ringlets. "It takes two hours to blow this out. And I can't go out in the sun if I want to maintain this pale shade." She pulled up her sleeve to reveal flesh with only a light tan. "But not being able to eat is the worst."

She turned in the direction of a glass cake stand on the counter, as if she'd caught a scent of it, her senses heightened. Half of the chocolate buttercream cake I'd made the day before was left over. "Did you make that? Can I have it?"

She started in on the cake, and in between bites spooned the green pistachio ice cream into her mouth. Soon there was nothing left on the cake stand but a smudge of frosting and some crumbs. After dieting, ravenousness can hit like a violent wave. It's a force of nature, more powerful than you. I feared Julia had been pulled under; I was watching from the shore.

When she finished, she sat at the table, flushed, rubbing her belly. "I feel sick."

I wasn't surprised. "Do you want me to make you some tea?"

She shook her head. "There's something I need to do. Give me a while."

Julia left the kitchen and I washed the dishes, which were strewn over the table and countertops. I couldn't tolerate disorder in my kitchen. When I turned off the sink, I heard Julia retching.

"Julia?" I said through the bathroom door.

"I'll be out soon," she said. It seemed as if she was crying. "Leave me alone."

The sound of her vomiting filled me with sadness. I couldn't listen.

No one knew the whole story, but Marlowe and Verena had given me enough fragments about Julia to piece together a narrative.

Each of the five Cole sisters had her domain: There was Julia at Austen Media; the eldest sister, Jacintha, was powerful in the entertainment division at NBC; the youngest sister, Jillian, was an executive at one of the largest advertising agencies in the country; Jessamine was the New York–based assistant of a legendary Hollywood director; and Josette had worked her way up to a senior position at Calvin Klein. Each sister had a network of spies and informants, small but well selected. Most of the informants were lower-level employees who had never heard of the Cole sisters; they sent their information through intermediaries.

What Julia and her sisters were doing with the information was a matter of debate at Calliope House. Julia had said different things to different people — "You must know your enemy before you can defeat them" and "We're going to bring them down from the inside." It was impossible to know whether she was simply delusional.

Thanks to Marlowe, I'd learned more about Julia's Austen exposé. As the manager of the Beauty Closet, she had her tentacles spread throughout the Austen empire — "the one thing they all need is makeup," she'd said. The people at Austen were convinced she was one of them. She sat in on meetings with magazine editors and television producers, secretly recording their conversations and meetings, which were often peppered with racist and sexist innuendos. She filmed the secret party where Austen editors fêted the elderly French scientist who'd invented cellulite. She was there when they dreamed up new problems for women to worry about, such as the day they coined the term "tit slide" to refer to the way that women's breasts move to the side and look flat when they lie on their back. *Avoid tit slide with these helpful tips!*, the cover of one Austen magazine had announced. She participated in the company-wide meeting at which editors created a fake evolutionary psychologist named Dr. Sapphire Liebermann, who "worked" at the University of Arizona and would be quoted in Austen publications stating that it was natural for men to cheat and for women to be overly emotional and like the color pink. "Dr. Liebermann" was Austen's top expert for months, but when a New York publishing house offered her a book deal, she tragically "died" in a rock climbing accident. One time, Julia even discovered an editor masturbating with tubes of lipstick in the Beauty Closet, which inspired the title of chapter seven: "Fucked by Revlon."

Julia said her book would blow them all away. She said it would be like a bomb taking down the Austen Tower.

After recovering from her binge and purge, Julia found me in my bedroom at my desk. She crawled onto my daybed and opened her massive handbag, pulling things out and placing them on the mattress in front of her — a pair of black high-heeled shoes, a hairbrush, and her phone, which she had claimed was in a landfill. Last, she removed a gun. The silver metal caught the reflection of the sunlight through the windows as Julia set it on the bed. She made no mention of it, but kept digging in her bag until she pulled out a roll of breath mints. "Finally," she said, placing a mint on her tongue. "Would you like one? They're the bulimic's friend."

"Why do you have a gun?"

Julia picked it up as if it were a toy. "It was a twenty-first birthday present from my father. Every Cole sister receives a gun on her twenty-first."

"Do you carry that around with you?"

"Not to work anymore, since the metal detectors appeared. It's a police state there and getting worse. Ever since Stanley Austen's name appeared on that Penis Blacklist

— ever since he became *penis non grata* — he's been on a rampage." She removed another mint from the roll. "You're full of questions and I know why. You're suspicious of me because of *her.*"

At last.

"I know you want to talk about her, but I already told you everything I know." Julia stretched, appearing ready for a nap.

"You haven't told me *anything.*"

"I didn't come here to talk about Leeta. I need to ask you for a favor."

"Forget it."

"But —"

"Not interested." I turned to my laptop. Three new messages from Kitty's readers dropped into my inbox, announced with a *ping.* I read them, pretending Julia's eyes weren't burning into me. I'd been waiting to talk to her for so long, and now that she was here I was straining to ignore her.

"I see what's happening," she said. "You want me to woo you."

I flashed her an irritated look. "I want you to stop being so full of shit and just talk to me for once. Leeta was important to me. I'm worried about her."

"My, my, it's not just your clothes that have changed. Love the tights and boots, by the way." Julia sat cross-legged on the bed, the straps of her tank top slipping down her shoulders, revealing the roses and thorns tattooed on her chest. She made no move to pull up the straps, but pointed to my wall, where I'd pinned the newspaper photo of Leeta. "Take that down and we'll talk. I don't want her staring at me."

I did what she asked, placing the clipping on the desk so that Leeta was only staring at me.

"I have many interns in the Beauty Closet, but only a couple *special* interns, if you know what I mean," Julia began.

"Spies."

Julia bristled at the word. "They're *interns.*"

I tried not to look at her chest, at the lack of breasts. "I know all about the exposé you're writing. That's why you need spies."

Julia didn't appear to be upset that I knew at least one of her secrets. "I have to trust my interns completely. I trusted Leeta right from the start and look where it got me. This whole thing has been disastrous."

"How did you meet Leeta, exactly?" I had never been clear on their origins.

"She was an intern at *Glamour Bride.* I knew she wasn't one of them. She'd come down to the Beauty Closet to pick up supplies, and the way she talked and dressed, her whole attitude, gave her away." Julia continued, explaining that Leeta confessed she was at Austen to spy. She'd moved to New York after finishing college in L.A. and was considering graduate work in women's studies, focusing on the media. She thought an internship at Austen would give her firsthand insight. "She was sneaky and I liked that," Julia said. "I told her what I was doing in the Beauty Closet, and when I invited her to be my intern, she said yes immediately. A person isn't good at finding out secrets unless they have secrets of their own. She obviously had many."

Julia crushed another mint with her molars. "I enjoyed working with her at first. I told her about Calliope House and she read Verena's book and then Marlowe's. I sent her to spy on you, but then things changed right after that." She found Leeta sobbing in the concealer aisle. "She told me she just found out that a young girl she knew had been raped, that she had jumped in front of a train. It was a horrible story, but the names Luz and Soledad meant nothing to me then. She flew to L.A. for the funeral and I didn't see her for a while."

"You knew about Leeta's connection to them all along?" I shouldn't have been surprised. Julia had clearly been lying when she said she knew nothing about Leeta's life outside the Beauty Closet. The rest of us had only recently learned about Leeta's friendship with Luz and Soledad, but Julia had known for much longer.

"I didn't know their connection was significant until later. When Leeta went out to L.A. for the funeral, this Jennifer stuff hadn't even started yet. Weeks passed before Luz's and Soledad's names surfaced in the media in relation to the Dirty Dozen, and by that time Leeta wasn't even working for me anymore."

"Why did she stop working for you?"

"She finally returned from L.A., but she was never the same. She acted strangely, almost haunted. She knew about my undercover work, and her erratic behavior worried me, so I told her that her services were no longer required. She handed in her Austen badge and I never saw her again. Well, not until her face was plastered all over the news. What a shock that was. My business is secrecy, yet I managed to find the one intern in all of Manhattan who would become an international outlaw. You could not make this up."

"When did the police come to you?" I wanted to see the timeline in my head.

"They showed up after her roommate

tipped them off. I confirmed that Leeta had been my intern, that she no longer worked for me and I had no information about her activities. I never mentioned Luz. I did not want to become further entangled in this mess."

"You lied to the police."

"Yes, so? They figured it out on their own. I knew Leeta hadn't done anything wrong. That roommate of hers is probably a liar."

"Then why would Leeta run away? That's what doesn't make sense."

"Who knows?" Julia uncrossed her legs and reclined on the bed, resting her head on my pillow. "I'm tired," she said. She rubbed her gnarled toes back and forth on my bedspread. "I swear, I should get disability for having to wear those horrible shoes to work."

I finally had her in front of me, but she was trying to wriggle from my grasp. *"Julia."*

"Hmmm?" Her eyes were closed.

My inbox pinged again, announcing four new messages. She asked what I was working on and I explained about my new project. If this was a day for answers, or at least partial ones, it was a good moment to ask her why she had wanted the spreadsheet months ago.

"I wanted to test you. I needed dirt on

Kitty for my book and thought you might be a useful source, but I didn't know if I could trust you."

"So you're not going to do anything with the email addresses?" I was on the verge of relief.

"I didn't say *that*. My sisters and I collect all sorts of information. We have no plans to use the email addresses now, but we can never know what might be useful in the future." She yawned, arching her back and sucking in air dramatically. When she deflated onto the bed, she said, sleepily, "Leeta took a copy of that spreadsheet," as if it were an afterthought.

I placed my hand on my chest. *"What?"*

"Don't worry," she said, glaring at me through one eye. "No one will trace it back to you. If anyone finds out, I'll say I gave it to her."

"What's she going to do with the addresses?" I was protective of Kitty's girls. *My girls.*

"Maybe Jennifer's army is looking for new recruits."

"You said you didn't think Leeta was involved."

"What I think is that you should stop obsessing about Leeta. I know she mesmerized you — she was like that, she had a certain magnetism — but she's gone now, who knows where."

"Forget her?" I could never forget the girl who woke me from my sleep. Even if I'd wanted to, her face was everywhere. "Did you know she's on a T-shirt?"

"Some of the editors at Austen have the book bag," Julia said. "Now listen: I need to ask you for a favor." She sat up and began searching through her bag again, which contained even more items. She pulled out a silver hard drive, which fit into the palm of her hand.

"What I'm about to say to you — actually, everything I've said to you today — is top secret. Do not breathe a word to anyone, okay?"

I nodded in agreement, but I was still stuck on the fact that Leeta had a copy of the spreadsheet. I had her red notebook and she had something of mine.

"You know about my exposé, so that saves me the trouble. This hard drive contains what I've been working on for years. At this point it's mostly detailed notes and sketches. There are also audio files, scans of secret documents, surveillance photos, contact information for my sources, everything. Plum, are you listening? This is important."

I looked up from the floorboards. "I'm

listening."

"I want you to write the book."

"Me?"

"It is entirely possible that something might happen to me," she said, pausing for a moment. "I've thought about it and talked it over with my sisters and we think it's best if you write my exposé of Austen. You worked at Austen. You know what it's like there. I think you're the right person for the job. Besides, I hate writing." She held out the silver hard drive, but I didn't take it. "The book will have both of our names on it," she said. "I already have an interested publisher."

"Back up. Why do you think something might happen to you?"

"The police could discover that I lied to them. What if they think I'm lying about other things? If they arrest me, they'll confiscate my computer, everything. Or maybe Jennifer will blow up the Austen Tower. Think of all those floors collapsing. I would be crushed to death in the Beauty Closet."

I pictured the Austen Tower aflame like a birthday candle. "That's a ridiculous thought," I said, but maybe it wasn't. "Julia, please tell me what's happening." She didn't reply. I wanted to grab her by the shoulders and shake her and watch her ringlets flail around until she begged for mercy.

"I feel uneasy, that's all. I wish you wouldn't be so suspicious of me." Her hand remained extended, the silver hard drive in the space between us, forbidden fruit. I looked from Julia to the hard drive, then reached over and plucked it from her palm.

"Thank goodness," Julia said, reclining again. "I can relax knowing you're on board. If I become incapacitated, those cocksuckers at Austen will still get what's coming to them."

She curled on her side, closing her eyes. I collected my laptop and moved quietly toward the door, eager to get away from her. I wanted time to sort out everything she'd said. As I crept past the daybed, her hand reached out and grasped my leg, her fingers warm on the inside of my thigh. "You know, I've always thought you were lovely," she said, fading into sleep.

Julia slept in my room all night. I opted for a guest room. When I went downstairs in the morning, she had already gone, though I didn't know which version of her had walked out the door. While cooking breakfast, I could think of nothing but my conversation with her. She'd seemed truly afraid of something.

As the Calliope women arrived in the kitchen to fill their plates with scrambled eggs and smoked salmon, I longed to tell them about Julia's visit, but everything we'd discussed was, in Julia's words, top secret. Sharing secrets with Julia made me feel distanced from everyone else.

I was glad when breakfast was over and the kitchen cleared out, but the morning wasn't peaceful. Huck was having a tantrum, his wailing filling the house from top to bottom. At the kitchen table, I plugged the silver hard drive into my laptop and peeked at the files it contained, but there were thousands of them. It was impossible to concentrate, given the noise, so I addressed envelopes and stuffed them instead. Girls across the country would soon open their mailboxes to copies of *Fuckability Theory* and *Adventures in Dietland.*

Huck's crying did not abate and when the police knocked on the door, announcing a bomb threat, I was grateful for an excuse to go outside. I filled two shopping bags with the puffy brown envelopes, then grabbed my satchel and joined the others in the evacuation. We were cordoned off on the usual benches at the end of the block, but since it was the middle of the day rather than the middle of the night, the ice cream shop was open. We bought cones and passed them around. Huck's face became a pastiche of vanilla ice cream and snot, but at least he was finally quiet. We licked our cones and watched the bomb squad do their work.

The beleaguered staff of the Bessie Cantor Foundation for Peace and Understanding stood in a circle nearby, trying to avoid the accusing stares of some of the neighbors. The owner of an Italian restaurant on our block was particularly incensed. It was the middle of the lunch rush when the evacuation order came, and so businessmen and women were sitting on the curb, plates balanced on their knees, trying to shovel penne and spaghetti into their mouths without spilling anything on their tailored white shirts.

Stopped at the light, a taxi driver shouted: "What'd Jennifer do now?"

"This ain't nothing to do with her," a cop shouted back.

Though it was only our block of Thirteenth Street and the one directly behind us on Twelfth that were closed, the chaos spread into the surrounding areas. The traffic on Sixth Avenue backed up, pedestrians and drivers stopped and gawked. It was New York street theater: the potential for disaster, which no one wanted to miss.

"The idea of a bomb threat is nonsensical, isn't it?" I crunched the last of my cone.

"What do you mean, hon?" Verena was wearing jeans and a T-shirt bearing the name of the Baptist Shakes, an all-girl punk rock band from Georgia.

"If the *big one* ever comes, do you think they're going to warn anyone in advance? Why would they want to blow up an empty building?"

"They're just lunatics," Marlowe said. "Making threats is the aim. The police take it seriously because they have to."

"But aren't you afraid that one day the house next door might actually blow up?" The women of Calliope House had lived with the bomb threats for so long that they seemed to forget there was the possibility of a real explosion, one that was likely to kill us all.

I stood up and paced in front of the bench. No one seemed interested in addressing my question, so I didn't pursue it. I supposed that the threat was better left at the back of the mind, where it could be ignored. Living at Calliope House was a choice that each of us had made, and we knew the risks. No one was forcing us to stay there.

"Speaking of lunatics, why did Julia stay over last night?" Marlowe asked. She and the others looked at me. I wasn't prepared with an excuse.

"She . . . wanted to ask for advice about her book, the Austen exposé. She's writing a chapter about Kitty." The lie came easily, but I hated telling it. I didn't want to be on Julia's side.

"Did she say anything about Leeta?" Marlowe asked. "I planned to talk to her, but had to leave early yesterday. I'd like to interview Julia for *The Jennifer Effect.*"

"I asked her about Leeta, but she clams up as soon as her name is mentioned."

A *New York Daily* truck rumbled past us, the message on its side enticing us to "Read the *New York Daily* for the latest on Jennifer."

"Did you hear what happened this morning?" Marlowe said at the sight of the truck. Every morning there was something new, and I was glad to move on from the topic of Julia. Marlowe explained that video game companies had been warned to stop producing games that featured women as sex objects and victims of violence.

"Aww, what are all the kiddies gonna play now?" Rubí said. "Half the fun of childhood is learning how to splatter a prostitute's brain with a baseball bat."

Sana read from an article on her phone: "In the wake of the threat, several gaming companies have seen their stock fall."

Marlowe shook her head, marveling, and handed Huck to Verena while she scribbled some notes. Verena held the sticky baby out in front of her.

"This morning I read about a bunch of teenage girls in Texas who've been traveling around to strip clubs," Rubí said. "The girls hang out in the parking lot and when the men go inside, they slash their tires and break their windows. The police chief in one of the towns said that his force didn't have the *manpower* to deal with an uptick in female offenders."

Sana leaned over and whispered in my ear: "He's talking about women like you." I elbowed her away, not wanting the others to hear what she was saying. Sana was the only one who knew about my recent activities.

More NYPD trucks arrived, so I knew we weren't going to be allowed back home anytime soon. I was being deprived of lunch and growing hungry and cranky, the ice cream cone not keeping my hunger at bay. I picked up my shopping bags. The long strap of my satchel crossed my chest, weighing on my shoulder because of the brick I still carried with me. "I'm off," I said. "I have errands to run." I'd been so busy sending books and emailing Kitty's readers that it had been several days since I'd spent an afternoon roaming the streets, but that's what I needed to do. Julia's visit had left me with excess adrenaline. I loved Calliope House, but I needed to get away for a few hours, to escape being enclosed.

"What kind of errands?" Sana asked, suspicious.

"Mailing books," I said, giving the shopping bags a jiggle.

"And what else?"

"Maybe I'll do some shopping."

"You mean you're actually going to *pay* for something?" She said it in a playful tone, but there was bite to it. Marlowe, Verena, and Rubí looked up at me, confused, but I slinked into the crowd.

I mailed the packages of books from the post office first so I wouldn't have to carry them around all day. The woman behind the counter stamped the envelopes, the name of a girl printed on each one. I wondered if Leeta was planning to write to them too, and if so what she would say, but email was probably tricky when you're on the run from the police.

After the post office, I ate a late lunch. My body was no longer accustomed to waiting for food, and I finished my cheeseburger in four big bites, then ordered another. Outside the restaurant window, I could see V — S — across the street, with the enormous poster of the lilac negligee woman, only this time she was wearing a pink bustier and stockings, her bare ladyparts shielded by the squeeze and tilt of her thighs. Bonerville. They could have put the poster over the doorway and the woman could have spread her legs, welcoming all of

Manhattan inside.

I stared at her while finishing my second cheeseburger, then left the restaurant, feeling the heat of the animal protein on my breath, tasting it on my lips. Standing before V— S—, I really wanted to steal that pink bustier. I was feeling jittery with energy that I needed to burn off somehow, and I felt like doing something reckless. I liked writing to Kitty's girls, but I missed the high that came from action. I walked back and forth on the sidewalk, considering my options. The cover of the *New York Daily* — with the faces of Leeta, Missy, and Soledad — popped up around me on the side of a truck, on a newsstand, in the hands of passersby, a swarm of black-and-white insects that I wanted to bat away so I could see clearly, so I could breathe.

I decided I couldn't return to the scene of my original crime, so I settled on a cosmetics store a half block away, a three-story extravaganza of face paint. Inside, I discovered a store that looked like a spaceship, with domed ceilings and bright lights and what seemed like an alien female staff, their hair wrapped tight in buns, giving them instant facelifts. It was like being in the Beauty Closet again, only Julia and Leeta were missing. I waited for an opportunity to slip something into my satchel, anticipating the rush that came with it, but there was a security guard watching me, as if she had a sixth sense. Pretending to be interested in a display of blushers, I picked up a compact of pink powder. I had always associated blushing with shame and embarrassment.

"Something to brighten you up?" A female voice pierced the drone of the spaceship. The saleswoman, wearing a white smock, was plump, a standout among her colleagues. Still being watched, I decided to buy something rather than steal. It would be an act of solidarity with the plump woman.

"What's the opposite of brightening up?" I asked. I caught sight of a display of eyeliners in shades of black. Leeta black. "I'll take the darkest one of those." I asked the woman to apply it for me right there in the store. She directed me to a stool, where I sat as she circled my eyes, but when I looked in the handheld mirror she had given me, the circles weren't thick enough. "More," I said. She circled my eyes again, adding another layer, but it wasn't enough. "More."

"Are you sure?"

"My goal isn't to look fuckable. The look I want is *Don't fuck with me.*"

She laughed nervously, unsure if I was

crazy. "I've never been asked for that before."

When she finished ringing my eyes, I asked to see dark lip-glosses. I picked through the small pots until I found something that appealed: Darkest Plum. I paid for my items, then applied the gloss with my pinkie, covering the taste of meat that had lingered on my lips. The saleswoman held up the mirror again and I admired my transformation. "I think it's important that makeup reflects the true inner self," I said, repeating a line I had once read in *Daisy Chain*.

On the bus heading back to my neighborhood, more people than usual stared at me. I decided I would wear the eye makeup every day.

I was close to home, but stopped at a bakery to buy a treat for the road. As I made my way over the crosswalk at Seventh Avenue, munching a cherry turnover, I passed a bike messenger who was stopped at the light, checking his phone. He began singing "Big Girls Don't Cry" and then laughed, a deep-throated cackle. I glanced over my shoulder. When he saw me looking, he sang his own version:

"Big girls eat pie."

I turned around and walked back toward him, stuffing the end of the turnover into my mouth. "Do you think you're funny?" A bit of pastry flew from between my lips.

"Miss Piggy," he said, cackling again, clearly disgusted by me, the exile from Bonerville. If there'd been a trapdoor beneath me, he would have opened it and sent me into oblivion. As far as he was concerned, if I didn't make his man parts happy, I had no reason to exist.

"Move it, lard-ass," he said. I didn't move, but stood so close to him that the tip of his front tire was wedged between my knees. I sucked a bit of cherry off my thumb. His little song had been intended as a drive-by, a shot fired into the anonymous fat girl as she crossed the street. It was intended to wound, but I wasn't wounded. It was the intention that infuriated me.

The man was wearing metallic sunglasses and a helmet, which covered his head and face in a kind of armor. Only his mouth and chin were visible, and the skin I could see was sweaty and rough with stubble. I imagined kissing him, the stubble ripping my skin, streaking me with blood.

"I asked you a question," I said. "Do you think you're funny?"

The light turned green and I felt the

whoosh of traffic around me, but I didn't budge. "Get the fuck out of my way," he said, but I wasn't going to get the fuck out of his way. He could have easily ridden around me, but he wasn't the type to back down when challenged, even if he had a schedule to keep. I squeezed my free hand into a fist, a wave of heat filling me from top to bottom, red moving up a thermometer.

"You wanna fight, big girl?" There was that cackle again. In that moment I hated him more than I had ever hated anyone. I reached my right hand into the satchel resting on my hip, the strap crossing my chest, and felt the brick inside.

"A fight is exactly what I want." This sentence escaped my mouth as if someone else had programmed me to say it. Something had overtaken me, but I liked it. I grasped the brick hidden inside my satchel, moving my fingers over its dusty surface. The man's face was covered in armor, but I could aim at his mouth.

Are you crazy? a voice inside my head said. It sounded like Sana's lilt.

The man stood up from his bike and swung his leg over it. This is it, I thought. He lowered his bike to the pavement. He was wearing shiny black bike shorts and a tank top, his arms muscled and tattooed. Still I didn't budge. I was willing to see this through, even if he punched me in the face and bashed my head into the concrete. Bring it on. I'd been punched in the face before during the New Baptist Plan and survived, but that time I hadn't fought back. A fight is what I'd wanted these past few weeks. Maybe now I was going to get it. It'll hurt, but it'll feel good too.

A Baptist isn't afraid of a little pain.

I gripped the brick, steeling myself. If there were butterflies in my stomach, some had broken free and were fluttering through me, pumping me up, urging me on. I wanted to open my mouth and release them in a roar. I pulled the brick from my satchel, but an arm came in between the bike messenger and me, the arm of a large black man.

"That's enough," said the man, who was wearing a security guard uniform. He seemed to be about my father's age. A crowd surrounded the messenger and me on the crosswalk, which I hadn't noticed from within my bubble of fury. The bubble popped.

The messenger held up his hands as if the police had told him to freeze. Big black guy trumped big white girl. He picked up his bike and got on it. "Crazy bitch," he said as he rode away. He'd backed down, but I hadn't.

I turned to the security guard, irritated. I hadn't asked to be rescued.

"I've been watching you," he said. "What the hell were you thinking?"

"That guy tried to insult me."

"Better to just ignore him."

"Says who?"

"Says somebody who doesn't want to see you get your ass kicked."

I was going to put the brick back in my satchel, but decided to carry it home in my hand. "I appreciate your concern," I said in a petulant daughter voice.

"You better watch yourself," the man called after me, but I ignored him and hurried along toward Calliope House, high on my encounter with the guy on the bike. When I opened the door, I was anxious to tell someone what had happened.

"Where've you been?" Sana asked, coming down the stairs. I was breathless, my face flushed.

"I almost just got into a fight with a bike messenger."

"What are you doing with that brick?"

"I've been carrying it around with me."

"Give me that," she said, snatching the brick away. She was still being prickly, just as she had been during the bomb threat, so I moved past her and went into the kitchen. I lifted a carton of apple juice from the top shelf of the fridge and poured myself a glass. Sana had followed me and watched me gulp it down.

"Nice eye makeup," she said.

"Thanks. I had a makeover."

"Have you *seen* yourself?"

I bent over and looked at my reflection in the microwave. The black eyeliner had bled beyond its borders. "Raccoon eyes," I said. Kitty had written a whole column about it once. I used my fingers to wipe off some of the greasy makeup, as black as a tire's skid mark.

"Do I need to worry about you, Plum?"

"I've never felt better in my life." It was the truth.

"Plum —" she started. I held up my hand, knowing what was coming, but Sana wasn't deterred. I knew she'd been saving this up and now it was flooding out: "You've been through a lot . . . You're not used to living without Y—— . . . You're upset about Leeta . . ." and on it went.

"I feel alive now in a way I never have before. I thought you were happy for me?"

"We're all happy for you, but how many

times could you have been arrested in recent weeks?"

"Several."

"What were you doing with that brick?"

"I fantasized about smashing someone with it, but in reality it's not so easy, I guess."

"Are you even listening to yourself right now?"

"People count on us to be passive. They deserve to be punished."

"The haters outnumber us by a large margin. Are you going to smash them all?"

This wasn't what I wanted to hear. I'd been enjoying my high, but Sana had extinguished it with her incessant scolding. I missed feeling high. In its place was agitation.

I excused myself to go to my room before our exchange could escalate. I'd save my anger for those who deserved it. I still wanted a fight, but not with her.

In my room, I took off my heavy boots and tossed them into the corner. My tights were dirty from touching the bike, so I brushed them off, moving my hands along the curves of my calves, feeling their bulk. It felt good to touch my body. It centered and calmed me.

I peeled off my tights and unbuttoned my

dress, which was sweaty under the arms and down the back. I took off everything else and climbed into bed naked, enjoying the chill of the sheets. I breathed slowly through my mouth, placing my hands on my stomach to experience the movement of air through my body, keeping a rhythm. My thoughts were zipping around in my brain. Unable to corral them, I kept focused on my breath.

Sana didn't know what it was like to be numb for so many years and then to feel again. Before quitting Y——, I'd been like a lamp that was broken, but now I was switched on, emanating heat and light. There was pleasure in feeling strongly. Even an emotion like rage could feel good — it was almost cleansing, the way it made me feel alive.

I ran my hands over my body, playing with my nipples, placing my hands between my legs, exploring. I wasn't like those women on the screens in the underground apartment, who had sanitized slits between their legs. Between my legs was a handful of flesh and hair. While on Y——, I had masturbated a couple times a year, but it was never worth the effort — all that stroking for a tiny pop at the end. Now merely rubbing my fingertips together aroused me. Without the drugs, my body was alert to touch.

Since I didn't want to be fuckable any-more, I focused on how I felt inside, not how I might have looked to an imaginary someone. I was anchored in the sensations of my body rather than living outside of it, judging it. Sometimes I thought about sex with a partner. Rubí went out all the time and offered to fix me up, but I wasn't ready. That step would come in time. I was content to be alone for now, to become acquainted with the body I had never liked to touch. I rubbed myself, the whole messy handful between my legs, my hand bringing me closer to what I wanted: pleasure and release.

I slept for a little while, then went down-stairs to make dinner, feeling mellow and balanced for the first time that day. Rubí was sitting at the kitchen table with a glass and a bottle of tequila.

"Bad day?" I said.

"The worst." She told me that Dabsitaf had been approved by the FDA despite how hard she and Verena had worked to stop it. "They said the dangers of obesity outweigh the potential dangers of the drug."

I placed my cutting board on the table across from her so I could chop vegetables and we could talk. "This isn't over. You'll raise awareness. I'll help you," I said, but she remained quiet. I sliced an eggplant as she finished her drink and poured another. After she set the bottle back on the table, she pointed to the television behind me, the sound muted. "Look at that," she said.

A breaking news banner appeared at the bottom of the screen, announcing JENNIFER REVEALED.

I dropped my knife on the cutting board and reached to turn up the volume.

"Thank the Lord on high," said Cheryl Crane-Murphy. "Yes, it's true. We finally know who Jennifer is."

Soledad

United States Army specialist Soledad Ayala was traveling in the Khost province of southeastern Afghanistan, riding in a convoy of Humvees to FOB Salerno, which they called Rocket City. She and another medic were the only two women in the unit, riding in the back of the last Humvee, dressed in dust-colored clothes and armed with M4 carbines.

The helmet strap circling her chin was going to cause a breakout; Soledad could feel the oil and sweat there, and so she reached up to wipe her skin. Outside the window it looked like Nevada or Arizona, which is what she wrote to Luz in her letters, hoping it would make them seem less far apart. Soledad told Luz about the monkeys and the sounds they made. These were details a child would enjoy, but Soledad feared Luz wasn't a child anymore, that she'd changed. There were warnings from school about truancy and smoking.

It'd been a mistake to join the reserves — Soledad had learned that too late — but after Luz's father died she was desperate for money and wanted to go to college. She'd earned two degrees, a bachelor's in sociology and a master's in women's studies, and now she was paying for them.

For hours the Humvee traveled the barren terrain and Soledad thought of Luz. She held her gun to her body, which was constricted by the uniform and the pounds of equipment strapped around her. She dreamed of taking it all off and letting cool water splash over her skin. Agnes, who was sitting next to her, remained silent, looking out the tiny window without a hint to what she was thinking. Soledad was grateful for the quiet, which she expected to continue until they arrived, but then there was a boom.

Pulse of light. Heat. Shattered glass.

Boom.

It seemed to be hours long, the boom, and she was trapped inside it, rolling around in it, feeling it echo and vibrate through her.

The boom finally stopped and in its place there was silence, a pause; outside the window she saw nothing but sand and smoke. Then she heard shouting, and men's voices, and the jackhammer sound of guns firing. She reached for Agnes's hands, which were trying to free her from the wreckage.

Outside the vehicle there were bodies in the dirt, and parts of bodies. Soledad left a trail of blood behind her in the sand as she looked for the wounded; she was wounded too, but walking. There was a soldier on the ground, his thigh cut to the bone. Agnes was fastening a black band above the wound as the man screamed. Soledad pinned his shoulders to the ground with her knees, her hands on his head, trying to still him as Agnes worked. They were engulfed in a cloud of choking black smoke and sand. The guns were firing, but she couldn't see them; she could only hear them. The dying soldier looked up at Soledad. Her face would be the last thing he would see in this world, but her face was nothing special.

"Mama," he said. He was only a boy.

Soledad wiped the sand and sweat from his forehead. She feared she was going to black out soon. The blood from the wound in her left shoulder had soaked the arm of her uniform into a deep scarlet. She returned to the truck for supplies, taking a moment to rest her head against the side of it. When she turned around a man was heading in the direction of Agnes, screaming in his nonsense language, the sounds flying from his mouth. Soledad's gun was strapped around her and she positioned it in front of her and shot at the man as he ran through the cloud. She missed and shot again, hitting him in the back. He fell to the ground, the enemy man, silent and still. Dead.

Look out! A voice in the cloud, an American voice, one on her side, was trying to warn her. Another enemy man was moving toward her, and she shot him in the chest.

When she awoke in the hospital three days later, she didn't remember much, but she could see the man in the cloud, falling into the dirt and landing on his back, his legs twisted beneath him. She had never killed anyone before, but it had been easy. That's what she remembered about it more than any other detail: how easy it had been.

In the hospital in Kandahar, Soledad was treated for a deep wound to the shoulder, blood loss, and infection. Her mind returned to the cloud, the choking black smoke and sand, the Taliban fighters she had killed. Several days passed before the doctors decided she was stable enough to learn about her daughter's rape. Luz was still alive then, but it would be more than a week before Soledad was allowed to travel, and by that time Luz would have jumped in front of the train. Soledad feared that Luz had been angry with her for leaving her with her grandmother, for not being there to make everything all right.

Where was this girl's mother? the people at home had said.

Until her weeping trio of sisters met her at the airport, Soledad didn't fully believe that Luz's suicide was real. When she arrived home, a photographer took a photo that ran across the wires: *Army reservist Soledad Ayala arrives home in Santa Mariana, north of Los Angeles.* Soledad went into the house and closed the door. Her mother was in bed, sedated and barely conscious, being tended to by relatives from out of town. She didn't want to see her mother, who had failed Luz.

Soledad sat in the living room, feeling unattached to her surroundings, as if she were viewing the scene from afar. She'd traveled back from the war, moving through time and space, but she hadn't completely crossed over. Her body was at home, but some part of her, some essential part, had been left behind.

She experienced the cloud of sand and smoke, the sound of gunfire, the killing of the Taliban men, the days she was unconscious in the hospital, and the news of Luz, raped and dead. It had all happened at once, in a flash; it was a big jumble, a black cloud, and she was caught inside it. She hadn't been due to go home for another four weeks; she hadn't prepared herself for the transition from that world of violence and death to her home in California. She learned after her first deployment that leaving the war meant crossing over from one state of mind to another, that there was a shift from soldier back to mother. Now she was only the mother of a dead girl.

Why wasn't this girl's mother supervising her? the people in town had said.

When the formalities of the funeral were over, she sent her mother to Texas with her sisters and the rest of her relatives. Two of the young men who'd raped her daughter were out on bail and they were going to die, she was sure of that. She'd killed before, it was easy. She was only a medic, and a woman, but she'd been trained to kill the enemy. That's what she'd done and would continue to do.

Leaving the war meant crossing over. The mind of a soldier wasn't the mind of a mother, but she wasn't a mother anymore. When she was in Afghanistan, something had crossed over in her, and when she went home, it didn't cross back.

A quiet settled over Calliope House the day after the Jennifer revelations became public, as if we were holding a moment of silence for the mother who'd lost her daughter, which was at the root of everything. The story was still taking shape; some questions were answered, but many others remained. Information about Soledad stuffed the papers and airwaves, much of it speculation. There was no news about Leeta, but she hadn't been lying when she told her roommate she knew the identity of Jennifer.

After a morning engrossed in the news, I had the kitchen to myself in the afternoon. I slid a tray of cupcake batter into the oven. That Leeta was connected to me and also to Jennifer — Soledad — was unreal. I didn't know how to think about something that was so far removed from anything I'd experienced. For the rest of the day I wanted to pretend that they didn't exist, but as I went through the messages in my inbox, I discovered I didn't have that option.

The messages were mostly from new girls who'd sent their addresses, requesting books. One girl suggested a high school edition of *Fuckability Theory,* an idea I said I would pass on to Marlowe, amused at the thought of her replacing every occurrence of *fuck* and its variations.

Working my way to the top of the inbox, I found two names I recognized, Hannah and Jasmine. They'd written several times to discuss Marlowe's book, so it wasn't unusual to see email from them in my inbox, but these messages were different. The girls explained that they'd received weird correspondence in recent days, each time from a different, vague email address, with subject headings such as "Revolution!" and "Rise Up!" In one of the messages, the girls were advised to cancel their subscriptions to *Daisy Chain* and donate the money to Reproductive Justice, a nonprofit group. In another, they were encouraged to skip school and engage in acts of civil disobedience. Hannah forwarded the most recent one to me:

From: account7
To: Hannah_hannaH
Subject: Fight Back!

The police and the "justice" system don't take violence against women and girls seriously. If you've been assaulted or harassed, take the law into your own hands. Form vigilante groups with other girls. Sign up for self-defense classes, but don't just use the skills defensively. Go on the offensive!

Hannah wanted to know if these messages were from me. "Oh my God," I said under my breath, slamming my laptop shut. I recalled Julia's response when I asked her why Leeta wanted the spreadsheet: *Maybe Jennifer's army is looking for new recruits.* No. I scoffed at my own wild thoughts. I was becoming paranoid like Julia.

And yet, something nagged at me.

As a woman being hunted by the FBI, Soledad had better things to do than email Kitty's readers, but her network was large and Leeta was out there somewhere. Maybe someone in the group wanted to reach out to these girls — at the heart of "Jennifer" was Soledad's own lost girl. There was a certain degree of logic to it. I wondered if this could be traced back to me or to Julia, and what would happen if it was.

"What's burning?" Sana was standing in the doorway, next to the refrigerator. I didn't know how long she'd been there watching my rising panic. I'd forgotten about my cupcakes and now opened the oven, a gush of smoke blinding me. I slid the pan of charred cakes onto the stovetop.

"Are you all right?" Sana said, a question she asked too often and not without reason. We were still slightly awkward with each other the day after our argument.

"I have a lot on my mind, you know, with all the stuff in the news." I used a knife to flick off the burned top of a cupcake, then pinched a chunk of the moist part underneath, blew on it, and ate it. I was hungry and I didn't want to face Sana, so I stuffed my mouth. She took the tray away from me and dumped the cakes in the trash.

"Things aren't so dire that we have to eat ruined food, are they?"

I licked the crumbs from my lips. She was waiting for me to say something, to explain why I was acting odd, but I would have to lie and I didn't want to do that. I couldn't tell her about the messages until I had more time to think about the situation. If I mentioned it to Sana it would become a brouhaha, and I couldn't deal with that. I needed to keep a lid on this and Julia's book and my suspicions about her. The lid on the pot was already rattling, about to blow off. Everything I worried about was linked to Julia.

"I'm still concerned about you," Sana said. "I'm just putting that out there, into the universe."

I wrapped my arms around her, squeezing her tight, hoping this would convey how much I appreciated her. She squeezed me back. I rested my cheek against her shoulder, the yellow of her blouse and the citrus scent of her soap transporting me away from this kitchen and away from thoughts of Jennifer, to somewhere simpler, like the lemon trees in my mother's yard. I was reluctant to let go of Sana and this reverie. We continued to embrace, no line between us. "I'm sorry I haven't been myself lately," I said, but this wasn't entirely true — I didn't know what it meant to be myself anymore.

When the hug ended, she didn't push me to say anything more, even though I knew that's what she wanted. She left the kitchen and returned to her desk, leaving me alone, my laptop on the table, unavoidable. I would have to open it again.

From: PlumK
To: JuliaCole
Subject: SOS

Julia,

I need to speak with you urgently. DO
NOT IGNORE THIS MESSAGE!

— PK

Within minutes, I received a reply — an
indication that something was wrong.

From: JuliaCole
To: PlumK
Subject: Re: SOS

Let's meet tonight at Café Rose. 10:00.
I need another favor.

J.

Of course.

When I arrived at Café Rose, Julia was sitting at a table in a back corner, drinking
espresso despite the late hour. She was the
Austen version of herself, with flawless
makeup and straight hair, pale skin, boots

with heels. I couldn't see what she was wearing underneath the trench coat, but I assumed it was her Austen uniform. I thought of her chest under that fabric, covered in roses and thorns.

"What's with the eye makeup?" she said when I sat down. "Taking beauty tips from our favorite fugitive, are we? That would make a great article for *Daisy Chain.* 'Get the Jennifer look!' "

I was conscious of the server hovering nearby. "The T-shirt already exists, so why not?" I said quietly.

"Jennifer as fashion statement, stripped of all the violence and bloodshed, available at Neiman Marcus."

"Camo will be in style soon."

"No doubt."

This banter seemed to be a relief for both of us. The server requested my order and when she was out of earshot, Julia and I both leaned in. "Someone is emailing *Daisy Chain* readers, telling them to revolt and rise up," I whispered.

"It's not a problem," she whispered back. When the server appeared with my wine, Julia and I straightened up, smiling at her pleasantly. I took a drink slowly, peeking at Julia over the rim of my glass.

When we were alone at the back of the

465

café again, Julia continued, explaining that the Austen network had been under sustained attack for weeks. "Email accounts have been hacked, subscriber information downloaded, everything. This works to our advantage. They will never connect those email addresses back to you and me. Don't worry."

I relaxed a bit, taking another sip. "But I've been emailing the same girls on my own. It might seem like an unbelievable coincidence."

"There's nothing criminal about that. You worked at Austen for years. You developed a connection with the girls, blah blah blah. Trust me, this is the least of our worries." That phrase — *our worries* — was loaded with meaning. I didn't know why I was included in it.

"What about this favor you want?" There was no reason to lounge by the pool — I dived right in.

"Not yet." She tapped her fingers on the table, surveying the café over my shoulders. I'd always laughed at Julia's paranoia, but now if she was scooped up in a net, I'd be scooped up too.

"Relax," I said, glancing around.

"I can't relax. The heat has been turned up."

"What heat?" She didn't answer but fanned herself with a menu. "What did you think when you heard the news about Jennifer?" I wanted to gauge her reaction.

"It's shocking," she said, still peering around, not appearing shocked.

"Was it actually news to you, Julia?"

Her focus returned to me, her eyes narrowing beneath her smudged charcoal lids, her Bambi lashes. She moistened her lips with her tongue, amused. "I remember when I first met you in the Beauty Closet," she said. "You were so timid. I remember you *blushing* when I asked you what color your nipples are. Now look at you." She reached over the table and picked up my drink. My bottom lip was imprinted on the glass, a furry caterpillar in gloss, just below the rim. Julia drank from the same spot.

"I remember that meeting as well. You were shifty then, as you are now."

She slid the glass back to my side of the table. "As much as I'm enjoying this conversation, it's time to discuss the favor."

I considered taking another drink from my glass, but didn't. "You should have *I need a favor* printed on your business cards."

"I trust you. I don't trust many people," she said, seeming sincere. "Meet me in the bathroom in two minutes." She stood up, straightening the collar of her trench and disappearing into the bathroom. I waited a couple minutes, then followed.

"At the end," Julia said from behind a stall door. There were three stalls. The first two were empty. I opened the door to the third stall and squeezed inside, which wasn't easy. Julia and I stood chest to chest in the cramped cubicle.

"I'm in deep trouble, Plum," she said, her usual swagger replaced with something like desperation.

I wanted to back away from her, but there wasn't room. "I'm not sure I want to know, Julia." I had wanted to know before, but in this moment I was afraid.

"Please," she said. "I need you to ask Verena for money, as much as you can get. Tell her it's for you. Make up a story. You can say you have debts."

I felt my stomach tighten. "Why do you need money?"

"It's not for me."

"Then who is it for?" I knew what she was going to say, but I needed to hear her say it.

"It's for *her.*"

If we weren't locked in the narrow stall, my emotions would have overflowed. "I knew it," I said, trying to stay measured. "I knew you were lying this whole time." I'd been on the margins of this, whatever it was, and now I was moving closer to the center. I reached past Julia to unlock the stall door.

"She needs your help," Julia said, blocking me, reaching out and placing her hands on my shoulders.

I thought of Leeta regularly, never suspecting that she might think of me too. "Is she okay?"

"No, she's not."

"Where is she?"

Julia shook her head. "It's better that you don't know. Knowing too much will put you in danger."

"You mean *even more* danger than you've already put me in?" It wasn't only my stomach that had tightened — every part of me was contracting. I reached for my throat, placing my hand at the base of my neck. "Why does she need money?"

"She needs to escape, make a run for it."

I leaned sideways, resting against the burnished metal wall of the stall, letting it absorb my weight. "Is this really happening?" I coughed a nervous laugh. *Wake up,* I said to myself. *This must be a nightmare.* I thought about my shoplifting, my brick, my arguments with strangers. That was the minor leagues.

"What has she done, exactly?" Everyone wanted to know the answer to this question. Cheryl Crane-Murphy alone had devoted weeks to the topic. Here I was, actually in a position to find out.

"Whatever she did, she did for Luz," Julia said.

"Tell me."

"I can't. It's better for you if you don't know. That's the truth."

"But, Julia, I can't help you if I don't know. You're asking me to be part of this."

The door to the bathroom opened and Julia placed her index finger on my lips. The sink turned on then off; the blower turned on then off. After a few minutes, the bathroom door opened then closed.

She removed her finger from my lips, the tip slick with my gloss. "Darkest Plum?"

"How did you know?"

"I know every shade of lip-gloss."

"Julia, you're changing the subject."

"Please don't ask me any more questions. Just know I never wanted to be involved in any of this. She came to me for help and I couldn't turn her away." There was a tremor in her, which left a tiny crack in the barricade. "I'm scared, Plum." She struggled to say this, her voice sticking, unaccustomed to emotion, to truth.

I worried she was going to cry. I'd seen her lose control before, and I was afraid of it happening again, of her becoming unhinged in the bathroom stall. "It's okay," I said. I brushed her hair back, looping it behind her ears. "I'm sure you're scared." I thought of the men with their guns, the helicopters, the dogs. I was scared just listening to her.

"Is Darkest Plum going to help us, or not?" *Us.* I had always thought of Julia and Leeta as a pair.

"I'll think about it," I said. This seemed to calm her. Her face was in front of mine; we were sharing breath. She moved in closer, placing her lips on mine, a soft, lingering kiss, so that Darkest Plum was now on both of us.

"Forgive me," she said, "but if something happens to me, I would always regret not doing that."

I felt my skin burn. "Soft Rose," she whispered. "I know every color of blush, too."

She unlocked the stall door. "Think it over," she said, and then she was gone.

Exiting the café, I welcomed the rush of night air, a splash of cold to my face. Julia had left me reeling, as always, but this time she had really outdone herself. Leeta was hiding and needed my help. I wondered whether Julia and her sisters might be sheltering Leeta in their apartment, but that would be too risky. Leeta was probably nowhere near New York.

I walked distractedly through the dark, looking down at my black boots as they hit the concrete, blocking out everything else. The taste of Julia lingered on my lips and I wiped it away, staining my hand with Darkest Plum. I could still wash my hands of Julia and Leeta. I could still extricate myself, since I hadn't done anything wrong or irrevocable, not yet. I had agreed to write Julia's book, but that wasn't a crime, unlike giving money to Leeta, which could land me in jail, my name plastered in the headlines, forever linked with Leeta's notoriety. I'd thought that I wanted to be an outlaw, but now I wasn't so sure.

I wished I could discuss this with Sana despite the risks of telling anyone else about it. She and Verena were having dinner with potential donors for the clinic, but I texted her and asked if she could meet me afterward at a bar near Calliope House. I didn't want to talk to her at home, where she'd be more likely to react loudly. She responded right away and agreed to meet me in an hour.

The bar was packed with college students, but I appreciated the buzz and the noise. I ordered a glass of wine and grabbed a good spot just as two women were leaving, squeezing myself into the narrow space between the tables. A copy of the *New York Daily* lay abandoned on the floor near my feet. The cover featured the usual photo of Soledad in her uniform, as well as Leeta and Missy. ARE MEN REALLY SO BAD? JENNIFER'S OVARY-ACTION, the headline read. I wouldn't bother reading the article, but I would save the paper for Marlowe, in case she hadn't seen it.

As I sipped my wine, I thought about Sana and how she would try to talk me out of helping Leeta. Maybe that's what I wanted, someone else to make the decision for me. I knew it wouldn't be fair to place this burden on Sana, just as Julia had placed her burden on me, but I worried that the decision was too big for me alone.

The bar was growing more crowded with students, who bumped into each other, spilling drinks and stepping on toes. Turning back to the newspaper and its ridiculous headline, I heard a disembodied male voice.

"Hey," the voice said.

I looked up from my glass and soon the voice had a face. "What are you doing here alone?" He was a generic white guy in his early twenties, holding a bottle of beer.

"I'm waiting for a friend," I said, meaning, *Go away, you're not getting my table.*

"Mind if I wait with you?" Before I could answer, he slid into the empty chair across from me, uninvited. "My name's Mason." He had the firmness of body and brightness of skin that only men who were recently boys had; he was like a flower that had just pushed its way up through the dirt. I wasn't attracted to him, but he had a glow.

"My friend will be here soon," I said, but my phone vibrated and made me a liar. A message from Sana: *running late, can we talk at home instead?* I sighed with annoyance.

"Stood up?" Mason said, putting the

amber bottle of beer to his mouth and sucking on it.

"I have to go. You can have the table."

"Don't go. I didn't even catch your name."

"I didn't offer it." I picked up my things. As I was about to leave, two large men moved away from the bar and I could see a table in a corner on the other side of the room. Three women and two men were crowded around it. They were looking in our direction, rising out of their chairs and straining to see, their merry brown and blond heads bobbing with laughter. When they noticed me looking, their smiling faces turned serious.

I asked Mason if the group on the other side of the bar were his friends. "Yeah, but they don't mind if I ditch them for someone as pretty as you."

I blushed for the second time that night — *Soft Rose* — but not because I was flattered. I sat back down. I had an important decision to make, but I couldn't let this pass.

"Tell me your name," Mason said again.

"My name's Jennifer." From the front page of the newspaper, Leeta's eyes were fixed on me. Mason had no reaction. "I'm Jennifer," I said again, but there was no alarm in his eyes. *Jennifers are our daughters, sisters, wives, and mothers.*

"You seem nervous," he said, sipping his beer. "Just relax, babe."

I didn't know his game, but I decided to play along. I wanted to see what he planned to do. He launched into casual conversation, as if we were old friends, as if I had wanted to talk to him, as if he were fascinating. He spoke about random things, like his love of baseball and his studies at law school. A chunk of his peanut-colored hair fell over his eyes regularly, requiring him to brush it away. It seemed like an inconvenient haircut, but I imagined it had its uses, allowing him to appear shy and cute around girls.

"So who's this friend you were waiting for?" he said, finishing his beer and sliding the bottle to the middle of the table.

"She dumped me. She must have met a guy. Men find her irresistible."

"I think you're irresistible."

"You don't mean that," I said, coquettishly. I wanted to maintain my pleasant demeanor, but I was growing angrier inside. I had left home that night in my brown and violet dress feeling confident and happy in my appearance, but Mason and his friends seemed to think I was a joke. *This is how it's going to be,* I thought. I had changed so much in the past few months, but the world hadn't changed along with me. Plum would always be a target. Giving up the hope of Alicia meant giving up the hope of ever blending in.

"I live not too far from here," Mason said. "My roommates are out. Maybe we could go back to my place and, I don't know, hang out?" He put his hand beneath the table and gently touched my knee, trying to signal something, perhaps that he was harmless, like a dog rolling over onto his back. When I didn't answer, he used his other hand to brush his finger along my arm at the border of bare skin and sleeve. He leaned across the table and whispered: "I like you."

There were murderous women about, slayings, kidnappings, castrations, but he wasn't deterred from his deviant plan, whatever it was. His was the face of a boy you'd see smiling back at you from a framed photograph on the desk of a doctor or insurance executive — the nonthreatening son, as bland as a vanilla cupcake.

Mason was waiting for an answer, and I wondered how hard he would work to win me over. He didn't expect me to be hard work. I was supposed to be grateful for his attention — that's what he was expecting: a round-faced girl desperate for male attention, brightening under the beam of his unexpected lust. Such a girl would do anything he wanted. He looked at me expectantly and I pretended for a moment that I was a generic woman. This is how it was, I thought. This is what people did. They went to bars and chatted with strangers and then went home and had sex with them. All those nights when I locked myself in my apartment, watching television and eating my Waist Watchers dinners, this is what people my age were doing.

"Come on, baby," he said. The lock of hair moved down into place. From the sound of his voice and the way he said *baby,* I didn't think he was from New York. Virginia, maybe, or a point farther south. Wherever he was from, it wasn't these parts. They didn't grow boys like him around here.

I finished my glass of wine in two gulps. "All right," I said. "I'm going to the ladies' room. You can tell your friends we're leaving." I picked up my satchel and the newspaper and brushed past him, moving toward the stairs that led down to the bathroom. Several people turned to look, more than usual. Were they all in on the joke? A feeling I used to know well but hadn't experienced for a while crept up on me: humiliation.

I didn't need to use the bathroom, but I needed a few moments to myself. When I went back upstairs, Mason and his friends might reveal the joke and laugh at me. I needed to be prepared for that. But there were other possibilities. Perhaps Mason would continue the charade, thinking he could take me back to his place for a free blowjob. After all, I was supposed to be desperate. Or perhaps he was attracted to fat women and used the joke as a cover so his friends wouldn't laugh at him. Picking up fat women for an ulterior purpose was a fairly common phenomenon, Rubí had told me. It was called *hogging*, which was a sport. Mason had decided to play, but he was going to lose.

For some reason, locked in my second bathroom stall of the night, I imagined Mason trying to pick up Alicia in a bar, not as a joke but because he liked her. She might have been flattered by Mason's attention. She might have gone back to his apartment and had sex with him. She couldn't see his true self. Stupid Alicia.

I left my stall and stood in front of the sinks, the newspaper still wedged under my arm. I held it in front of me and stared at Leeta on the front page. Her eyes were fixed on me, as they'd always been. She was out there somewhere, thinking about me, in need of my help. "I've been chasing you," I said, running my hands over the newsprint. This was my moment.

I went back upstairs and found Mason sitting at his friends' table. None of them were laughing now. Sana would have advised me to go home, arguing that I couldn't confront all the shitty people in the world. She was right, but I forged ahead. Mason deserved to pay. I would be swift and brutal.

"I don't want to go home with you," I said to Mason in front of his friends. "I think you're ugly."

It took him a moment to register what I was saying. "Huh?"

"You're fucking ugly," I said. "Hideous, in fact."

Mason's friends, the three women and two men, looked at each other. This hadn't been part of the plan.

"*I'm* ugly?" Mason tried to laugh for his friends. "I'm fucking ugly? Have you ever looked at yourself in the mirror, fatty? You're disgusting. No man in his right mind would ever lay a hand on you." No more *baby* for me.

It felt good to hear him say this, to know the charade was over. "You laid a hand on me. You seemed to be enjoying it."

"Because I wanted to win a bet." He laughed again, glancing around the table for support, but the men and women at the table were silent and expressionless, unsure how to react. The big blob had spoken. It could speak. They had always relied on the blob to be quiet, to absorb their taunts and snide remarks and slip quietly through the cracks of life. Now the blob was angry.

Uh-oh.

"You say I'm disgusting, Mason, but I think we both know what gets you off: a nice big fat girl like me. You just don't want your friends to know."

Before he could reply, I reached for their table and lifted it, sending bottles of beer spilling everywhere. They leapt from their seats to escape the splashing liquid and crashing amber glass. "You stupid cow," one of the women said. They scrambled to get clear of the table, but Mason slipped on the wet floor and hit the back of his head against the wall on the way down. He was dazed, lying on his back in a pool of beer, blinking his eyes slowly. His friends didn't help him.

I placed my foot on his chest so he couldn't move. My black boots. My colorful tights. I could do this.

"You need to learn some fucking manners!" I shouted.

"Hey, come on," Mason said. There was a

crowd gathering. "I'm sorry, okay? I think you're pretty, Jennifer. I do."

"What?" I asked loudly over the clatter of the bar, wanting him to repeat it.

"I think you're pretty."

I couldn't help but laugh. "You think I'm *pretty*?" Of all the things he could have said, this was the least expected. A deep roar came up from my diaphragm. The laugh was so sudden, so *vast,* that I feared it might rip me apart.

"Say it again."

"You're pretty, Jennifer. I mean it."

I continued to laugh. The laugh was long enough to stretch from the earliest days of my childhood till now, like a shooting star leaving a long trail of light. The trail wrapped itself around all the kids who'd tormented me when I was a girl and all the boys who'd ignored me when I was a teenager and all the young men who'd withheld their affections from me as an adult and all the women who'd excluded and harassed me until now, when Mason told me he thought I was pretty. Finally, I had what I wanted! When the laugh caught up to the present moment, the tail slipped out of my mouth.

Silence.

Mason thought he could throw a crumb

in the direction of the fat girl and it would make up for everything that had happened to her in her life, most of all what had happened that night. Telling her she's pretty was the pot of gold at the end of the rainbow, the winning lottery number, the healing hand of Christ on top of her head. He had been made to believe he had such power. It had been given to him by women like her.

I leaned over and looked at him closely. He wasn't Mason anymore; he was *them.* Looking at him, looking at *them,* the behavior of my whole life was suddenly inexplicable. The years of Waist Watchers, Baptist Weight Loss and plans for surgery, the hours and hours that added up to years of my life spent sitting at home afraid to go outside, afraid to be laughed at and shunned and rejected and stared at by faces like the one looking up at me now, one of the generic, mass-produced, ordinary, follow-the-crowd, hateful faces. At another time, at home alone, I would have wept to think about it. I wished I could go back to the beginning of my life and start again.

I removed my foot from his chest. I didn't want to fight with him. He didn't matter. I turned to leave, pushing my way through the onlookers. No one tried to stop me. The police hadn't been called. Mason's friends seemed to have disappeared.

As I walked away from the bar, the sky above was clear and black. Somewhere up there was the laugh that had escaped from me, the long trail of light that was now part of the universe. I couldn't see it, but I knew it was there. I would only have to look up to remember it.

My breakfast the next morning was a poached egg, rye toast with butter, melon, and tea. I didn't spend my morning in the kitchen making omelets and stacks of waffles for myself and everyone else. A normal breakfast satisfied me.

When I finished eating, I remained at the table, fixated on Eulayla's fat jeans hanging on the red wall. I still hadn't deposited the $20,000 check from Verena. I had also never canceled my surgery. I called Dr. Shearer's secretary to make it official. After hanging up the phone I didn't feel a sense of loss. I felt proud.

Sana had asked why I'd wanted to talk the night before, but I told her I had been bored and thought going to the bar would be fun. She didn't seem to suspect anything. I had decided not to tell her about Julia's request for money. I'd been relying on the women of Calliope House, particularly

Sana, for support and community, but this was a decision I needed to make alone. It wouldn't be fair to implicate them. Leeta had never been part of their lives, and they didn't understand my connection to her. She was my problem.

While I considered what to do about Leeta, I decided it was time to return to Swann Street. I'd abandoned my apartment in Brooklyn months before and needed to face it again. On my way there I mailed about fifty books to my girls, as the requests kept coming in. After the post office I went to my bank and deposited the $20,000.

On the subway to Brooklyn, descending into the dark tunnel, traveling back to my own netherworld, I prepared to see my old home again. I arrived at the brownstone, opening the familiar street door and stopping at the wall of copper-colored mailboxes in the entryway before going upstairs to my apartment. Mail was stuffed into my box, and there was a notice from the post office saying they'd stopped delivering it. I shuffled through the bills and junk mail, throwing most of it in the recycling bin. One letter was from Austen Media, dated from the summer. It stated that I'd been fired for *gross misconduct* for deleting Kitty's email and was not allowed back in the slim chrome tower. I was about to throw the letter away, but then decided I might frame it instead.

I inserted the key into the front door of my apartment, and when I opened it, I saw my living room, my desk, the kitchen, just the way I'd left them. At the sight of my old home I felt a twinge, a plucked guitar string of memory that reverberated from head to toe. I flicked the light switch and was relieved the electricity was still on. My coffee mug, still half full, sat on the kitchen counter. Everything was covered in dust, a gray powder like time made manifest, the time that had passed since I'd left this life.

There was barely any food inside the refrigerator. The cupboards were mostly empty, aside from a box of crackers and a few cans of soup. In the freezer there was the stack of Waist Watchers entrées that I'd made, wrapped neatly in foil, the two-star and three-star meals. I recalled my empty belly and the lethargy, sometimes even paralysis, that had resulted from existing on those meals. I'd moved slowly back then, when I'd moved at all.

In my bedroom, I removed Alicia's clothes from the closet, the dresses that didn't fit me and never would. I called Sana and asked if she might need clothes for the girls at the clinic when it opened. I explained that the outfits weren't likely to be the girls' style, but they would work for job interviews and court appearances. She was enthusiastic, so I packed the clothes in the two black suitcases that were stored under my bed and arranged for a courier to pick them up and deliver them to Calliope House.

The clothes I used to wear every day were in piles on the floor and stuffed into the dresser. I put them in the trash. Over the next several days, I slept in my old bed and awoke each morning to continue sorting through my belongings, going through my books and mementos, my whole life in New York. I discovered empty bottles of Y——, as well as piles of Waist Watchers literature and copies of *Daisy Chain*. Most of that went into the recycling bin. The copy of *Adventures in Dietland* that Leeta had given to me went into the box of things I would always keep, with my family photo albums and souvenirs.

As I continued sorting my things and packing, I would go out to withdraw cash from the bank. I considered visiting the café while I was out, but Carmen was still on maternity leave and she was the only part of it that I missed.

Movers came to collect my furniture and boxes and take them to a storage unit in Queens, where I'd leave them while I was living at Calliope House. Then the apartment was empty, except for the bedroom where my cousin Jeremy's boxes were stored. I called him in Cairo to let him know that I was moving out of his apartment. I offered to continue paying rent until a new tenant moved in, but he told me not to worry. With me moving, he said it was likely he would sell. I understood that he would have sold years before if not for me, and I was grateful for the time he had allowed me to live in a nice place, one that I wouldn't have otherwise been able to afford. The apartment on Swann Street had made the other difficulties in my life easier to bear.

On my way out, I took one last look around. The apartment was smaller than I remembered it, in the way that everything looks smaller after you've left it behind.

The next morning, I awoke in the buttery light of my bedroom back at Calliope House and realized that it wasn't simply another day. It was the tenth of October, the day my weight-loss surgery had been scheduled to take place. Lying in bed, I instinctively placed my hand on my bare belly and ran

489

my fingers over the terrain — soft to the touch despite the lines and crevices. I was grateful for what was missing: the violent eruption of an incision. Beneath the expanse of flesh, my stomach was nestled among my other organs, healthy and whole, not stapled and clamped shut. I knew I had Leeta to thank for leading me to Verena and the others, for this morning spent snug in my bed, not under the blazing lights and masked faces of an operating room.

The money I'd been withdrawing from the bank for Leeta was in a neat stack in my bottom dresser drawer, but she would need much more than that. I knew Julia would contact me soon; at any moment I'd receive a frantic email or phone call and she'd demand to know if I was going to help fund Leeta's escape. Until that moment came, I would put it out of my mind. What I wanted now was to celebrate how far I'd come.

I decided to throw a party, with food and lots to drink. The previous weeks had been intense for all of us — the women had their work, I had my personal struggles, and through it all was Jennifer. We continued to refer to Soledad and the attacks by this single name, its origins not yet clear. Jennifer had made up seem like down, had left us all spinning and dizzy, had set the world on fire, and she was still out there.

I climbed out of bed and headed out to shop for groceries and booze. In the afternoon, I baked a three-layer chocolate ganache cake and prepared vegetable curry and rice for the main course, the perfect warming meal for an October evening. I didn't bother to tell the others we were having a celebration. It didn't need to be a formal occasion; I would let it bloom before their eyes.

As the curry and rice simmered on the stove, I cleared the stolen lingerie out of my bedroom closet and carried it downstairs in two plastic bags. In the tiny backyard, Verena kept her gardening tools in a tall metal drum, which I emptied onto the ground. I dumped charcoal into the drum, drenched it with lighter fluid, and set it ablaze. When the fire was glowing and flames shot out the top, I opened one of the bags and pulled out a few thongs and padded bras, dropping them into the drum, which made the fire pop. I'd always known the underwear would serve a purpose — it had just taken me a while to discover what it was.

When it was time for dinner, I was joined by Verena, Marlowe with baby Huck, Rubí, and Sana. We ate curry and rice in the kitchen, followed by cake. I was pleased that

I no longer needed voluminous amounts of food to feel satisfied. I was learning to listen to my body's hunger cues and desires, which helped me know when I needed to eat, and what, and how much. Rubí said my metabolism was ruined from years of dieting and it would take time to heal and get back in touch with my natural rhythms. I would never restrict myself again or do math before eating. I would give my body what it needed and wanted — nothing more, nothing less.

After dinner we carried our drinks outside to where the fire was burning; the drum was positioned in the middle of the concrete slab that was our yard, ringed by trees bright with autumn gold. I kept the fire going, but everyone was eager to help. "Let me," said Sana, dropping a lilac negligee into the flames, and then a pair of striped boy shorts. We watched them sizzle.

"This lingerie is from Bonerville, right?" said Marlowe. I told her it was and she asked why I had two bags full of it.

"Long story," Sana said, directing the conversation elsewhere.

We were running out of drinks, so Rubí went inside to mix another pitcher of mojitos. She brought it outside and refilled our cups. The backyard was only a small patch, but we were all crammed together, drinking, watching the fire, and, inevitably, talking about Jennifer. It was the festive atmosphere I'd wanted, but then I saw through the kitchen window that Julia had arrived. She sliced the cake and ate some of it with her fingers. I excused myself to go inside, closing the door behind me.

"What are you doing here?" I asked. The last time I'd seen her was in the café bathroom. At the sight of her, I imagined my wrists in handcuffs.

Julia moved around the table, stuffing her mouth with curry and rice. "Have you made a decision?" she whispered.

"I'm not sure yet. I need more time anyway. I can't withdraw too much money from the bank at once. It'll arouse suspicion."

"So you have access to money?" she asked with frantic hopefulness.

I nodded and Julia closed her eyes. "Thank God," she said. "I need it on Friday. I'll come by at noon. I can't wait any longer than that." Friday was two days away.

"I told you, I'm not sure. I want to know more about Leeta."

"Shhhh," Julia said. "For crying out loud, do not say that name." She peered at the women outside. Through the glass, Marlowe

493

waved. Julia didn't bother to wave back. "Did I mention this is a matter of life and death? I'm not bullshitting." Her acrylic nail tips were chipped, as if she'd been biting them. "You have no idea what I'm going through."

"Because you won't tell me."

She ignored me, focused completely on the food, an animalistic glint in her eyes. I missed the vulnerable Julia from the café bathroom, but assumed that version was rarely let out of its restraints. She piled her plate high, then composed herself before opening the door to go outside. "Let's try to act normal," she said over her shoulder.

Julia approached the women around the fire and I followed. "What is this, a party?" she said, announcing her arrival. I took my place on the opposite side of the drum, between Rubí and Sana. Everyone looked at Julia, her mouth so full that she struggled to chew and swallow. "Since you're all here, I might as well tell you that I've quit my job at Austen. Tomorrow is my last day."

"Whoa! End of era," said Marlowe.

"What are your plans?" asked Verena.

"I'm going to travel for a while. You won't be seeing much of me in the near future." Julia looked at me over the flames. Was she going on the run as well?

"You're going to *travel?*" Verena said in a tone of disbelief. "What about your under-cover work?"

"I can't do it anymore. This charade is too much," she sputtered, shoving more food into her mouth. Bits of rice fell down her top. "I'm so goddamn hungry all the time, you have no idea what it's like." She began to choke on something stuck in her throat. She clasped her neck with one hand, coughing loudly, flinging her dinner plate into the bushes. Rubí handed her a drink, which she downed at once. "I'm a wreck, I apologize," she said when she recovered, her eyes watery from the curry and the coughing, and perhaps there were tears as well. She looked at me again over the flames, their orange tongues giving her a devilish glow.

Rubí reached into the bag and dropped a few bras into the fire. "So what's the special occasion?" Marlowe asked me. "We don't get to burn underwear and eat curry every night. You're spoiling us." She handed Huck a pair of lacy pink crotchless panties, which he threw into the drum, giggling with de-light.

"My surgery was scheduled for today," I said, drinking rum and mint from the plastic cup, enjoying the feeling of community. "I wanted to celebrate."

"I had no idea," Verena said.

Sana and Rubí put their arms around me, squeezing me between them. "I want you to know she's gone," I said to Verena. "The thin woman inside me, the perfect woman, my shadow self."

"Alicia?"

"No, I'm reclaiming her. That perfect woman, that smaller self, was only ever an idea. She didn't really exist, so she doesn't need a name." *Alicia is me, Alicia is me.*

Verena blew me a kiss from across the fire. "Virginia Woolf once wrote that it's more difficult to kill a phantom than a reality," she said. And so it was, but at last my phantom was gone. I knew my life would never be easy, but this must be what Sana had meant. I had crossed over and would never go back.

I turned my face away from the fire, burying my head in Sana's shoulder, a moment of escape from the heat of the blaze and my emotions. When I looked up again, Verena was standing on the other side of the drum, holding the framed pair of Eulayla's fat jeans. She hit the frame against the metal drum, shattering the glass. With the jeans freed from the frame, she hugged them to her body.

"Verena, what are you doing?" Marlowe asked. She spoke for all of us. The jeans had always been a sacred object, untouchable.

"I've been inspired by Plum," she said. "This feels right."

She held the legendary jeans out in front of her, the jeans that had obsessed me as a teenager, the jeans that had launched a million diets. "The New Baptist Plan really worked," I said, staring at the iconic denim. "I'm completely transformed. You guaranteed it."

"Born again," she said.

"No calorie counting and no weighing," I said.

"No pain, no gain."

"Results not typical."

"Feel the burn." Verena tossed her mother's jeans into the fire. *"Burst!"* she said as they sank into the flames.

Who is Jennifer?

Soledad Ayala was born in Mexico in 1973. When she was eight years old, her family moved to South Dakota for five months, then to Iowa for six months. In each place, the other children made fun of her for being chubby, for having an accent and a weird name: *Soledad.*

Dad! Daddy! Soleduddy!

When her family moved to Wyoming and she started another new school, she told the teacher her name wasn't Soledad but Jennifer. The girls named Jennifer whom Soledad had met weren't like her. They were blond or brunette and pretty. They didn't have accents or dark skin. They had nicknames like Jenny or Jenna, names that no one laughed at. Soledad didn't want to be laughed at. She wanted to blend in.

For a few years, every day on the first day of school, the teacher would call out the name

Soledad Ayala and Soledad would raise her hand and say, "Everyone calls me Jennifer." Throughout her elementary school years she was known as Jennifer Ayala. Even her parents called her Jenny, but she knew in her heart she wasn't a real Jennifer; she wasn't like the American girls, she was only an impostor. She liked to think that by calling herself Jennifer, Soledad would disappear, but whenever she looked in the mirror Soledad was still there.

When she and her family settled in California, she started junior high; her guidance counselor, Miss Jimenez, told her that she shouldn't pretend to be someone else. "Soledad is your real name," she said. "That's what we should call you." Soledad was unhappy at the thought of giving up Jennifer, but she didn't want to disappoint Miss Jimenez. The nickname faded away, consigned to Soledad's early childhood, but her mother sometimes called her Jenny for fun when they were reminiscing about old times.

"Who's Jenny?" Luz had asked when she was little and first cognizant that her mother had a name and it was Soledad, not Jenny.

"Jenny is a girl I used to be," Soledad had told her daughter, but that wasn't true. She had never been Jenny; she had only been an impostor.

■ ■ ■ ■

Soledad had a firm alibi for the night that two of her daughter's rapists, Lamar Wilson and Chris Martinez, disappeared. The police assumed the men had jumped bail, but given the high-profile nature of their crime, a thorough investigation was necessary in order to rule out other possibilities. They began with Soledad, who'd been recorded on CCTV at multiple locations in Santa Mariana on the night in question, including the local shopping mall, where she stayed for several hours, browsing aimlessly and having dinner with friends from church; and the supermarket, where she carefully loaded her cart with a week's worth of food for herself, now that she was alone. For days afterward she was observed in town by neighbors and police, doing nothing out of the ordinary. The police were confident that neither she nor any members of her family had plotted revenge against Wilson and Martinez — Soledad's father and husband were dead, she had no brothers; her sisters, mother, and other relatives were back in Texas. The investigation moved on.

Weeks later, after Wilson and Martinez were dropped into the desert along with the rest of the Dirty Dozen, Soledad cooperated with federal authorities, agreeing to speak at a press conference. FBI agents were impressed with the bereaved mother's courage, but they began to investigate her anyway, lacking confidence in the Santa Mariana police. They soon discovered that Leeta Albridge had been a volunteer at the women's clinic where Soledad had once worked training rape crisis counselors. The FBI knocked on Soledad's door again, to address what couldn't be a coincidence, but there was no answer. A neighbor told them she'd gone to Mexico City to care for a sick aunt.

While Mexican law enforcement officers tried to locate Soledad, FBI agents in Houston visited her mother in the hospital, where the old woman would soon die from pneumonia. In her delirium she was insistent that her daughter was innocent of any wrongdoing and said she wasn't running from the police but had killed herself. "She had a gun," her mother said, describing the days before Luz's funeral. "She was upset. She was drinking." Soledad's sisters, who were in the hospital room while their mother was being questioned, pleaded with the agents to leave her alone, but they refused.

"She's a good girl," Soledad's mother repeated many times through her tears, and then she added: "My Jenny wouldn't do anything wrong."

Soledad's three sisters rose from their chairs in unison, demanding the interview be terminated, but it was too late. The agents had heard what their mother said.

After her connections to Leeta Albridge and captain Missy Tompkins were uncovered, federal agents interviewed Soledad's other friends and her associates from the army. In the Inwood section of Manhattan, FBI agents searched the apartment of specialist Agnes Szydlowski and her husband. As medics in Afghanistan, Agnes and Soledad had saved each other's lives. Agnes drank coffee and smoked cigarettes at her kitchen table as the agents dusted every surface in her home for fingerprints. "I love Soledad like a sister," Agnes said, "but you're wasting your time. She's never been in my apartment."

Investigators later discovered that Agnes and her husband owned a motorcycle, the same make and model as the one witnesses in Times Square described on the night Stella Cross and her husband were murdered.

"That motorcycle was stolen months ago," Agnes said. She said nothing else until she had a lawyer.

Across the Atlantic, authorities in Scotland

began to investigate British Army captain Gwendolen Campbell at the request of the FBI. During Gwendolen's first deployment to Afghanistan, the Taliban shot down a helicopter she was riding in, leaving her blinded in one eye and missing several fingers. Despite her injuries and the deaths of her fellow soldiers, she survived the attack thanks to American medics on the ground — Soledad and Agnes. Rarely did a day pass without Gwendolen thinking of the two women who had saved her life. When she heard the news that Soledad's daughter had died, Gwendolen felt wounded, as if it had happened to her own family. She traveled from her home in Glasgow to California to attend the funeral. After she returned home, her family and friends reported that she fell out of touch, which wasn't in keeping with her normal character. No one had been able to find her.

Investigators searched every residence associated with Captain Gwendolen Campbell in England and Scotland. They received a tip about a Highlands farmhouse not far from the village where the Empire Media CEO's nephew had been found wandering one morning weeks earlier, released by his kidnappers. There was no direct evidence that Gwendolen had been in the farmhouse, and the nephew could not identify her, but there was a knife in the kitchen with traces of blood and blond hairs on it, which were later proven to be a DNA match for the CEO's twin brother. On the bathroom mirror was a message written with red lipstick: *For Jennifer, with no regrets.*

Gwendolen's passport had recently been logged at the airport in Buenos Aires. Since then there had been no sign of her.

Soledad Ayala (Aliases: Jennifer Ayala, Jenny Ayala) was placed on the FBI's Ten Most Wanted list, the only woman there, with a promise of a $100,000 reward for information leading to her capture.

In an interview with *The Nola and Nedra Show,* Cheryl Crane-Murphy said, "Before we send a lynch mob after this woman, might I remind everyone that Soledad Ayala earned the Silver Star for bravery in Afghanistan? She was not able to collect her award at the White House *for obvious reasons,* but she still deserves our respect."

"Might one call her an American hero?" asked Nedra Feldstein-Delaney.

"One might," said Nola Larson King.

On Friday, I was awakened by the music: *". . . your mama's in the trunk of Daddy's car / no baby, she's not gonna wake up / you see, Mama could never keep that big mouth shut . . ."*

I placed the stacks of cash in white envelopes and stuffed them into a paper bag that Julia could take with her should I decide to give her the money. As I was folding up the bag, my phone rang.

"Change of plans," Julia said, nearly breathless. "Come to the Beauty Closet right away."

"Why can't you come here?" I preferred Julia on my turf. Besides, I wasn't allowed back in the Austen Tower.

"I'll explain when you get here. Ask for me at the desk. We have all new security staff, so they won't recognize you. Use a fake name. Hurry."

I rushed to shower and dress. While lacing

up my boots, I heard the doorbell ring. "Bomb threat!" Marlowe shouted from downstairs. I was ready to go. I'd folded the paper bag into a firm rectangular parcel, which I now stuffed under the waistband of my oatmeal skirt, where it stayed pressed against my belly. I put on a loose jacket and draped a scarf around my neck to hide the extra bulk.

"Bomb threat!" Sana yelled, leaving three rapid knocks on my door. A bomb was the least of my worries. I was more concerned about being mugged.

I followed the women out the front door, careful to avoid eye contact with the police-woman who was shepherding us out. If something went wrong, it was possible I wouldn't be returning to Calliope House. I looked at it over my shoulder on my way to Sixth Avenue, its plain brown exterior belying the beating red heart inside.

The other women took their places on the benches, but I hailed a taxi. "Just where do you think you're going, Sugar Plum?" Sana said. "Bomb threats are a group activity."

"She's abandoning us," Verena said.

"You're going to miss out on ice cream," Marlowe added.

I slipped into the back seat of a waiting taxi. "I'm not abandoning you," I said before closing the door. "I have errands to do and then I'll come home. I promise." Driving away, I watched them through the back window: Verena and Rubí, Marlowe and Huck, Sana — the usual gang, my friends. For them it was an ordinary day.

In Times Square, crowds on the sidewalks stood still, gazing up at Soledad's face on the jumbo screen, as if toward some celestial event. It was too soon to know whether Jennifer — Soledad's all-American girl who had morphed into something else — was an out-of-control blaze leaving only destruction or a controlled burn intended to purify. I patted my stomach as I weaved through the people, feeling the money under my clothes, as well as my thumping pulse. I entered the Austen Tower and went through the metal detector. I gave the guard a name, not my real name, and waited for Julia. When she arrived, I saw that her façade was already crumbling. A bit of flab hung over the waistband of her pants; her straightened hair was beginning to frizz and coil; her makeup had faded, leaving nothing but a faint outline of her features, her face that of an old china doll that had been bleached in the sun.

She didn't speak until we were in the

elevator. "Can you believe they offered to throw me a goodbye party this afternoon?" Julia snorted.

On the outside of the door to the Beauty Closet was a sign that read INVENTORY IN PROGRESS. ENTRY FORBIDDEN! Once we were inside, Julia locked the door and disarmed the keypad. The Beauty Closet matched Julia in its disarray. Hundreds of tubes of lipstick and mascara had crashed to the floor, as well as bottles of a perfume called Hussy, which had shattered, leaving liquid and glass everywhere. There was a stench, the sweat of a thousand hussies, which made it painful to breathe.

"How much money did you bring?"

"Twenty thousand," I said, gazing at the door, longing to open it and flee.

"What did you tell Verena?" Julia was stuffing files from her desk into her bag.

"I didn't tell Verena anything. This is my money."

Julia opened her mouth as if to speak, then reconsidered. Her lips, in Muted Rose, turned into a half-smile, and she nodded. "I'm sorry I've lied to you, but I didn't want to involve you unless it was absolutely necessary. When she came to me, I had to help her. You understand, don't you?"

"I'm here, aren't I?"

Julia attempted to tame her wild hair, smoothing it with her hands, but it made no difference; each flattened curl sprang back up. She was serious and fearful. She didn't even flirt with me. Crushed cakes of purple and blue eye shadow bruised the white floor around her. "Come with me," she said.

I followed her down the Lips aisle, left at Mascara, right at Concealer, to the end of the Blush corridor. Julia wasn't wearing her heels, just simple brown flats, and I had never seen her move so quickly. I struggled to keep up.

At the end of the corridor was a pile of boxes sitting in front of a blank space of white wall. Julia pushed the boxes aside, grunting and puffing. Once the boxes were cleared away, I saw a cutout line in the drywall. Julia wrenched it open with a crowbar, revealing a hidden space.

The space was glowing with yellow light coming from two lamps balanced on a steel beam; beyond the lamps it was black. Julia bent over and stepped inside. She motioned for me to follow, but my limbs were heavy. I couldn't move.

"You wanted the truth," she said. "It's in here."

I entered the space. A figure was sitting

atop a sleeping bag in a dim corner to my right. As I moved closer I saw she was wearing a gray tracksuit, her arms and legs pulled tight around her, headphones dangling around her neck. Her dark hair was nearly shaved off. She squinted up at me, a tiny, startled creature.

"Leeta?"

Julia moved one of the lamps so I could see her better. Her face was scrubbed and pale. Without the long hair and eye makeup, without the colorful tights and boots, she was pared down, almost naked.

"It's Plum."

"I know who you are, Louise B." Her voice was raspy, unused. She scooted out from the corner where she was sitting, moving into the light. She wasn't the looming figure I'd seen on the screen in Times Square, but I was finally beginning to recognize her face, that face that had haunted me for so long.

"It's really you."

Behind me, Julia was sweeping up the concrete floor, trying to remove all possible traces of Leeta from the hiding space. "Go on," she said over the broom handle. "She won't bite."

I unbuttoned my jacket and wriggled out of it, leaving the paper bag under my waistband, and maneuvered myself onto the hard floor to face Leeta. "Your hair is so short," I said.

She turned away, fidgeting, reaching for the locks that were no longer there. "I'm not what you expected. I'm being hunted like an animal, so I've become one." She backed into her corner again, pulling the gray hood up over her head. The face that peeked out at me from beneath the heavy fabric, now darkened by shadow, had been spotted all over the country, all over the world, but Leeta had been hiding beneath fifty-two stories of Stanley Austen's media empire the whole time. I thought of the barricades outside the building and had to smile. The enemy was inside.

"Did you bring money?" she asked.

I kept staring at her, only semi-aware that she had asked me a question. She asked again. "Money. Did you bring it?"

I reached under my shirt and removed the paper bag, but I didn't hand it to her. Julia wheeled a large brown crate into the hiding space. "Five minutes," she said.

Leeta bounced her legs up and down, slipping her hand beneath the hood to reach for her hair again, then moving her hand to her mouth and nibbling one of her fingers. She eyed the crate. "I want to see the sun.

Even if they capture me or shoot me, at least I'll have a taste of freedom one last time. Nothing feels as good as freedom."

The playful girl from the café was gone. Leeta, stuck in a dark cave for months, hunted by the police with their guns and dogs and helicopters — she was the reality of everything that had been happening. I worried about what they would do if they found her. She seemed so alone down here, as if she'd been abandoned.

"What happened to Soledad?" I felt an almost electric charge saying the name to someone who knew Soledad, the woman whose grief and rage for her daughter burned as brightly as a star.

"All the women have scattered. I don't know where."

"How did you meet Soledad?" I knew what I'd heard on the news, but the details had been vague.

Leeta was silent, as if she'd closed up in her dark corner, but then she began to recount the story. In college, she was required to sign up for a community service project. She volunteered at a women's clinic; Soledad worked there and trained Leeta to become a rape crisis counselor. The clinic offered abortions and birth control in addition to rape counseling. "Working there was intense," Leeta said. "Bulletproof windows and an armed guard outside. Women had to pass by a guy with a gun just to get rape counseling, which is fucked up. Working there, it was easy to feel that it was us against the world — and the world didn't care. Sometimes me and Soledad would go for drinks after our shift, to cope with hearing so many awful stories and seeing so many women cry." Soledad was used to it, but Leeta said she struggled with the job.

Soledad's house in Santa Mariana was an hour away, but Leeta went there for barbecues and movie nights sometimes, which is when she spent time with Luz. "When I got homesick, Soledad mothered me. How embarrassing to need a mother at my age, right?" Leeta's eyes, which had been wide and alert, softened. She blinked slowly. "Do you want to know what I did for Luz and Soledad, Louise B.? I think you need to know."

"Tell her," Julia said as she continued cleaning. I was still holding the paper bag and set it down on the floor next to me, wiping my palms on my knees, conscious of my colorful tights and boots, wondering if Leeta thought me a fool.

She explained that after Luz's funeral,

Soledad insisted that her relatives return to Texas right away. Alone at home in Santa Mariana, she invited Leeta over and told her that her friend Missy was going to kidnap Wilson and Martinez. They couldn't get to the other rapists, who were locked up, so the two ringleaders would pay for all their sins. "I asked Soledad why she wanted to kidnap the men — I was stunned at what she was suggesting — but she just said they were going to get what they deserved. This wasn't the Soledad I knew." Leeta tried to talk her out of it for Soledad's own sake, so she wouldn't risk going to prison, but she'd made up her mind.

Soledad couldn't be directly involved in the kidnapping because she would have been an obvious suspect, so she asked Leeta to go to the bar where Wilson and Martinez hung out and lure them to a vacant lot, where Missy would be waiting for them. "I would be the bait in a short dress and blond wig," Leeta said. "I wasn't in my right mind then. What'd happened to Luz was the worst thing that'd happened to anybody I'd ever known. I just kept thinking of her and all those crying women at the clinic and how this was never going to end. Despite my shock at Soledad's plan, I began to wonder if she was right. Maybe we needed to go to the source of the problem."

It wasn't difficult to lure the men from the bar. They followed Leeta to the car, eager and excited at the thought of sex, and she drove them the ten miles to where Missy was waiting. "Being in the car with them made me sick. Those two scumbags killed Luz, each of them and the other men taking a piece of her, and I wanted to pull the car over and run into a field and scream, but I couldn't do that, so I drove and screamed in my head. The men were talking to me in the car but all I could hear was my screaming."

When they arrived at the darkened lot north of town, Missy was waiting with a black van. "They suspected something was wrong. They were scumbags but they weren't stupid." Leeta said they were reluctant to get out of the car. When they finally did, Missy Tasered them and tied them up. Leeta helped Missy load them into the back of the van and then Missy told her to drive away and keep going, out of Santa Mariana and as far away as she could get.

I had no idea how to reply. Leeta stared from beneath her hood into the darkness that surrounded us. I could only imagine the scenes that played in her mind, that would always play. In my head I saw the

Dirty Dozen dropped into the desert, the Harbor Freeway interchange, and all of the other attacks linked to Jennifer. "Did you know this was the beginning of something *bigger*?"

Leeta said she didn't. Days after the abduction, she called Soledad from the desert motel where she'd taken refuge and asked again what she was going to do with the men. "She said she'd let them linger for a while, that they weren't going to be first. I didn't know what she meant by *first*. I didn't ask. That's the last time I talked to her." After the Jennifer attacks began to unfold, the first publicized attack with its link to the military, Leeta wondered if they were connected to Soledad and Missy. She tried to contact Soledad again, but it was Missy who replied. She and Leeta talked on the phone and through email, but Missy never admitted to anything. After Wilson and Martinez were killed with the rest of the Dirty Dozen, she knew for certain. "Missy was worried that I'd go to the police, so she wanted to keep tabs on me. I didn't go to the police, but I told my roommate I knew who Jennifer was. I just couldn't keep it inside anymore." Leeta knew she'd made a mistake by telling her roommate. That's when she went underground.

"How have you coped with hiding down here?" I asked, tugging on my collar. Finally, I was getting the answers to my questions, but what I really wanted to do was leave the suffocating hiding space. Leeta and I had both been underground — she in the Beauty Closet, me in Verena's basement. New York was full of these dark places.

"During the day I know Julia is on the other side of the wall, but at night . . . sometimes there's that screaming in my head again."

"Why don't you turn yourself in? Your sentence might not even be that long." I was out of my depth, but this seemed like the sensible thing to suggest. Prison couldn't be worse than this hiding space.

"The police wouldn't believe anything I'd tell them. They're out for blood. They'd want me to turn against Soledad, and I'm not going to do that. The truth is, I'm scared."

Whether she ran or turned herself in, she was headed for a life of confinement. I wanted to reach out to her, to say it would be all right, but that would be a lie.

"Almost ready?" Julia said. Leeta struggled to stand up and so did I.

"I understand if you don't want to give me the money, Louise B."

"You *need* the money," Julia said.

"It's her choice. I don't want her to do anything she's uncomfortable with. She could get into trouble."

I knew I could get into trouble, but I wanted Leeta to see the sun. "This money was given to me for a reason, but that reason no longer exists. You helped me," I said. I wanted to say, *You saved me.* "Now it's my turn to help you."

She took the paper bag and stuffed it under her jacket. "I was right about you. You're not like them." She nodded upward toward the fifty-two stories on top of us.

"No, not like them."

She pushed back the hood so I could see her face more clearly. She grabbed my hands, grasping them hard. "That time I spent spying on you was the last happy time in my life," she said. "I've thought of you often while I've been down here. Julia has given me updates on how your life has changed, and that's offered some rare moments of joy. Wherever I end up, just know that I'm on your side."

She looked at me for several seconds more and then she walked away, inserting the earbuds and pulling the hood back up. Music blasted, muffled to me but deafening for her. I stared at the back of her, at the outline of her body against the hole in the wall and the light from the Beauty Closet. I'd imagined her for so long. In reality, I didn't know her, but we lived in each other's memories, each of us what the other needed us to be.

Julia removed the lamps from the hiding space, so the only light was coming from the other side of the hole in the wall. We helped Leeta into the crate. Once inside, she stepped into her sleeping bag and pulled it up so it rested under her arms like a strapless dress. She lowered herself into the crate and lay on the bottom in the fetal position, her face positioned near one of the air holes. Julia and I dropped eyebrow pencils on top of her and she didn't flinch. We filled the crate with pencils, all the way to the top, until there was no sign of a person underneath. Julia attached the lid.

After we wheeled the crate out of the hiding space, Julia sealed the hole shut, pushing the boxes back in front of it. We moved down the Blush corridor toward the exit.

"Am I allowed to ask where you're taking her?"

"New Mexico," Julia said. "I'll hand her off to someone there. She has to keep moving."

We took the service elevator to the parking level and pushed the brown crate to the back of a small white delivery van that Julia had rented. I looked over my shoulders, exposed and scared. "Act normal," Julia whispered. "There might be cameras."

There were no windows on the sides of the van or in the back doors. With great effort, we lifted the crate and wrestled it into the hold. Once it was secure, Julia locked the doors. I wanted to say *Be careful* or *Good luck,* but nothing I could say would have been adequate.

"Write the book," Julia said, and I told her I would. When she was in the driver's seat with the door closed, I placed my palm against the glass and Julia did the same on her side. That's how we said goodbye.

I followed the signs back to the lobby and rushed to get away before I ran into someone like Kitty. When I stepped outside I wanted to cry or scream or beat my fists against the Austen Tower, but I couldn't. Other people would see. Wherever I went, I was seen.

After being in the hiding space, I found everything outside to be beautiful, even the concrete barricades and the neon lights. I headed toward Broadway. The white van was out there somewhere, but I didn't see it. As I walked I stripped off my jacket and scarf and dragged them behind me. I pushed my way through the masses of tourists and began to run faster than I had ever run before.

Leeta was right. It felt good to be free. With unexpected power in my legs, I kept going, racing ahead with the wind and the sun on my face, taking a leap into the wide world, which now seemed too small to contain me.

Burst!

ACKNOWLEDGMENTS

Alice Tasman, one of my lucky Alices, was the only literary agent in New York brave enough to take on *Dietland*. I am grateful for that every day. I am also tremendously lucky to have the other women at the Jean V. Naggar Literary Agency, and all my international co-agents and publishers, in my corner. I cannot possibly thank all these lovely people enough.

Lauren Wein, my editor (and admirer of my *Dietland* spreadsheets), shared my vision for the novel from our first phone call. Heartfelt thanks to her for helping me give Plum and company the editorial makeover they needed while always remaining true to them. Thanks also to Nina Barnett and Alison Kerr Miller for their help with improving the manuscript, and to the whole team at Houghton Mifflin Harcourt. I am so appreciative of their efforts, I could just *burst*.

The generous and talented writers I met

in the Bennington College MFA program continue to inspire me all these years later and will always be my writing community. In particular, I would like to thank William Vandegrift for his friendship, and Alice Mattison, my original lucky Alice, who encouraged me in the beginning and helped me reach the end.

For their valuable editorial feedback, I would like to thank Susanna Jones, Michelle Walker, and my French editor, Aurélien Masson.

During my London years, which were equal parts exhilarating and traumatizing, three scribbling women — Lindsay Catt, Theresa Lee, and Carol McGrath — provided friendship and support when I needed it the most. I would also like to thank the Fat Studies community in the U.K., whose ideas and fellowship enriched my life and work immeasurably.

Callie Khouri used the term "crossed over" in her brilliant screenplay for *Thelma & Louise,* which I shamelessly adapted for my own purposes in the spirit of sisterhood and consciousness-raising.

The Virginia Woolf line "It is far harder to kill a phantom than a reality" appears in her essay "Professions for Women."

This book owes a debt to second-wave

feminists, those women who changed the world in such a profound way. I don't have space to list the writers who have been so important to me, since that would require pages and pages, but I would like to make two acknowledgments: Sandra Lee Bartky, whose essays completely altered my reality, and the feminist novelists from the 1970s and early 1980s, whose work I turned to when I feared I might lose my nerve.

An early and important source of inspiration for *Dietland* was *Fight Club,* Chuck Palahniuk's novel and the film adaptation directed by David Fincher. I would like to think that *Dietland* would exist even if *Fight Club* hadn't provided that initial spark of an idea, but I'll never know.

Big love to my family, especially my parents, J^2, and my late maternal grandparents, and to all the friends and mentors I don't have room to mention here. Thanks to the many kindhearted people — some of whom I have never met — who offered encouragement and research help during the millions of years it took me to complete this novel.

Finally, thanks to Alicia Plum. She never abandoned me.

ABOUT THE AUTHOR

Sarai Walker worked as a writer and editor for *Our Bodies, Ourselves.* Her articles have appeared in national publications, including the *New York Times.* She earned her MFA in creative writing from Bennington College and her PhD in English from the University of London. She lives in Los Angeles, CA.

The employees of Thorndike Press hope you have enjoyed this Large Print book. All our Thorndike, Wheeler, and Kennebec Large Print titles are designed for easy reading, and all our books are made to last. Other Thorndike Press Large Print books are available at your library, through selected bookstores, or directly from us.

For information about titles, please call:
(800) 223-1244

or visit our website at:
gale.com/thorndike

To share your comments, please write:
Publisher
Thorndike Press
10 Water St., Suite 310
Waterville, ME 04901